John Jarrett

DEMPSEY AND THE WILD BULL

The Four-Minute Fight of the Century

Dedication

For my wife Mary, she's a knockout!

First published by Pitch Publishing, 2015

Pitch Publishing
A2 Yeoman Gate
Yeoman Way
Durrington
BN13 3QZ
www.pitchpublishing.co.uk

© John Jarrett, 2015

A CIP catalogue record is available for this book
from the British Library.

ISBN 978 178531-031-7

Typesetting and origination by Pitch Publishing

Printed in Malta by Melita Press

DEMPSEY AND
THE WILD BULL

Contents

Preface

I T happened more than 90 years ago and is still called the most savagely exciting fight for the world heavyweight championship of all time. Friday 14 September 1923, Polo Grounds, New York City, Jack Dempsey, the Manassa Mauler, defending his title against Luis Angel Firpo, the Wild Bull of the Pampas, a huge crowd of 82,000 with gate receipts at $1,188,603, the second biggest live gate at that time. All for a fight that lasted three minutes and 57 seconds. Nobody asked for their money back!

In the first round, Dempsey floored Firpo seven times and was decked twice himself, at one time flying out through the ropes to land on the press benches. He climbed, or was pushed, back into the ring, barely inside the ten seconds and survived the round. Making a remarkable recovery, Dempsey came out for round two and dropped Firpo twice for the finish of a fight they would never forget.

Boxing was almost unknown in Argentina when Luis Angel Firpo began abusing his fellow men in the prize ring, winning the South American title before setting sail for New York City, the Big Town and the big money. A shaggy-haired giant with a right hand like a hammer, he managed himself into a dollar fortune, fighting off the big-name managers eager to cut themselves in on his earnings, taking most of it home to become one of the richest men in the Argentine where he had become a national hero.

Jack Dempsey, whose savage fists took him from the hobo jungles all the way to high society, was boxing's biggest box-office attraction in the Roaring Twenties. He was one half of the first five million-dollar fights in ring history, managed by the legendary Jack 'Doc' Kearns and promoted by ace showman Tex Rickard. Yet in 1920, his first year as champion, Dempsey was targeted as a draft-dodger, having claimed to be the support of his family (which he was), while thousands of his fellow citizens went off to France to fight in World War I. The 'slacker trial' (in which he was exonerated) would hound him until he lost his title to Gene Tunney in 1926 on a rainy night in Philadelphia. They loved him after that one and he would become one of America's greatest sporting legends.

In 1950, the Associated Press's mid-century poll of 374 sportswriters and radio sportscasters ranked the Dempsey–Firpo fight as the top sports drama of the previous 50 years.

This is the story of Dempsey and Firpo and their sensational punch-up at the Polo Grounds on a Friday afternoon in September 1923. Get your ticket here!

Acknowledgements

ALTHOUGH I am the sole driver for this thing, it wouldn't even be on the road but for the backing and invaluable support of my team of mechanics and advisers…my son Jeffrey and his daughter Rachel for technical backup, my daughter Glenda, husband John and children Alex and Matthew for advice and assistance, my friend Bob Mee for being there with advice and encouragement, and the people at NewspaperArchive.com for their wonderful service.

Thank you.

1

Day Of The Fight

O N a January day in 1922, a husky young fellow walked into the United States consulate in Buenos Aires and asked vice consul H.G. Waters to visa a passport bearing the name Luis Angel Firpo. The holder's occupation was given as 'boxeador'. When Waters asked the purpose of the visit to the United States, the big fellow calmly said he was going up to get a fight with Jack Dempsey.

'You think you can lick him?' queried the vice consul, with a wry smile.

'That's what I'm going for,' the fellow replied quietly.

Waters entered in his ledger the object of Firpo's visit as 'training for boxing.' In the margin he pencilled, 'says he's going to lick Dempsey – *vamos a ver'* (we'll see.)'[1]

Precisely one year and nine months later, 14 September 1923, the world would see what Luis Angel Firpo, labelled the Wild Bull of the Pampas by columnist Damon Runyon, could do as he prepared to challenge world heavyweight champion Jack Dempsey, the Manassa Mauler, for his title at the Polo Grounds in New York City. The Big Town newspapers made pretty dismal reading that Friday morning for Carlos Vega, whose daily task was to read the sporting news to Señor Firpo, who did not speak English.

'Seldom, if ever,' reported the Associated Press, 'in the history of the world heavyweight championship, will a challenger go in a

---

1   *Charleston Daily Mail* 14 September 1923

ring with less backing among experts than Luis Angel Firpo when he opposes Jack Dempsey tonight at the Polo Grounds.'[2]

'Jack Dempsey is supremely confident that he will whip Luis Firpo tonight,' wrote Frank G. Menke for the *King Features Syndicate*. 'Luis Firpo is hopeful of victory. And that difference in the mental attitude of the rival warriors seems to forecast better than anything else, the outcome of the international clash.'[3]

Menke pointed out that the people behind the Argentine were supremely confident in the fight's outcome, but they had never seen Dempsey in action. On the other hand, the champion and his handlers were certain of victory, because they had seen Firpo in action. The fighter himself admitted that he was being sent against Dempsey a bit too early; that he really needed another year of experience against first-class fighters in the United States.

'There are too many "ifs" to be overcome in doping this fight,' wrote United Press sports editor Henry L. Farrell, 'and there is too little known about how much Firpo can take and as far as that goes it has never been established how much Dempsey can take.'[4] In picking Dempsey to win inside seven or eight rounds, Farrell conceded that the longer Firpo was on his feet the better were his chances.

Universal Services syndicated columnist Damon Runyon was concerned over the drop in betting odds against Firpo, to 2/1. 'There is no reason for the change in the odds,' he wrote. 'On what the men have shown in their training camps, the odds should lengthen not shorten. Firpo should be 10/1 – 100/1 if the majority of boxing experts who have been watching the two men are correct in their views.'[5] Runyon believed that Firpo was more dangerous to Dempsey than his fellow pundits gave him credit for, but still picked the champ to win as easily as he won from Jess Willard.

In his fight preview, International News Service sports editor Davis J. Walsh wrote of 'the heavyweight championship meeting tonight between Jack Dempsey, as vindictive in action as a jungle tiger and every inch a champion, and Luis Angel Firpo, a human grizzly capable of all the savagery of his primitive forebears. The bout

---

2   *Oakland Tribune* 14 September 1923
3   *Steubenville Herald Star* 14 September 1923
4   *Eau Claire Leader*, Wisconsin 14 September 1923
5   *Davenport Democrat and Leader* 12 September 1923

is scheduled to go fifteen rounds but few look for such an ending and none hope for it.'[6]

Current and former ring champions were given space on the sports pages to forecast the outcome of the fight. Former heavyweight champion James J. Jeffries didn't waste words, saying, 'Dempsey will stop Firpo in a few rounds.' Another former champion, 42-year-old Jess Willard, who had the unfortunate distinction of being stopped by both Dempsey and Firpo, penned a syndicated series of articles with NEA sports editor Harry Bradbury.

'The Dempsey–Firpo fight will be a slugging match with the result a toss-up,' Jess stated. 'A grizzly bear will rip into a gorilla. A pile-driver will crash against a buzz-saw. They talk about the wallop in Dempsey's punches, but I want to tell you that Firpo hits the hardest. I know.'[7]

The old boxing master Jack Britton, former welterweight champion, believed Dempsey a certain winner over Firpo. 'Dempsey will win inside of three rounds,' he declared. 'Firpo has nothing but a right hand swing. Dempsey is a two-handed fighter who can hit harder with either hand than Firpo can with his right. Dempsey has forgotten more than Firpo will ever know. The Argentine will be nothing but a chopping block.'[8]

World lightweight champion Benny Leonard was also dismissive of the South American's chances. In a series for the North American Newspaper Alliance, Leonard picked Dempsey to knock out Luis Firpo inside of five rounds. 'If an Army mule were in a match with Zev, our champion three-year-old, would you bet on the former?' asked Benny. 'Then don't bet on Firpo…I liken Firpo to an Army mule because he has got the kick of one, but not the speed of Zev, which is Dempsey.'[9]

Having said that, the 135lb Leonard travelled a few rounds with the 216lb Firpo in the privacy of the challenger's living quarters in Atlantic City and admitted the Argentine was better than he had shown in his public training drills. 'He showed me that he had a good left, as well as a right. He hit shorter and cleaner with it.' But Benny still couldn't see him surviving against Dempsey. 'I would not be surprised if it ended in a round or two,' he wrote.[10]

---

6   *Logansport Pharos Tribune*, Indiana 14 September 1923
7   *The Lima News*, Ohio 3 September 1923
8   *Cumberland Evening Times* 14 September 1923
9   *Bridgeport Telegram* 13 September 1923
10 *Oakland Tribune* 11 September 1923

There was a glimmer of hope for Firpo from the old-time lightweight champ, Jack McAuliffe. One of the few undefeated champions in boxing history (42 bouts) the 57-year-old McAuliffe had been assigned by United Press to cover the fight. The veteran saw enough to predict Dempsey's downfall, writing from Firpo's camp, 'There is no doubt about it – Dempsey is on his way. Sporting writers might just as well get out the champion's obituary because next Friday night there is going to be a new heavyweight king. From what I saw at Saratoga watching Dempsey do his stuff, I should say this South American is a certain winner.'[11]

In Los Angeles, where Dempsey had made his home, his Hollywood friends were with him all the way. Movie actress Mary Pickford told United Press, 'Dempsey will win but Firpo is courageous in coming to a strange land and almost reaching the top.'

Husband Douglas Fairbanks saw his pal winning with ease, saying, 'Dempsey ought to knock Firpo through the ropes by the third round.'

Charlie Chaplin, 'the Little Tramp, was for the champ. 'Dempsey will win but I'd sure like to see Firpo in action.'[12]

From Buenos Aires, Firpo's hometown, AP reported, 'If Argentina's 9,000,000 inhabitants could influence with their thoughts or good wishes the result of tonight's battle at the Polo Grounds, Luis Firpo would surely come home with the heavyweight championship of the world.'[13]

Even the sensational news of the uprising in Spain ran second on the front pages of the newspapers with the dispatches from New York being more eagerly and widely read than the bulletins from Madrid and Barcelona. United Press correspondent Miles W. Vaughn wrote, 'There probably will be a lot of candles burned before the shrines of a lot of saints and a lot of prayers said in a lot of Spanish and Portugeze dialects all the way from Panama to Punta Arenas and the Amazon to Terra Del Fuego, for all South America wants Luis Angel to win.'[14]

Firpo's big-fight strategy was actually being planned in Buenos Aires by Señor Felix Bunge, his backer and mentor. He said that he would announce what he had in mind after the fight, together with the plan of combat which Firpo will follow, a plan which Horatio

11 *Oshkosh Daily Northwestern* 12 September 1923
12 *Daily Globe*, Ironwood, Michigan 14 September 1923
13 *Oakland Tribune* 12 September 1923
14 *Oakland Tribune* 13 September 1923

Lavalle, Firpo's manager, took with him when he left for New York. According to Bunge, the plan has been shown by Lavalle to Benny Leonard who gave it his hearty approval. 'I sent Firpo his final message today,' Bunge added. 'It was a message of encouragement and a caution not to forget to keep himself covered. I await the good news of his triumph in all confidence.'[15]

When INS sports editor Davis J. Walsh wrote that into his column, he added, 'Laugh, now, and show your ignorance.'[16]

A couple of days before the big fight, columnist Bob Dorman was at Firpo's camp while Carlos Vega, the fighter's friend and interpreter, was reading an article by a leading sportswriter in which the fight with Dempsey was called a farce on account of Firpo's supposed weakness on defence. Turning to Vega, Luis said, 'So Señor Dempsey will cut me to pieces. Look at my face carefully. Look at my ears. Do you see any scars? Are my ears what you call cauliflower? No? Perhaps Luis' face does not take the full force of those blows. Perhaps his face is moving away when they land.'[17]

Fight promoter Tex Rickard, playing down the negative forecasts of the gentlemen of the press, announced, 'I look for a slashing fight with the odds of victory about even…Dempsey may have advantages in speed, experience and generalship, but he is not the superman that a lot of critics would make him seem. He will have the hardest fight he has ever had to keep the championship.'[18]

Rickard, the old-time Yukon gambler, had won every gamble with rain in his career as a fight promoter but he was still prepared, should inclement weather change his luck for Dempsey–Firpo on Friday, to hold the fight on Saturday. He had more immediate worries a couple of days before the fight, reported in the press under headlines of 'BOGUS TICKETS FOR BIG FIGHT'. The article read, 'Six men were arrested in a Duane Street print shop and police confiscated $50,000 worth of counterfeit tickets for the Dempsey–Firpo title match Friday night. Some of the tickets, police said, had been put in circulation. The men were charged with acting in concert in printing and distributing them.'[19]

15 *Syracuse Herald* 13 September 1923
16 *Ogden Standard Examiner* 12 September 1923
17 *Bridgeport Telegram* 14 September 1923
18 *Evening Independent*, Massillon, Ohio 13 September 1923
19 *Steubenville Herald Star* 14 September 1923

Rickard announced that another shop had been raided and plates confiscated before the alleged counterfeiters had had time to start printing. The tickets printed were of $5.50 and $27.50 and Rickard said they bore resemblance to the originals down to the minutest of details.

Another thorn in the side of the promoter had been the application of heavyweight contender Harry Wills for a temporary injunction against the big fight. Wills charged that he had been unjustly discriminated against by the New York State Athletic Commission and that his challenge to Dempsey more than a year ago had been ignored, but the court ruled that he had put forward no basis for interference with the forthcoming bout. Wills alleged that a contract he signed with Dempsey shortly after filing his challenge gave him a prior right to oppose the champion, but the court pointed out that this agreement left either principal to engage any other opponent in the meantime. 'The threatened legal entanglements were brushed aside in Supreme Court today when Justice Hagarty denied the application.'[20]

However, with that threat removed at least for the time being, a bigger crisis reared its ugly head early on the Friday afternoon when Jack Dempsey and Luis Angel Firpo attended the official weigh-in at the offices of the State Athletic Commission in the Flatiron Building at Madison Square. The estimated crowd of 5,000 milling around the entrance, eager to catch a glimpse of the fighters, was blissfully unaware of the drama about to unfold upstairs.

Dempsey weighed heavier than at any time in his championship career, the scale settling at 192.5lb. Firpo had not put in an appearance by the time Jack stepped off the scale and got dressed. He was given a tremendous ovation when he left the building behind a troop of policemen who wedged an aisle through the crowd for him.

Firpo had arrived half an hour late, wearing a broad grin as the crowd cheered him. Stripped and on the scale, he made the indicator tremble at 216.5lb, 24 more than the champion. He stepped over to be measured, his height being officially recorded as 6ft 2.5in, one inch taller than Dempsey.

What happened next was recalled by *Ring* magazine publisher Nat Fleischer in his 1958 book *Fifty Years at Ringside*. 'Dr William A. Walker was at the weigh-in to examine the rivals. William Muldoon, Chairman of the Commission, objected to the presence

---

20 Nat Fleischer *Fifty Years at Ringside* (New York: Fleet Publishing Corporation 1958) pp.122–124

of newspapermen in the room, but after considerable persuasion, he permitted Jimmy Dawson of the *New York Times* and myself to remain.

'Dr Walker, while placing the stethoscope over Firpo's chest, accidentally bumped into the challenger's left arm. Instinctively, Luis threw the arm upwards. Thinking this a queer reaction, the doctor ran his fingers over every part of the arm, squeezing it here and there as he tested for a fracture. Firpo was smiling as Doc Walker's probing fingers reached his elbow, but under the smile were lines of pain.

'Muldoon called Rickard over. "What's the trouble?" inquired Tex. Walker tapped Firpo's elbow. "This," he said. Rickard turned pale… His face grew ever grimmer as he heard Doc Walker say to Muldoon, "Firpo seems to have a dislocated fracture of the left arm." Firpo, who spoke no English, burst into a torrent of Spanish.

'The challenger laughed and said he was all right. Muldoon thought otherwise. Firpo waved his arms violently. And then he screeched in Spanish, "I can beat Dempsey. It is nothing." Then, as if to prove it, this man of iron courage raised his left arm and brought his fist down upon the table. The doctor was horrified, for he knew, more than the rest of us, how terrible the agony of that gesture must have been.

'But Firpo, with gritted teeth and a wild look in his eyes, smiled. Then Tex's hard shell of calm left him…He swore at Firpo in Spanish, threatening him with God knows what. Muldoon laid a restraining hand on Rickard, saying, "Tex, I'll see what we can do. From my examination, I think it's a simple dislocation without a break." Muldoon asked Firpo to put out his left arm, and when he did, suddenly jerked it forward, snapping the bone back into position.

'That, to me, was the moment when Luis proved his absolute gameness. Firpo, with the arm tightly bandaged, remained in the doctor's care for the next few hours. The swelling was reduced, but when it came time for Luis to go into the ring, I knew that he was in agony with every movement of his arm.'[21]

Although Fleischer didn't mention the incident in his 1949 book *The Heavyweight Championship,* he recalled the episode in a March 1962 issue of his *Ring* magazine stating that there was another newspaperman in the room at the time, Dan Lyons of the *New York Globe.* Yet in an article attributed to Firpo which appeared in the December 1931 issue of *Ring,* the fighter stated that, 'The only

---

21   *Ogden Standard Examiner* 14 September 1923

persons in that room at that time were Mister Muldoon and Tex Rickard besides the doctor and myself. "Mister Rickard," I remarked. "I will fight tonight provided you will get me a return contest." "I'll do that, Luis. You'll surely get it if you're licked tonight. I'll tell the newspapers about the arm after the fight."'

When Firpo did emerge from the building later that afternoon, the crowds were still there and they gave him a great cheer. Some citizens gave him something else. It was learned later from his secretary what the process servers were aiming at when they changed his smile into a frown as he appeared on the street. 'They had waited along with the crowds and, as he stepped on to the sidewalk, they tipped their hats and made him a present of a batch of papers which he took smilingly. He did not know they were process servers until they had run so far no one could catch them.'[22]

An interpreter said the papers were warrants for $54,206.25 against the reported $160,000 Luis was to receive for fighting Jack Dempsey. They were served for Andrew D. McCorkindale who asserted that he managed Firpo in previous fights and was to manage him during his stay in the United States. Similar warrants were also served to promoter Tex Rickard.

On that Friday in September, Tex Rickard had other things on his mind. He had a million-dollar promotion unfolding at the Polo Grounds where he had arranged seating for 90,374 persons. Early in the afternoon, the crowd waiting outside the arena was nearly large enough to take all of the 5,000 $3.30 seats that would be available at 4.30pm when the gates would be opened. However, when the ticket wagon opened for business, there were only 3,500 pasteboards available and suddenly there were 20,000 wildly excited fans wanting them.

The wagon was overturned and a line of mounted policemen had to charge in wielding their clubs. Reserves were quickly sent for and a fire engine turned up, hoses were quickly plugged in, and Associated Press reported the prospect of a cold shower in the chilly air was more effective than the threat of the policemen's clubs. Order was restored after half an hour.

It seemed as though the entire population of the city wanted to see this fight. Police were kept busy when a riot broke out on the viaduct approaching the Polo Grounds. Several hundred fans attempted

---

to break through the police lines but were dispersed after a lively encounter in which clubs were used freely. Lines were tightened after this episode and none without tickets were allowed within several blocks of the arena.

A dispatch out of New York reported, '"One-Eyed" Connelly and other famed gate crashers will be up against it when they try to edge into the Dempsey–Firpo fight at the Polo Grounds tonight. Several hundred patrolmen will see that there is no disturbance and that no one without a ticket passes the cordon they established at 4 o'clock outside the grounds.'[23]

It wouldn't be a world title fight without the world champion gatecrasher, James Leo 'One-Eyed' Connelly, a native of Lowell, Mass. The jovial Irishman spent his life travelling coast to coast, attending the great sports events of the day without ever buying a ticket. He was on first-name terms with all the boxing celebrities and sportswriters, known to Tex Rickard, Jack Dempsey, Damon Runyon and a host of others, not to mention the 'dicks' and 'fly-cops' of the nation.

Billy Hamilton of the *Boston Herald* was settling into his press seat at the Polo Grounds ready to cover the Dempsey–Firpo fight when Connelly appeared at his elbow. 'I carried in a trunk for a ticket taker,' he explained, 'and then took one of the newspaper guy's coat down to the ringside.'[24]

Former heavyweight champion Jess Willard had a hard time getting into the arena, arriving at 9.00pm after a 45-minute wait to get to the gate. He should have followed Connelly.

'By seven o'clock the horseshoe, topped with its ring of American flags, was fairly well filled…Bare-armed workmen, apparently careless of the chilliness, stretched the three strings of white rope taut around the ring. Two sombre workmen dropped some great chunks of resin into the canvassed floor and then ground them to powder with their heels.'[25]

At half past seven, the lights were turned on in the stands, and shortly afterwards the great battery of 1,000-watt lamps, 36 white and four blue, to give a scientifically blended synthetic daylight, flooded the ringside. Half an hour later, the first preliminary fighters stepped into the ring.

---

23   *Salt Lake Tribune* 15 September 1923
24   *Lowell Sun*, Mass. 15 September 1923
25   *New York Times* 15 September 1923

The first bout was over before the fighters had a chance to warm up as English heavyweight Dan Bright flattened Leo Brown of Australia with a swinging right to the jaw, just 58 seconds after the opening bell. That woke the crowd up and they cheered when Charley Nashert, a Jersey City light-heavyweight, dumped Frankie Koebele on the canvas twice before taking the judge's decision. The Brooklyn fighter had been soaking up Firpo's heavy right hands in sparring and he could have done without the aggravation.

Mike Burke of Greenwich Village battered Al Roberts of Staten Island into defeat in the third preliminary of six rounds. Roberts absorbed terrific punishment about the head and was barely able to keep his feet in the last round as, bloody and groggy, he reeled about the ring under a fusillade of blows. There was disappointment in the crowd with the non-appearance of Gene Tunney in the semi-final bout of 12 rounds. The American light-heavyweight champion, matched against Leo Gates, a Mohawk Indian living in Harlem, was forced to withdraw because of an old injury to his right hand.

Bartley Madden of the West Side was brought in to meet Gates and proved too strong for Leo who took a pounding throughout. By the time the final round commenced, the fans had lost interest, one reason being the arrival at ringside of Luis Angel Firpo, escorted by a posse of policemen. He wore his checkered bathrobe of purple and yellow, a heavy stubble covering his chin. Behind Luis came the portly figure of his rubber, Dan Washington, closely followed by Horatio Lavalle, the wealthy Argentine sportsman who had been his right-hand man during training, Hughie Gartland, one of his business representatives, and Guillermo Widmer.

Before Firpo left his dressing room, Carlos Vega read to him a dispatch out of Buenos Aires that brought a smile to his grim countenance. 'After a frog fishing expedition into the swamps near the city, Enrique Firpo, father of the South American champion, returned to his home this morning and started the day by praying for his gladiator son…"Dempsey will not last four rounds with my boy," he said later, and refused to comment any further.'[26]

It was 9.55pm as the challenger reached the ring, where the last round of the Madden–Gates fight was ticking towards the final bell. A spectator in the first row gave up his seat to Firpo. A couple of minutes later he took his own seat, in the south-eastern corner of the ring.

---

26 Charleston Daily Mail 13 September 1923

Then a tremendous wave of sound gave birth in the upper tiers of the stands and rolled down over the vast crowd to engulf the ringside as the champion came into the ring, dressed in white silk trunks with a new white sweater. Smiling, he crossed quickly to Firpo's corner and shook hands with the man he had never seen before. Firpo touched gloves but he didn't smile and Dempsey crossed to his corner, sat down and an army blanket was draped over his knees. With the champion were Doc Kearns, trainer Jerry Luvardis, and stablemate Joe Benjamin.

Both fighters were photographed with their handlers before returning to their corners and announcer Joe Humphreys called for quiet as he introduced the judges, Billy McPartland and George Partrich, and the referee, Johnny Gallagher. The weights of the fighters were announced – Dempsey 192.5lb, Firpo 216.5lb. Then Humphreys got Dempsey to his feet, proudly proclaiming, 'The champion of champions, our own champion, Jack Dempsey!'

As the applause died down, Humphreys introduced, 'The pugilistic marvel of Argentina, the recognised champion of all South America, Luis Angel Firpo!' There was polite applause from the crowd anxious for the first clang of the bell. Referee Gallagher called the fighters to the centre of the ring for their instructions at precisely four minutes past ten, New York time. The Battle of the Century was about to begin.

2

The Journey Begins

IT was a long road from the Argentine Pampas to the Polo Grounds in New York City. The road began in the industrial city of Junin in Buenos Aires province, and for Luis Angel Firpo it began on 11 October 1894 when he was born to Italian-Spanish parents. His father, a native of Genoa, Italy, emigrated to the Argentine as a young man. Enrique Firpo was small in stature, but his wife, born of Spanish parents in the Argentine, was of much larger build and it was from her that young Luis inherited his physique.

The size of the Firpo family was variously reported as being three, four and five siblings. In his 2006 book *The Heavyweights,* Bob Mee states that Firpo was 'the son of an Italian father and Argentine mother who took their family of four children to the capital city when Luis was nine'.[27]

In an April 1922 interview with sportswriter Bob Dorman, Luis is quoted as saying, 'My family objected at first to my becoming a pugilist, but my success won them over. My four brothers have become regular fight fans.'[28]

An Associated Press story in September 1923 reported, 'The mother died several years ago leaving an older brother and a younger sister, besides Luis.'[29]

In a Henry L. Farrell column dated 13 October 1923, Firpo is quoted as saying, 'My mother is not a noblewoman. We are just

27   Bob Mee *The Heavyweights* (Stroud UK: Tempus Publishing Ltd 2006) p. 96
28   Bob Dorman *Iowa City Press Citizen* 22 April 1922
29   *Sioux City Journal* 2 September 1923

common stock.'[30] His statement implied his mother was alive at that time.

Aged 13, Luis already stood six feet tall. At school he devoted much of his leisure time to athletics, showing a natural aptitude and physical qualifications. But it was boxing that grabbed the young man's attention, as he related to Bob Dorman early in 1922. 'I was going to college when Harry Wills, Sam Langford, and other American fighters came to Buenos Aires to give boxing exhibitions. I went to most of the bouts and became so enthusiastic that I couldn't stay out of the game. I have been in some thirty fights in my own country, twenty of which I won by knockouts. There is no future there for a fighter. Here in the United States are all the champions.'[31]

A few weeks before he was due to fight Dempsey, a news dispatch out of Buenos Aires told of, 'The days when this giant of the Argentine had built himself a shack which he called a gymnasium and spent long hours each day at a bag…all he would say was, "I am doing all this so that one day I shall bring to the Argentine the fighting championship of the world."'[32]

Felipe Zunga, a trainer of Chilean boxers who gave Firpo his first lessons, recalled, 'This man was made for boxing. He was made for it not only physically but morally and intellectually. Firpo is docile and when a suggestion is made to him he accepts it and puts it into practice. Moreover he possesses tranquillity which is not often seen in boxers.'[33]

When Firpo first made his way to America in 1922 he couldn't speak English, and some of the newspaper hacks looking for a story made it up as they went along. Luis was said to have worked as a cowboy, store clerk, butcher, and brickmaker. They wrote of the young giant, born in near poverty and reared in near poverty, practically unknown beyond his immediate family circle, the brickyard where he had laboured and the chemist store where he served, not as a druggist but as a porter.

Some press agent stories said that Firpo was the son of a wealthy railroad builder and a Cantilonean noblewoman. United Press sports editor Henry L. Farrell was on hand when the fighter himself explained to a writer, 'My father is a railroad builder, but he builds

30   Henry L. Farrell *The Daily Clintonian*, Indiana 13 October 1923
31   *Lowell Sun*, Mass. 27 April 1922
32   *Emporia Gazette*, Kansas 1 September 1923
33   *Boston Evening Globe* 8 May 1922

with a pick and shovel.' He also ridiculed a story circulated by the New York correspondent of the Buenos Aires newspaper *La Nacion* that he walked across the Andes mountains in the middle of winter to box in an amateur tournament. 'I rode across the mountains,' said Firpo, 'and the only discomfort I suffered was from the lack of food as I had little money and a very great appetite.'[34]

Global contractor Jim Tuck was a tremendous fight fan who knew everybody in the fight game. In a magazine article, he wrote, 'Firpo was not a *pampero* but a city boy. Far from being a *gaucho* Firpo actually toiled at the extremely prosaic profession of clerking in a drugstore before he abandoned prescription-filling for pugilism.'[35]

'Before turning to pugilism,' reported Associated Press, 'Firpo had a variety of occupations, doing odd work as a stevedore for some time. He also earned a little as a boot black and had another job as a bottle-washer in a drugstore.'[36]

It was all honest toil and kept the brawny young man out of trouble but it was not what he wanted to do – he wanted to be a fighter. 'After college,' he said, 'I took lessons in boxing and finally entered the ring as a professional. I am half-Italian, half-Spanish. I never heard of that combination in the ring before.'[37]

The raw power encased in Firpo's big right hand was first unleashed in the professional ring on 10 December 1917, just two months after his 23rd birthday, at the Internacional Boxing Club in Buenos Aires in a ten-round bout against Frank Hagney. From Sydney, Australia, Hagney was 33 years old, ten years older than the local boy, and had several sporting careers on his résumé. He was a champion cyclist and renowned sculler, one of the best in the world. His ring career was something else.

In a recorded nine fights the Aussie would lose eight of them, seven by knockout, but if there was something fragile about his chin there was nothing wrong with his heart. First time out he faced Canadian Arthur Pelkey, who had boxed 27 times against men like Tommy Burns, Gunboat Smith, Sam McVey, Jess Willard, and Luther McCarty. He drew with Burns, the former world heavyweight champion and he fought the giant Willard before he won the title from Jack Johnson. Luther McCarty died after being knocked out in the

34   Henry L. Farrell *The Daily Clintonian* 13 October 1923
35   Jim Tuck *Boxing & Wrestling* January 1969
36   *Sioux City Journal* 2 September 1923
37   *Iowa City Press Citizen* 22 April 1922

first round by Pelkey. No disgrace then for Hagney being knocked out by the Canadian.

Frank was in Havana for his second fight, facing fellow Australian Colin Bell who had won 34 of his 47 bouts. Hagney was in Cuba as sparring partner to world heavyweight champion Jack Johnson who was preparing to defend his title against Jess Willard. He was beaten in four rounds by Bell who had fought a 15-round draw with the redoubtable Sam Langford and gone 20 rounds with Joe Jeanette, another feared black fighter.

A few months later Hagney was in the United States where he earned $115 being knocked out inside three rounds by Larry Williams. The Aussie was knocked out in one round by Al Reich who had been a sparring partner to Jack Dempsey. 'A clout on the chin brought slumber and when Frank was brought out of his coma he was resting on the rubbing table in his dressing room. His first question was, "When is my bout with Reich going to start?"'[38]

A couple of weeks later Hagney was bounced off the canvas again, this time by Charley Weinert. Frank was saved by the bell in round one and the Newark heavyweight wasted no time in ending the bout in round two. A 39-fight veteran, Weinert had fought men like Gunboat Smith, Battling Levinsky and Jack Dillon.

So when Frank Hagney was selected as Luis Firpo's first ring opponent two weeks before Christmas 1917 he looked a safe bet for the young Argentinian…knocked out in each of his five fights. But the Aussie had to be happy facing a novice after the guys he had been in with, and the sparring he had done in his travels with heavyweight champion Jack Johnson stood him in good stead against Luis Angel Firpo. He was able to avoid the kid's heavy-handed rights after sampling a few but his spoiling tactics brought an end to the contest in round six when it was declared No Contest.[39]

Disaster struck the young Firpo in his next fight, in January 1918, when he travelled to Montevideo in Uruguay for a ten-round bout with local hero Angel Rodriguez at the Teatro Casino. Born Angel Daniel Rodriguez Caridad on 21 July 1891, Angel would lose only one of 50 contests in a 15-year career and would rack up a staggering

---

38 *The Portsmouth Herald* 22 January 1916
39 On *Wikipedia* website result changed to a win for Firpo. In Nat Fleischer's *Ring Record Books* 1957, 1961, 1965, 1972, 1978 the Hagney bout is not listed in Firpo's fight record. It is shown as a No Decision bout in record of Firpo and Hagney on *BoxRec.com* also on *CyberBoxingZone*.

44 knockouts. He had won the light-heavyweight championship of Uruguay, knocked out the Argentine claimant to the title and beaten William Daly in a contest for the vacant South American title. Going against Firpo, Rodriguez was unbeaten in 25 bouts, all but one inside the distance.

The Argentinian had all the physical advantages; a massive 50lb in weight, 4.5in in height and three years younger. He towered over Rodriguez when referee Federico Siepcke called them together for round one. But once the bell rang it was Rodriguez who towered over Firpo, his accurate thudding punches putting Luis on the canvas four times. When he staggered to his feet for the fourth time it was too late. Señor Siepcke had signalled the knockout before the first round had run its course. It was a chastened Luis Angel Firpo who made his way home to Buenos Aires.

In September 1923, as Firpo prepared to challenge Jack Dempsey for his world heavyweight title in New York, an Associated Press dispatch from Buenos Aires made interesting reading in newspapers across the country. Angel Rodriguez, holder of the South American light-heavyweight title, was visiting the Argentine capital and he recalled his fight with Firpo, saying, 'I honestly believe that this knockout was the key to Firpo's success. Instead of being discouraged, as many young boxers might have been, he was all the more determined. He realised that he did not know how to box and from that moment proceeded to learn.'[40]

The learning process began in September 1918, eight months after the Rodriguez disaster, and it began away from home, across the Andes Mountains in Chile, the longest country in the world, running 2,700 miles down the western coast of South America. Chillan is some 232 miles south of Santiago, the capital, and that was where Luis Angel Firpo began to rebuild his fledgling boxing career. Opponent William Daly was a native of Chile with only three fights on his dance card, spread over eight years.

On New Year's Day 1910 he dropped a ten-round decision to Adolfo Morales in Santiago. When they boxed a rematch 21 months later, Daly hammered his man to a knockout in round sixteen. Morales hadn't fought since their first meeting and he never fought again, dying of his injuries later that night. The tragedy affected Daly and he didn't step into a ring again until September 1917, six years later.

---

40 *Sandusky Register* 11 September 1923

With a 1-1 record he had somehow qualified for a contest against the unbeaten Uruguayan fighter Angel Rodriguez for the vacant South American light-heavyweight title. Rodriguez brought a résumé to the ring of 24 straight wins, all but one inside the distance. He got rid of Daly in round three to claim the title.

One year later, Daly stepped into the ring to face Luis Angel Firpo, the boy wonder from Buenos Aires. Firpo outweighed his man some 40 pounds and in round seven of a ten-round bout he outpunched Daly to rack up his first knockout.

Six weeks on, Firpo was in Santiago to fight Ignacio Sepulveda ten rounds for a purse of $80. It was Sepulveda's first bout and Firpo convinced him that he was in the wrong line of work. A thudding right to the jaw saw Ignacio back in the dressing room halfway through the second round, hanging up his gloves with the rest of his gear. He never fought again. A few weeks later, the Santiago promoter matched Firpo with Calvin Respress, a travelling American from Macon, Georgia, who for a time had been trainer to world champion Jack Johnson. After four fights Calvin was still looking for a win, and he didn't get it against the big Argentinian, being disqualified in round two.

A couple of months later, in February 1919, they were back in the Santiago ring and this time Respress used his ring smarts to stay clear of Firpo's heavier punch and at the end of 15 rounds he was still on his feet, but Luis Angel Firpo had his fourth victory. Calvin liked the look of Luis and agreed to teach him a few things. They journeyed to Montevideo where Firpo's big punches sent Fernando Priano off to the showers in round four. Two weeks later in the same ring, American Arthur Manning was dispatched with a right to the jaw in round three.

The opposition was poor but Luis was knocking them over and with six straight wins he was being noticed. In Santiago, he was booked to meet Dave Mills over 15 rounds for the vacant South American heavyweight championship on 1 November 1919. From Oakland, California, the 33-year-old American had a 5-6-6 pro record and had tangled with guys like Big Bill Tate, John Lester Johnson and veteran Sam Langford. He was too-ring wise for Firpo and took the decision and the title.

Four months later, Firpo regrouped in the coastal town of Valparaiso where he had a date with a Spanish heavyweight named Andre Balsa. Back home, Andre had gone into the bullring with a cape and a sword but decided it was healthier to go into a boxing ring with gloves on his fists. It was somewhat ironic that Balsa would face the man who would become renowned as *El Toro Salvaje de las Pampas*, 'The Wild Bull of the Pampas'. Andre should have gone into the ring against Firpo with a sword in his hand, but they tied gloves on his hands and he was cut down by Firpo's heavy right hand in round six.

The Santiago promoter made Dave Mills an attractive offer to defend his South American heavyweight title against Firpo and the Californian readily accepted. Having boxed the big Argentinian off for 15 rounds in their first fight to win the decision, he was confident that he could do it again. He couldn't. Dave was 34 and nearing the end of his career, Firpo was 25 and coming on strong. He came on so strong in the opening round that day in April 1920 that Mills didn't last three minutes. The winner by knockout in round one and new heavyweight champion of South America, Luis Angel Firpo. It was time to go home.

The good citizens of Buenos Aires turned out in force to welcome their new hero, greeting his train at the railroad depot, following the car as he rode through the flag-bedecked streets to his home for a joyous family reunion. A few weeks later they packed the Club Universitario and raised the roof with their cheers as Luis destroyed Antonio Jirsa inside the first round with a blasting right hand to the jaw.

The June 1920 issue of the Argentine sports magazine *El Grafico* carried his photograph on the cover, proclaiming 'LUIS ANGEL FIRPO, ARGENTINO, CAMPEON SUR AMERICA'.

After a ten-round outing with novice Alberto Coleman of Chile in Mendoza, Firpo agreed to give Dave Mills a rubber match with his heavyweight title on the line. They met at the Club Universitario in Buenos Aires on 11 December 1920 and Firpo kicked off the Christmas festivities a couple of weeks early as the local citizenry celebrated his crushing one-round defeat of Mills to send the American into retirement.

In the spring of 1921, Firpo's name was being linked with that of 'Gunboat' Smith, and his followers, especially American and English residents of the Argentine, reckoned the big boy was stepping out of his league. They knew Ed 'Gunboat' Smith was an Irish-American heavyweight from Philadelphia who came by his nickname from his shipmates in the United States Navy who likened his size 11 feet to gunboats.

Now he was 34 years old, and vastly experienced against the leading heavyweights in the world, guys like Jack Dempsey, Jess

Willard, Frank Moran, Georges Carpentier, and Harry Greb. In March of 1921, the Gunner was facing retirement with 139 fights under his belt, but he still figured to be too much fighter for Firpo.

Undaunted, Luis made the journey across to Chile to Valparaiso, where the fight was to be held. Next day, the people of Buenos Aires rejoiced at the shock news bulletins that told of Firpo's victory by a decision over 12 rounds. Still unbelieving, the Anglo-Saxon contingent called for a rematch to be held in Buenos Aires. They had to see this with their own eyes.

A few weeks later they jammed the Club Universitario to see the fight. Firpo was cheered to the rafters when he entered the ring. Minutes later, Smith made his way to the ring and climbed through the ropes, waving to the crowd as he walked to his corner. In that crowd were quite a few fans who had seen Gunboat Smith fight before.

'Gosh!' they gasped when they saw this scrapper introduced under his name. 'That ain't Gunboat Smith.' He was as black as the ace of spades! 'You've forgotten how he looked,' suggested others, to whom the original Smith was unknown. 'Well, the last time we saw him he was white,' answered the doubtful ones.[41]

He is in the book as Black Gunboat Smith and when he faced Firpo that April day in Buenos Aires he had won eight of his 16 fights and been in with guys like Jeff Clark and Kid Norfolk. He was a native of Barbados but was a resident of Panama, a smart boxer with a good left hand and a solid right cross. In their first fight he had taken the Argentine big man the full 12 rounds and this time around he was doing okay.

But Firpo was stronger and bigger and he kept bulling his way in and by the final round Smith was exhausted. Firpo shoulder-charged him into a corner, then unloaded a powerful right hand that sent Smith crashing to the floor, out cold. He was out for ten minutes before coming out of the fog. Back on his feet, he walked over to Firpo and congratulated him. 'You're a good fighter,' he said. 'You're wasting your time down here.'

Those few words of encouragement from the guy he had just knocked out stuck with Firpo, and, after ending the brief career of Fernando Priano with a two-round demolition job in Tucuman, Luis Angel Firpo began entertaining thoughts of conquering North America the way he had south of the equator.

---

41   Charles P. Stewart *The News Palladium* Benton Harbor, Michigan 10 August 1923

Jack Dempsey was the heavyweight champion of the world and Firpo read of the purses he was earning; $27,500 beating Jess Willard for the title in 1919; $100,000 for knocking out Bill Brennan in New York in 1920; $300,000 for beating Carpentier in July 1921, boxing's first million-dollar gate. The big boy from Buenos Aires liked those numbers. He recalled Smith's words to him – 'You're wasting your time down here.'

By January of 1922, his mind was made up. He was 27 years old and in four years as a professional fighter he had won 13 of 17 fights, ten by knockout. He was the heavyweight champion of South America. It was time. Passport clutched in his massive right fist, he walked into the United States Consulate in Buenos Aires and applied for a visa. He was going to New York City to fight Jack Dempsey and win the world heavyweight championship for his beloved Argentina.

3

Runyon's Wild Bull Of The Pampas

THE arrival in the United States of South American heavyweight boxing champion Luis Angel Firpo hardly merited a single line of type in the country's most obscure newspaper. It was a non-event. Yet just a few months later, in the spring of 1922, his name was in the sports pages of every newspaper in the land. It made a good story, even if the boys with the pencils told it in a different way.

'Meet Luis Angel Firpo, a giant from the Argentine who would like to meet Jack Dempsey,' ran a paragraph in one paper. 'He stands 6ft 3.5in in height, is husky otherwise, and has seen 25 summers. Firpo claims to have scored 26 knockouts in 30 fights in three years fighting in South America. Cal Respress, former Negro heavyweight and for a time trainer of Jack Johnson, has Firpo in tow. He says he's the goods, of course.'[42]

Some of the big guns of the sporting pages, such as Damon Runyon and United Press sports editor Henry L. Farrell, went along with the Cinderella story of the South American giant. 'One of the features of the story of Luis Angel Firpo,' wrote Runyon, 'is that he came to the United States penniless, friendless and forlorn.'[43]

---

42   *Iowa City Press-Citizen* 25 March 1922
43   Damon Runyon *Davenport Democrat & Leader* 24 March 1924

Farrell would write in February of 1923, 'Just a year ago, Firpo slipped into New York from the Argentine looking for a meal. He thought he could fight...Firpo wasn't known then. He couldn't get matches and his money was low, so he had to train in a cellar.'[44]

In a magazine article years later, Hal Henessey described Firpo as standing on the steerage deck of the ship that had brought him to the Unites States as being, 'over six feet tall and weighing 215 pounds, his black hair was shaggy and uncut, it curled down over a tall celluloid collar that squeezed his 17-inch neck.'[45]

In March of 1924 a somewhat belated letter arrived on Runyon's New York desk from former Philadelphia promoter Fred Douglas, who was then running a gym in Brooklyn. 'Firpo was in this country six months before the time the writers say he arrived here,' claimed Douglas. 'He came to this country as guest of the captain of the *Southern Cross*.'[46]

Douglas related how Firpo was brought to his Philadelphia gym in a limousine accompanied by two captains of ships that sailed between the United States and South America. The big fellow had plenty of money at his disposal and had drafts on several local banks. Talking to Firpo through an interpreter, Douglas found him well educated and was impressed with his ability in the gym. Luis said he had received instruction from a big Chicago heavyweight, Frank Childs or George Byers, he couldn't remember which.

Douglas contacted local sportswriter Dick Kain, telling him he had Dempsey's next opponent in his gym, and he told former light-heavyweight champion Philadelphia Jack O'Brien and manager Leo Flynn that he had a big fellow 'who could make Bill Brennan jump out a window!'

Douglas also claimed that while Firpo was at his gym he received an offer of $1,000 to go to Chicago and sign a contract.

A somewhat different tale came in a news agency report that had former Firpo opponent Calvin Respress convincing the fighter he was wasting his time in South America and that his future was in New York. 'The matter of getting together passage money for the two of them was not easy, but they landed here just the same to seek their fortune...Firpo became acquainted with a New York business man

---

44   Henry L. Farrell *Mexia Evening News* 5 February 1923
45   Hal Henessey *Boxing Illustrated* November 1960
46   *Davenport Democrat & Leader* 24 March 1924

who lived in Nutley, New Jersey, and through that connection wound up in Newark boxing circles.'[47]

Firpo and Respress were at the Laurel Gardens in Newark one night watching the fights when they got into conversation with Robertson Ward, a local leather manufacturer. As Firpo spoke no English, Respress told Ward that Firpo was anxious to begin training and asked if he knew somewhere that wouldn't cost any money 'since the problem of eating was becoming serious'.

Ward directed them to an old roadhouse near his leather plant where a few fighters had knocked a gym together and were working out there. Firpo was soon into a strenuous training routine with guys like Young Bob Fitzsimmons and middleweight Eddie Nugent. They soon found out what Luis had in his right hand and finally prevailed upon Firpo not to try to kill them every time they sparred. But if Firpo didn't throw that right hand, he looked pretty bad.

Not being known to the Jersey promoters, Luis couldn't get any bouts. Respress, because of his colour and lack of connections, was unable to convince the club owners that they had the next heavyweight champion in their midst. So Robertson Ward stepped in again and arranged for Firpo to be seen by Nick Kline, who ran the Broad AC in Newark. Kline was not too keen even when Ward offered to pay him $200 to put Firpo on one of his cards.

The promoter agreed to watch Firpo training, telling Ward, 'Just because you want to pay for the chance, Firpo must have something.'

Kline worked with Harry Blaufuss and Babe Culnan putting fights on at the Laurel Gardens in Newark. But when Blaufuss and Culnan expressed no interest in 'the big bum' Nick went ahead anyway. He was attracted by the novelty of a South American heavyweight and promised Luis $125 for a bout on his next show. The big fellow was so delighted he took Kline in a bear hug that almost broke a couple of ribs.

Kline lined up local heavyweight Sailor Tom Maxted to test Firpo, the date 20 March 1922. The Sailor was giving Firpo 30lb but he had a gimmick. Across his broad back Maxted had a graveyard tattoo with rows of crosses cut in from his shoulders to his hips. Just before the opening bell, he would turn his back so that his opponent got an eyeful of the graveyard scenery. Maxted reckoned it never failed to affect the other guy's nerves and he had sunk his last two opponents without trace to prove his point. That night in the Laurel Gardens,

---

47   *Bridgeport Telegram* 20 January 1923

Señor Luis Angel Firpo was not impressed with Maxted's artwork. He had a brawl on his hands for a few rounds as Maxted sailed into him with all guns firing.

But by the end of round six the Sailor was out of ammunition. As round seven opened, Firpo tore into his man with both hands and after 65 seconds a thunderous right exploded in Maxted's face and he went down and out. Luis Angel Firpo had arrived in America.

Local newspapermen who saw and reported the fight weren't very kind to the new kid on the block. They said he had two left feet, floundered all over the place, was pot-bellied and had a baseball bat. But Firpo had one friend at ringside that night. Al Mayer was foreign correspondent in New York for *La Nacion*, Argentina's leading newspaper. The stuff he sent to the paper was usually high-brow; polo matches at Meadowbrook and Davis Cup tennis matches at Forest Hills. Boxing was not high on the agenda.

'Then one day I received a cable from my editor,' recalled Mayer. 'It said that a big guy named Luis Angel Firpo was on his way to New York. "Make him boxing champion of the world, it will boost circulation," the cable read.'[48]

'For his match with Maxted,' said Mayer, 'we installed special leased telegraphic wires direct to Broad Street main cable office. A special wire was rigged up from Buenos Aires to the Editor's desk so he could follow the fight and write up the story. We cabled thousands of words that night...at 50 cents a word!'[49]

That March night in 1922, Buenos Aires was hit by Firpo fever. Crowds of people gathered at the *La Nacion* building, blocking traffic. Police reinforcements were hastily summoned but could do little as the excitement mounted with each bulletin. When news of the knockout was flashed to the waiting throng, they paraded through the streets shouting and singing and for many the party was still going strong when dawn streaked the morning sky.

The Maxted fight revealed several things about Luis Angel Firpo. As a fighter he was something of a rough diamond; wild and unorthodox, but he had a punch in his right hand like a sledgehammer. When it landed, the other guy usually lost interest. A knockout.

Firpo not only had a big punch, he had a big appetite. An enormous appetite. A local butcher had promised him a 7lb steak

---

48   Al Mayer *Boxing & Wrestling* July 1957
49   Al Mayer *Boxing & Wrestling* June 1953

if he could beat Sailor Maxted. After the fight Luis insisted that the butcher, who had been a ringside spectator, open his shop and cut him his steak. He took it home with him to 135th Street in Manhattan, where he lived and did his own cooking.

Al Mayer would recall taking Firpo to lunch one day at a restaurant on 47th Street, owned by John Perona, who would later become owner of Manhattan's famous El Morocco. Mayer had invited newsmen and photographers to watch Luis demolish a mountain of spaghetti covered by dozens of meatballs. The pictures were published in newspapers coast to coast.

Robertson Ward had arranged the Maxted fight after seeing Firpo down two large bowls of soup, a loaf of bread, 4lb of rare steak, a whole apple pie, ice cream and four pints of milk. With his food bill hitting $40 a week, Ward made a quick decision, 'Young man, it's time you went to work!'

Then there was Luis Firpo the businessman. Nick Kline, who promoted Firpo's fight with Maxted, would recall, 'Firpo made two demands for that fight. He asked for $125, I gave it to him. He also asked for the moving picture rights. That gave me a laugh. Movies of an Argentine dub against the third-rater Maxted! But Luis wanted the rights, and he got them.'[50]

Firpo negotiated a price of $175 to have his American debut recorded on film, which he sold to a distribution company in Buenos Aires for a sum reported as $25,000 plus 40 per cent of the gross receipts. It was shown wherever a silver screen or a blank white wall could be found and the people flocked to see Firpo's sensational knockout of Sailor Maxted. One overzealous publicity man even billed Maxted as 'the heavyweight champion of the world, the man who knocked out Dempsey.'

In April 1923, in a news item out of New York, 'Luis Angel Firpo was made defendant in a suit for $50,000 filed by Thomas A. (Sailor) Maxted who was defeated by Firpo…Maxted declared that motion pictures had been taken of the bout without his consent, and that Firpo had been enriched from their exhibition in New York and abroad.'[51]

Maxted told the court that Firpo promised him a share of the receipts, which Luis denied, saying, 'I promised him nothing. The films were made at my expense. You can't profit from an investment

50 *Steubenville Herald-Star* Ohio 27 July 1923
51 *Ogden Standard Examiner* 26 April 1923

without investing.'[52] But Maxted had a case as decreed by the Supreme Court and Firpo was pressed for settlement. Luis never did like parting with money and it was later believed that Tex Rickard, once he realised Firpo's potential, settled out of court with Maxted.

Two weeks after the Maxted knockout, Nick Kline matched Firpo with local heavyweight Joe McCann back at the Laurel Gardens in Newark. This time Luis asked for a guarantee of $1,250 but the promoter compromised on $1,000. By this time Firpo had a bona-fide trainer and a good one at that. Little Jimmy De Forest had trained Dempsey for his title victory over the giant Jess Willard, now he was training a giant who hoped one day to fight Dempsey for the title.

'I was asked to go over to Jersey and look over a heavyweight prospect,' De Forest recalled. 'I had looked over a million prospects but I went over anyway and found Firpo working out in a cellar with a big black boxer. It didn't take more than a glance to tell that he had a lot of stuff and I consented to take him over.'[53]

In his preview of the fight, Sparrow McGann wrote, 'Joseph McCann is the man who will provide Luis Firpo with a chance to climb the second rung of the ladder to fame. McCann, after a workout in a Newark gym today, announced that he fully intended to shove Firpo off the dock. Certainly he walloped his sparring partner, Hughie Cartland, good and properly.'[54]

After looking McCann over, the writer visited the gym where Firpo was training under the supervision of Jimmy De Forest and was impressed with the big man's improvement since the Maxted fight. Firpo showed a stiff left jab while his powerful right uppercut was not nearly so crude as it was a week ago.

There was a story that De Forest had received an offer of $10,000 a year to bring Firpo into championship form but that he countered with a gambler's proposition. The proposition was that De Forest work for no set sum but that when his man began to go against the good fighters he should share in the purse. De Forest told McGann that Firpo had as much power in his fist and arms as the champion, but of course he didn't yet know how to apply all his power. De Forest said that his job was to teach Firpo, just as he showed Dempsey how to take advantage of the muscular development of his forearms. He had taken about ten pounds off Firpo who now weighed 220lb, and hoped

52   Stanley Weston *Boxing & Wrestling* April 1956
53   *Waukesha Daily Freeman* Wisconsin 31 May 1922
54   *Ogden Standard Examiner* 2 April 1922

to bring him down to 210, taking most of the weight off his legs. That Tuesday night in Newark, sports columnist 'Fair Play' was ringside to report, 'In putting away Joe McCann, Firpo did a workmanlike bit of work. Joseph Albert, a third rater, is no setup and he has a hard wallop. More than that he has a concrete jaw and very seldom has taken the count.'[55]

Going in with Firpo, McCann carried a record of ten fights, only one defeat and seven knockouts. 'In the third round, he crashed a right to Luis's jaw that would have knocked out almost anybody else. Firpo tried to grab McCann, and partly succeeded, but he went down to his knees. McCann thought he had his man, but he was fooled, for the big fellow got to an upright position before a count was taken on him. He held on for a moment to clear his head momentarily and then set sail for McCann. All his Latin fury was aroused and he fought hard from that time on. McCann was doomed.'[56]

Firpo's victory over McCann was the signal for another celebration in Buenos Aires. Reporting from there, a United Press correspondent sent the following back to New York City: 'Nobody doubts that the Spanish language is a fine thing for serenades, but it never was meant for prize-fighting lingo. The newspapers play him [Firpo] up alongside the German conference and the national elections. They devote whole columns to him, but the poor editors are having a terrible time doing it.

'When Firpo put McCann out at the end of the fifth round lately, one newspaper's translators got out all the dictionaries in the shop and achieved the following, "First round: The two adversaries abandon their corners with decided gestures and fall on guard. Some feints are produced. Firpo appears decided to handle matters with prudence, at least during the initial moments as if before resolving with respect to the tactics to adopt, he desired to study his adversary…McCann enters violently with a right placing a good swing on the jaw. It does not seem that Firpo has felt greatly the violence of the blow, but it cannot be doubted that this has been really hard since at the lips of the South American champion there hangs a drop of blood.

'"The Finish: Towards the end of the round [fifth] things acquire an aspect still worse for the champion of New Jersey. Energetic always, Firpo forces the combat. McCann tries to shear off the blows of his

55 'Fair Play' *Decatur Review* 5 April 1922
56 *Salt Lake Tribune* 16 April 1922

adversary by making a play with his legs that does not neutralise except in the smallest degree the blows...Firpo places a series of violent hooks from right and left to the jaw and McCann doubles up finally and slowly spreads out over the ring. In the midst of deafening shouting, in which the people, standing, acclaim Firpo the conqueror, the referee begins to count, but after a few seconds there is heard in the vast hall the sound of the bell that announces the termination of the round. The seconds of McCann take charge of caring for him immediately, trying to make him react, but it is visible that the champion of New Jersey is already done for.'"[57]

Firpo was a big rough fellow and his fights with Maxted and McCann prompted the New Jersey boxing commission to announce that they had banned the rabbit punch as well as the kidney punch since Firpo used the rabbit punch on Joe McCann and Sailor Maxted and laid them up temporarily.

'Firpo has this punch down to perfection,' wrote 'Roundy' in his column for the *Capital Times*. 'With his six foot six [sic] he is well able to use this Dempsey punch. Take it from me, this punch is a crippling one. Jess Willard, when he was training for Dempsey, used it a lot on his sparring partners and intended to use it for the first time in the ring against Dempsey. But Jess, one day about a week ahead of the fight, used it on his sparring partners. Jim Savage, one of them, got dangerously sick after Jess cracked him with it a couple of times, and Jess got scared to death and cut out the punch right there for good.'[58]

Willard, the giant cowboy, had already caused the death of one opponent, as Nat Fleischer recorded in his 1949 book *The Heavyweight Championship*. On 22 August 1913 he met Bull Young at Vernon, California. 'On this occasion,' wrote Fleischer, 'Willard, spurred by the reflection that his career was at stake, fought with unusual venom and such deadly effect that Young was knocked unconscious in the eleventh round. The loser remained in a state of coma. It was impossible to revive him, and he died after an emergency operation.

'Willard was arrested on a manslaughter charge and promptly exonerated. But he brooded greatly over this tragic accident, and there is no doubt that for a while he was more cautious than ever when in action.'[59]

---

57 *Waukesha Daily Freeman* 13 May 1922
58 'Roundy' *Capital Times* Madison, Wisconsin 16 May 1922
59 Nat Fleischer *The Heavyweight Championship* (New York: G.P. Putnam's Sons 1949) p.161

An Associated Press dispatch reported, 'Luis Firpo's pugilistic success in the United States has had the effect of making him a national hero in his native Argentina. Music stores in Buenos Aires are advertising tangos composed in his honor and shop windows everywhere are displaying photographs of Firpo and Jack Dempsey surrounded by exhibits of boxing gloves, punching bags and other paraphernalia of the fistic art.

'The aristocratic Jockey Club and a number of other organisations have cabled Firpo congratulating him on his victory over Joe McCann Tuesday night in Newark. One newspaper yesterday published a cartoon representing Firpo in the act of knocking over the dozen top stories of the Woolworth Building. Not more than ten years ago boxing in Argentina was an unknown sport.'[60]

Former heavyweight champions James J. Corbett and Jack Johnson tagged on to this exciting new fighter who was beginning to make headlines. Johnson, still fighting at 44, won a 15-round decision over Pat Lester in the Mexican town of Nogales. Immediately after the fight, Johnson announced that he would accept a challenge delivered at the ringside by a representative of Firpo for a fight between himself and Firpo.

Corbett quite fancied himself a newspaper columnist. Why not, the name was still good. In an April 1922 column, Corbett wrote, 'A dozen men connected with pugilism tried to grab off Firpo and manage him. But Luis said that he could do all the managing himself. Then a few promoters tried to stick him in with Fred Fulton. But Luis again showed real shrewdness by ducking that sort of fight. "Fulton may not be as great as he was, but just the same," said Luis through an interpreter. "I do not think I have had enough experience yet to fight him."

'Firpo, in the opinion of those who have seen him in action, is a good looking prospect, but he has a great many things still to learn. He is very weak when involved in infighting, he is rather slow in thinking out plans, and he has only rudimentary science. But he can hit – that's one thing that everybody agrees upon.'[61]

Firpo was ready and willing to fight for Nick Kline again in Newark. When he knocked out Sailor Maxted, he had asked Kline for a three-bout deal. He hammered McCann for a purse of $1,000

---

60   *Reno Evening Gazette* 7 April 1922
61   James J. Corbett *Fort Wayne Journal Gazette* 16 April 1922

and when a fight against Italian Jack Herman was proposed to the Argentinian, he offered the match to Kline. The promoter was not attracted to the match and shook his head. So Luis Angel Firpo prepared for his debut in the big time. Dave Driscoll, matchmaker for Ebbets Field, home of the Brooklyn Dodgers, announced that he would hold his first open air show on the afternoon of Saturday 13 May 1922. Firpo would meet Italian Jack Herman of Newark in one of the star bouts over 12 rounds.

'Though Firpo got his real start in New Jersey,' reported the *Bridgeport Telegram*, 'he seems to be on the point of deserting that state because of the referees he has encountered in the two fights in which he has engaged in this country. Luis' apparent lack of decision at times, especially in the clinches or coming out of them, is due, he says, to his fear of having a foul called on him, and it interferes with his work. He says he could have knocked out both Sailor Maxted and Joe McCann much earlier if he were confident of the referee.'[62]

Born in Italy on New Year's Day 1898, Herman's real name was Emilio Buttafochi. The family moved to America and when he signed for the Firpo fight, Italian Jack was living in Yonkers, New York. Aged 25, he had won two and lost four of his six pro bouts. A boxer rather than a fighter, Herman would be giving Firpo 25lb.

According to a report in the *Boston Evening Globe,* 'Luis Angel Firpo is torn between two emotions as his elbows bounce the punching bag at Young Bob Fitzsimmons' gym at Nutley, New Jersey, in preparation for his bout with Jack Herman in Brooklyn next Saturday. One is to return to South America as the hero the home folks think he is, but isn't; the other is to stay in the United States and be that hero.'[63]

Firpo stayed for the Herman bout anyway. From ringside Norman E. Brown reported, 'The Rip Van Winkle punch. That might be the name to the deadly blow that Luis Firpo, Argentine heavyweight sensation, packs in his hairy arms. The other day he added prestige to his name by knocking out Jack Herman in the fifth round at Ebbets Field, Brooklyn, and hit Herman so hard that Jack was dead to the world for fifteen minutes before he regained consciousness. Many ring fans believed him to be really deceased.

'As Luis climbed into the ring against Jack he would have made a perfect study for a painting of "The Primitive Man". His black hair

---

62 *Bridgeport Telegram* 12 April 1922
63 *Boston Evening Globe* 8 May 1922

fell over his forehead. His face was covered with a short stubble of beard. His chest and arms were covered with a heavy growth of hair. And when he swung into action! He struck from any and all angles with pile-driving force. He bored in like an angry bull, head low and bellowing. He used the rabbit punch, barred in most ring circles, not because he wanted to violate the rules of ring etiquette but because he did not know what the rabbit punch was. He knew only that he could beat a man down by striking him at the top of the spine with a hooked blow.

'That Herman stood up as long as he did under the cave-man tactics of Firpo was a marvel to ringsiders. Then Firpo, seeking another way to drive at Herman, drove a right from the hip up, a terrific uppercut. It caught Herman on the jaw with the crunching thud of a battle axe and Herman dropped like a barrel of tar. Firpo did not know when the blow started that it was due to connect. It was one of scores of terrific punches that he had let go with the same intent, of knocking his man cold. But it did the job. As mentioned before Herman had a beautiful nap of fifteen minutes.'[64]

Another report stated that Herman 'forgot to duck in the fifth. A Firpo right landed on his jaw, then a left sent to the inside found the point of his chin. He was raised a foot off the floor and landed flat on his back…When he woke up he asked, "Was anybody else hurt?"'[65]

The *Boston Daily Globe* correspondent observed, 'Firpo seemed bewildered for a moment, the blow was so sudden. It was not until the referee announced he was the victor that he smiled. The fight which was Firpo's all the way, was watched by a crowd of about 10,000, made up largely of residents of New York's Spanish colony.'[66]

Firpo was very pleased with his end of the purse, $3,000. Trainer Jimmy De Forest was not so pleased when he learned later, 'that some of the South Americans in New York had told Firpo that De Forest was a friend of Dempsey's and was being paid by the world champion to teach him the wrong way to fight. "He didn't have a thing to learn about the wrong way," De Forest said.'[67]

'When I found this out, I refused to go farther with him,' said Jimmy, 'but I promised the Argentine consul that I would work in the corner whenever he fought. When he knocked out Jack Herman

64 Norman E. Brown *Ada Evening News* Oklahoma 18 May 1922
65 *Benton Harbor News Palladium* 31 August 1923
66 *Boston Daily Globe* 14 May 1922
67 Henry L. Farrell *Dunkirk Evening Adviser* 23 August 1922

recently, one of his South American friends approached me and asked what I thought about him. I told him I knew Firpo was a good prospect and I could make something out of him if they turned him over to me. He said, "Ah, but you are a friend of Dempsey's."[68]

For Luis Angel Firpo, it was time to go home. The *New York Times* on 1 June 1922 informed its readers that the South American heavyweight champion 'sailed yesterday on the steamship *Southern Cross* for his home in Buenos Aires. Firpo took with him the winnings of three prize fights and several motion pictures, a five-foot secretary and two sparring partners.

'His secretary, Samuel Cerda, said that the word Firpo used most was "tomorrow" and that with this word he held off the promoters who have been trailing him ever since he reached the United States. Firpo said he would return here in four months.'

By the time Luis Angel sailed out of New York harbour, the big names on the press bench were already finding him a suitable subject for their columns. Damon Runyon had christened Firpo the 'Wild Bull of the Pampas' although an article in *Ring* in June 1957 credits veteran boxing writer Hype Igoe as being the first to hang the tag on Firpo. Grantland Rice wrote, 'The main reason that Luis Firpo is taken seriously in some boxing circles is his possession of the punch. The South American can sock. And only a socker of top proportions is going to halt Dempsey at any soon date. Most of them have hit him but they haven't hurt him much.

'Some of Firpo's friends might take a portion of that $450,000 they have offered for a Dempsey fight to engage some man like Jack O'Brien for a year's instruction. Then Firpo might have a chance. It would be a good investment, or at least a good gamble. And it is remarkable how much more important South America would be to a great many if it harbored the world's heavyweight champion.'[69]

After the Herman fight, writer-satirist William O. McGeehan wrote, 'He is not ready to go against even moderately good heavyweights, but suggests much power. He is an unharnessed pugilistic Niagara. There is in that right hand enough drive to drop Dempsey. There is suggested in the way he moves enough speed to make a splendid boxer.'[70]

68   *Waukesha Daily Freeman* 31 May 1922
69   Grantland Rice *Boston Sunday Globe* 28 May 1922
70   William O. McGeehan *Boxing Illustrated* November 1960

4

Tex Finds Another Jeffries

THE dispatch from Montevideo on 19 June 1922 stated, 'Luis Angel Firpo, heavyweight pugilistic champion of South America, arrived here Saturday from the United States…Deep appreciation of the reception given him by the American people was expressed by the fighter when he landed. Firpo said he had signed a contract to meet the winner of the forthcoming bout between Joe Beckett and Frank Moran. The battle will take place in London, he said, but the time has not as yet been determined. He added that he had made arrangements with a promoter to meet an unnamed opponent in Havana, probably in October.'[71]

From the Uruguayan capital, Firpo continued the journey to his beloved Buenos Aires, 125 miles across the estuary of the Rio de la Plata, the River Plate, the world's widest river. When he reached the city, his mighty chest swelled with pride at the rapturous welcome that awaited him. Men, women and children thronged the streets and the wide boulevards, cheering and chanting his name, fighting their way to the front in the hope that they may be able to touch him as he passed in an open touring car. He waved his great fist and his normally grim expression broke into a wide toothy grin.

This was so different from that day a few months ago when a few friends saw him board the ship that would take him to the New

---

71   *Greenfield Daily Recorder Gazette* 19 June 1922

World, their best wishes laced with words of caution about those slick hucksters who ran the fight game around New York City. Their fears were unfounded as Luis Angel Firpo blasted his way to three knockout victories and, for him, a small fortune, close to $5,000. 'There is a surprising amount of silent work going on to get control of the South American's affairs,' the *Bridgeport Telegram* had reported, 'but he still insists on doing his own business through an interpreter.'[72]

In his brief sojourn in the United States, Luis Firpo had demonstrated that he was a rough, tough fighter with a punch like a runaway locomotive, that he possessed a gargantuan appetite, and that he had a way with a dollar, a peso or any other form of legal tender. In his syndicated column, United Press sports editor Henry L. Farrell quoted the *Buenos Aires Standard*, an English language newspaper, 'The fight game in Argentina is sure booming now, thanks in no small degree to Firpo's mighty (?) achievements. Firpo has been having a glorious time since he returned to Argentina. They've been presenting him with illuminated parchments, gold watches, medals about the size of dinner plates and they've even gone so far as to pour champagne into his innards.

'Lots of fellows who made the trip back on the ship with Firpo are terribly peeved with "Lu". They almost killed the giant with kindness and, naturally enough, expected that Firpo's gratitude would be expressed in golden dollars for parties at the end of the trip. Luisito, however, stalked off the ship without unloading a ruddy dime. We figure that if Lu doesn't manage to capture the heavyweight title, he's at least certain to become a magnate.'[73]

Included in Firpo's entourage on that return journey was a black heavyweight named Charles Ware, also known as William Ware and in the fight game as 'Rough-House' Ware. From New Orleans, Ware started fighting in 1912, losing more than he won. But he did fight for the Panamanian heavyweight title three times in 1915 and for the colored light-heavyweight title against Lee Anderson in 1921. 'Ware, a dusky gym fighter,' wrote Farrell, 'will furnish evidence if anyone doubts that Firpo is thrifty.

'Ware was engaged to go to Argentina to act as Firpo's sparring partner. Thinking that a peso was worth about five dollars, Rough-House thought that he had stumbled into Paradise when Firpo offered

72 *Bridgeport Telegram* 12 April 1922
73 Henry L. Farrell *Dunkirk Evening Adviser* New York 23 August 1922

him fifty pesos a month for his end. He nearly starved when he found that a peso was worth about fifty cents.'[74]

Some of the game's top managers tried to sign Firpo to a contract but soon found themselves out on the sidewalk shaking their heads. The little Frenchman Francois Descamps had put Carpentier in the championship ring with Dempsey only to see his beloved Georges destroyed inside four rounds. This new kid from the Argentine looked a better proposition, he was bigger than Dempsey and he could punch. Monsieur Descamps presented Luis with a new Packard automobile and hand-made suits which the fighter gratefully accepted. But when a contract was waved under his nose, Luis shook his head. Descamps flew into a rage and called Firpo 'a rapacious monster, undeserving of life.'

'William A Brady, a theatrical producer who had also had an important hand in the affairs of James J Corbett, Bob Fitzsimmons and James J Jeffries, called on Firpo one day and spread out his credentials like a line of Fuller brushes,' wrote John Lardner in his 1947 book *White Hopes and Other Tigers*. 'He spoke of Corbett, Fitzsimmons and Jeffries, and the success that those champions had enjoyed under his care. Firpo, a student of boxing history as well as of money, though of almost nothing else, had called his secretary from the stove where he was cooking beans, to interpret. After considering Brady's statement, Firpo said, "Fitzsimmons is dead, Jeffries has no money, Corbett is all through." The reply was translated for Brady, and the interview came to an end.'[75]

Luis Angel, still an eligible bachelor, was living as a guest in the home of one of the richest men in South America, a magnificent mansion in the city suburbs surrounded by extensive grounds. His every need was catered for; Buenos Aires was an open city for him, yet he took no part in the throbbing nightlife of the city. He was in bed by 10pm. He was the most popular man in the country next to the president, but he was a fighter, and his people wanted to see him fight. Firpo used his popularity to obtain a permit from the Argentine government for a boxing match with Jim Tracey to be held in Buenos Aires on 8 October 1922.

As usual with Firpo, it was business before boxing. He sold the permit for $25,000 to Señor Augusti, a former bank clerk who would

---

74   Henry L. Farrell *Iowa City Press Citizen* 23 August 1922
75   John Lardner *White Hopes and Other Tigers* (Philadelphia: J.B. Lippincott Co. 1947) p.141

be promoting his first fight. Associated Press reported, 'Great interest is being evinced in the coming 15-round bout between Luis Angel Firpo and Jim Tracey, the Australian. The men will fight on the afternoon of 8 October in a huge open-air amphitheater which is now under construction. No referee has yet been selected but the man who will act in this capacity will speak English as well as Spanish. If Firpo should win this bout, promoter Augusti plans to bring to the Argentine Bill Brennan or some other American fighter to meet him.'[76]

To whet their appetite, Firpo delighted his fans by appearing in a four-round exhibition bout in the city with Joe Boykin, an American heavyweight from Dallas who had travelled south with Firpo as one of his sparring partners. Joe had boxed a few times in Philadelphia and New York before joining the Argentine strongman and he made sure Luis looked good before his adoring fans.

They flocked to his training sessions which were held in downtown Buenos Aires and Luis charged them 20 cents for admission, making regular announcements that he would bring the world championship to Argentina. He did his roadwork late in the afternoon when the boulevards were crowded and on that Sunday afternoon in October some 20,000 of them jammed into the arena to see him fight the Australian.

Sportswriter Jack Keene wrote, 'Luis Firpo, who hits like a steam hammer, is slated to meet the Australian heavy Jim Tracey in Luis' homeland of Argentina. Tracey must have lost all desire to live, if this be so.'[77]

Aged 25, Tracey was born in South Africa but grew up in Sydney, Australia, where he started fighting in 1914. In 1916 he beat George Cook over 20 rounds but was stopped by Colin Bell. In May 1922, he made his United States debut at Madison Square Garden against perennial contender Bill Brennan. In what one newspaper recorded as an awkwardly-fought match that had fans laughing all the way, Brennan landed a left-right combination in a neutral corner to stop Tracey in round eight.

Now Tracey was in Buenos Aires to fight Luis Angel Firpo. With a professional record of ten wins, ten defeats and two draws, Jim had been fighting at light-heavyweight and, although the same height, was

76 *Ogden Standard Examiner* 27 September 1922
77 Jack Keene *Olean Evening Herald* New York 5 June 1922

probably some 30lb lighter than the local hero. Tracey had impressed in training, though hardly enough to worry Firpo's fans.

An Associated Press reporter cabled from the Buenos Aires ringside, 'Luis Angel Firpo, heavyweight champion of South America, this afternoon knocked out Jim Tracey, the Australian fighter, in the fourth round. There was practically an even give-and-take in the first two rounds. Firpo's superior strength and punching ability showed in the third round, in which he had considerable advantage. In the fourth he landed a hard right and left to the head, and Tracey went to the floor, where he remained until the count of nine. He was badly dazed when he got to his feet again. A terrific right to the jaw knocked him out. About twenty thousand persons saw the fight.'[78]

A follow-up report the next day stated, 'Luis Angel Firpo, the big Argentine fighter who on Sunday retained his title of heavyweight champion of South America by knocking out Jim Tracey of Australia in the fourth round of what was to have been a 15-round bout, said today that he desired to return to the United States, but that he might take on several other heavyweights in Buenos Aires before making the voyage north.

'Firpo's work in the ring yesterday came as a surprise to the sporting writers and the public. The writers in their articles of today dilate on the improvement the boxer showed as compared to his skill prior to his visit to the United States. Sunday's fight has created stronger interest in boxing than had prevailed heretofore. The fine arrangements for handling the huge crowd at the arena are praised in all quarters. Neither before nor during the contest was there any confusion.'[79]

Promoter Augusti was delighted with his initial venture in the fight game although he refused to divulge any figures. George Lawrence, the manager of Tracey, said that a couple of weeks before the fight he learned that the advance sale was about $64,000. Lawrence estimated the total receipts as close to $150,000. Of this amount Tracey received little as he worked on a flat guarantee but Firpo obtained a liberal slice of the spoils. 'His share of the purse and the $25,000 he received for the permit brought his end up to a small fortune.'[80]

But if everybody was happy with the big fight in Buenos Aires, the city council was somewhat less than happy. Associated Press reported

---

78   *New York Times* 9 October 1922
79   *New York Times* 10 October 1922
80   *Salt Lake Tribune* 21 January 1923

from the city, 'Whether any more pugilistic encounters similar to that recently engaged in by Luis Angel Firpo and Jim Tracey, the Australian heavyweight, are to be permitted in Buenos Aires is a question which is engaging the attention of the local sportswriters, due to the opposition expressed at a recent meeting of the city council against special permission having been granted Firpo by which he might meet Tracey.

'Socialist members of the council said permission was granted Firpo due to misapprehension; that it was not supposed he was going to participate in a public prize fight, but would merely give an exhibition of his fistic ability. Boxing enthusiasts fear that the permission granted Firpo will be withdrawn by the council owing to the strength of the Socialists in the council, and that no more public boxing will be permitted. This will confine fights to the precincts of clubs, which has always been permitted.'[81]

A week later the news was bad. 'After a lengthy debate the city council revoked the special permission granted to Luis Angel Firpo to stage boxing exhibitions in this city. This means that there will be no more boxing bouts scheduled in Buenos Aires. The opposition to the staging of bouts in Buenos Aires came from the Socialist members of the city council according to dispatches last Thursday.'[82]

However, in an effort to save the day for the growing number of boxing enthusiasts, the Argentine Boxing Federation sent a petition to the city council asking it to annul the ordinance which prohibits prize fights from being held in public. It would appear that the ban was lifted as in February 1923 former Firpo victim Sailor Tom Maxted fought Alex Rely, billed as 'The Peruvian Brown Panther', at Avellaneda, Buenos Aires. 'Maxted claimed a broken wrist in the seventh round and the crowd of 25,000 rioted. Mounted and harbor police came to the rescue and both fighters were suspended by the Argentine Boxing Federation for what was called a sham fight.'[83]

The wave of euphoria that swept South America after the Firpo–Tracey fight did not have the same impact north of the border. A typical reaction appeared in the *Oelwein Daily Register* on 23 October 1922. 'After his four rounds victory over Jim Tracey, South Americans figure their heavyweight champion is ready for Dempsey. They have never seen Dempsey and they think that Tracey is a first class

81   *Salt Lake Tribune* 21 October 1922
82   *Bridgeport Telegram* 26 October 1922
83   *BoxRec.com* 22 February 1923

heavyweight. Americans who know the former Australian champion cannot begin to take Firpo seriously yet, when it required four rounds for Firpo to knock Tracey out.

'Tracey outpointed Firpo in the first two rounds, confirming the judgement of good American boxing critics who claim that any heavyweight who is at all clever and who packs a good punch would have no trouble beating Firpo. Firpo evidently can take it. He is built like a cave man and it would take a Wills or a Dempsey punch to put him down for the count.'

A few weeks after putting Jim Tracey to sleep, Luis Angel received an offer from New York promoter Tex Rickard for a fight with the winner of a contest between veteran Bill Brennan and Floyd Johnson, a young Iowa contender, scheduled for 12 January 1923.

On 6 December, Firpo cabled Rickard saying that he would return to New York in the near future 'ready to fight'. On 14 December, a dispatch out of Buenos Aires stated, 'Luis Firpo, South American heavyweight champion, has booked passage on the *Ebro*, sailing 10 January for the United States. He is willing to meet winner of Brennan–Johnson bout.'[84]

Firpo didn't actually leave on 10 January. It was 1 February 1923 when he embarked on the steamship *Southern Cross*, calling at Montevideo, Santo and Rio de Janeiro, stopping for a few hours at St Thomas in Barbados where Firpo would have a chance to do some roadwork before resuming his journey, scheduled to arrive in New York three days later.

By that time, the Brennan–Johnson fight had already taken place before a record crowd in excess of 14,000 at Madison Square Garden on 12 January. From Des Moines, Iowa, the 22-year-old Johnson was tagged the 'Auburn Bulldog' and brought a 27-2-7 record into the Garden ring against Brennan. The Chicago veteran, pushing 30, was having bout number 100 in a long, hard career against the best in the business. Among the ringsiders were former champions Jim Corbett, Jack Johnson and Jess Willard, who received by far the longest ovation from the crowd when introduced from the ring. Promoter Rickard liked that because he was hoping to stage a rematch between Willard and Dempsey.

Johnson won a bruising 15-round battle over an ill-conditioned Brennan, who was 10lb overweight. Wrote Davis J. Walsh from

84 *Sandusky Star Journal* 14 December 1922

ringside, 'Johnson showed such unfamiliarity with the accepted tenets of the Marquis of Queensberry's favorite pastime that it is now a matter of doubt as to whether he could acquire this knowledge in sufficient quantities to stand off a rough man like Firpo.'[85]

Watching the fight, promoter Rickard knew his plans had to change. When Firpo arrived in New York, his fight would be with the loser of the Johnson–Brennan scrap, not the winner.

The *Bridgeport Telegram* carried the following item on 16 February 1923, 'Wireless advices received by the Munson Steamship Line yesterday from the steamship *Southern Cross*, indicate that the Argentine heavyweight boxing champion is training hard on board the Munson liner, and expects to arrive in New York a week from today in excellent condition.'

'Several times in the past year he has been reported as on his way to the United States,' wrote Sparrow McGann, 'but this time he will come.'[86]

'Like "Tattered Tom", the poor hero of the paperback novel, Luis Angel Firpo is coming back to New York as somebody,' wrote UP sports editor Henry L. Farrell. 'He's a "card" at the most opportune time when the heavyweight class is coming into its greatest period of activity in years.'[87]

Luis Angel Firpo arrived in New York City on 22 February after a voyage of 21 days from Buenos Aires. He was accompanied by his secretary Alfredo Guerrieri, a sparring partner, light-heavyweight Carlos Scaglia, and an interpreter. The fighter was greeted by a party of his fellow countrymen headed by Argentine consul-general Earnest C. Perez, and he faced a battery of cameramen at the pier for more than an hour before waiting cars took the party to Madison Square Garden for a conference with promoter Rickard. He had already set the publicity wheels grinding out the news that the Firpo–Bill Brennan fight would take place at the Garden on 12 March.

Herbert A. (Hype) Igoe was 'probably the best-informed writer on boxing that ever lived', according to Damon Runyon. Igoe was in Rickard's office when Tex first laid eyes on the big man from south of the border. Tex spoke to Firpo through an interpreter, and as Luis prepared to leave, Rickard stopped him in the doorway and turned him around so he could see his back. 'I saw Tex mentally whip a

85   Davis J. Walsh *Waterloo Evening Courier* 13 January 1923
86   Sparrow McGann *Syracuse Herald* 21 January 1923
87   Henry L. Farrell *Iowa City Press Citizen* 5 February 1923

tape measure all over Firpo,' recalled Igoe. "'Hype," he said, "he and Dempsey will make the greatest fight you ever seed. [sic] He's the nearest thing to Jeffries I ever looked at. It will be the greatest fight in the world."[88]

One reason for the promoter's happiness was the fact that he had agreed with Firpo that he would box for nobody but Rickard for one year, and his first assignment would be against Bill Brennan at the Garden on 12 March. Chicago Bill had seen his best days in the ring but he was still a name and it was a step up for the big South American.

After announcing that he would begin active training at the Garden gymnasium, Firpo told the press, 'I know Brennan will give me the hardest fight I've ever had, but I'm sure I can whip him. Mister Rickard has promised me a match with Dempsey if I defeat Brennan, but I am willing to fight other contenders before meeting the champion.'[89]

Rickard stated that he regarded Firpo as the most promising of the younger heavyweight contenders and looked for him to emerge as a logical contender for the champion's crown.

'If he beats Brennan,' said Tex, 'I may match him with the winner of the Floyd Johnson–Jess Willard contest, scheduled at the Yankee Stadium on 12 May.'[90]

Rickard further stated that Firpo resembled Jim Jeffries, former heavy champion, more closely than any other fighter he had ever seen. That was high praise indeed, for Jeffries was Rickard's idol. He would argue back and forth with Hype Igoe on the merits of Jeffries and Dempsey with Hype, the sportswriter who had seen them all from the Corbett–Fitzsimmons fight, adamant that Dempsey would have beaten Jeffries and Rickard, who owed his fortune to Dempsey, still calling Jim Jeffries the strongest, greatest puncher in the game.

When Firpo started his training sessions at Max Levy's gym in Madison Square Garden, one of the first to cast a jaundiced eye over his performance was syndicated columnist Damon Runyon, who wrote, 'We went there expecting to a see a big clown. We came away with the thought that we had never seen a man who impressed us more strongly than Firpo.' Noting the comments of fight veterans on the obvious defects of Firpo's style, with which he agreed, Runyon

88   Hype Igoe *Ring* January 1931
89   *Danville Bee* Virginia 23 February 1923
90   *Twin Falls Daily News* Idaho 24 February 1923

added, 'There nonetheless came over us a feeling that this is a most formidable man.'[91]

'Leo Flynn…is convinced he made no mistake in matching his heavyweight against Luis Firpo,' recorded the *Syracuse Herald*. 'He had several scouts watching Firpo in his workouts and since then these spies have not been seen in the Garden gym. This is because Flynn is well satisfied with the reports in hand.'[92]

In the *Bridgeport Telegram*, 'Fair Play' quoted Flynn as saying that Brennan was going to upset the dope and give the South American the beating of his life. The writer agreed, stating, 'Unless Luis improves, this is precisely what he will get. Sizing up after two afternoons spent in looking him over, he may be described as a big, husky heavy-set sort of a chap…We do not see him as a contender for Dempsey's crown. Not this year anyway.'[93]

Columnist Westbrook Pegler observed, 'Scowling as though somebody had sold him the Brooklyn Bridge for cash, Luis Angel Firpo daily goes through his workouts…The Jamaica Kid was to have been Luis' sparring partner but he went away very suddenly when he saw Luis knock a punching bag into a pair of shoes, size 9E, with one blow.'[94]

One thing Firpo had going for him was the appearance of Jimmy De Forest in charge of his workouts. The veteran American trainer in the little old white cap had appeared in the ring behind Dempsey, Charley White and many other famous fighters.

De Forest told writer Sparrow McGann, 'I'll tell you the difference between Dempsey and Firpo. Jack is a natural born fighter and Firpo has to be made. I don't believe any man living can beat Jack right now, but he is at his peak and what with inactivity he will be on the downgrade within a year.'[95]

Promoter Rickard was mildly upset when he was informed of an injunction to be filed by Frank Harris, attorney for the Pioneer Athletic Club of 155 East 24th Street, claiming that his client had an agreement with Firpo for first demand on his services. Harris had failed to convince William Muldoon, chairman of the New York State Athletic Commission, of the complaint, so had applied to the courts.

---

91   Damon Runyon *San Antonio Evening News* 28 February 1923
92   *Syracuse Herald* 26 February 1923
93   'Fair Play' *Bridgeport Telegram* 28 February 1923
94   Westbrook Pegler *Galveston Daily News* 1 March 1923
95   Sparrow McGann *Ogden Standard Examiner* 24 February 1923

But the injunction was denied by Supreme Court Justice Erlanger on the grounds that the Pioneer Club had insufficient evidence to support its claim. The decision removed the last legal obstacle in the way of the Firpo–Brennan match. Luis Angel Firpo of the Argentine would meet Bill Brennan of Chicago over 15 rounds for promoter Tex Rickard at Madison Square Garden on Monday 12 March 1923.

5

Main Event At
The Garden

AS a heavyweight prizefighter, Bill Brennan was a mystery to the
media. The *BoxRec.com* website gives his real name as William
Schenck, birthplace Chicago, Illinois, hometown Louisville,
Kentucky. A *New York Times* article dated 12 December 1920 mentions
his birthplace as being County Mayo, Ireland. When he was shot
and killed in 1924, *The Atlanta Constitution* dated 15 June stated
that Brennan was born in Ireland. On 16 June, the *Chicago Herald
Examiner*'s report of his death said that Brennan was a Chicagoan, real
name Bill Shanks which was changed to Bill Brennan by manager Leo
P. Flynn. Writing in the October 1954 issue of *Boxing and Wrestling*,
Stanley Weston described Brennan as 'a big powerful fellow out of
County Mayo, Ireland'.

To further muddy the waters, Roger Kahn's 1999 book on
Dempsey stated, 'Brennan was born William Shanks in Louisville,
Kentucky and his forebears were German. When he started boxing
at the outset of World War I he changed his name; the cause of the
Kaiser was never popular in America. He came up with a fictional life
story that made him a native of County Mayo.'[96] He did in fact move
to Chicago as a young man where he became a tough street fighter.

What was indisputable was Brennan's talent. He was a hard-
punching, world-class fighter who fought 102 professional fights

---

96   Roger Kahn *A Flame of Pure Fire, Jack Dempsey and the Roaring Twenties* (New York:
      Harcourt Brace & Co. 1999) p. 215

against the best heavyweights of his generation in a decade of prizefighting. What was never disputed was the fact that he gave Jack Dempsey two of his toughest fights, in 1918 and 1920. Their first fight, in Milwaukee, had a somewhat bizarre ending, Brennan being knocked down in round six. He fell awkwardly and suffered a broken ankle yet he was still trying to stand up. But his fight was over.

A year later, Dempsey annihilated Jess Willard to become world champion, and in December of 1920 the Manassa Mauler gave Brennan a crack at the title in Madison Square Garden. He respected Brennan as a fighter and as a man, saying, 'When he was a top fellow and I was a bum, during that first trip I made to New York, he gave me work as a sparring partner, at fifty cents a day. He helped me eat and get a flop.'[97]

Dempsey was on a $100,000 guarantee while Brennan was happy to take home $30,000 for his end. He would have fought for nothing to get the chance to be world champion. He almost made it. In a terrific non-stop battle, Brennan almost knocked Dempsey out and when Jack found the knockout punch in round 12, his left ear and his title were hanging by a thread.

Back in action in January 1921, Brennan fought 18 times against second-rate opposition, although he did fight Billy Miske to a newspaper decision and he beat Bob Martin twice, Englishman Bandsman Rice and Jim Tracey. By January 1923, Des Moines heavyweight Floyd Johnson was coming up strong with 27 wins in 36 fights and they put him in with Brennan at Madison Square Garden over 15 rounds. The winner would fight Luis Angel Firpo, reportedly on his way back to New York looking for a fight with Jack Dempsey.

Johnson's victory over Brennan was decisive but not too impressive. 'Johnson proved he was a better man than an ill-conditioned Brennan, 10 pounds overweight and fighting on his nerve after the sixth round; whatever else he proved, however, was not to his credit. The Iowan is as open as Clancy's side door for a right cross and a good rugged infighter will tear him apart.'[98]

However, the man from Associated Press wrote, 'Floyd Johnson, Iowa heavyweight, loomed today as a dangerous contender for Jack Dempsey's crown...Fighting a crafty, rugged ring veteran, Johnson showed that he has all the equipment of a first class title contender. He

---

97 Jack Dempsey with Bob Considine & Bill Slocum *Massacre in the Sun* (London: William Heinemann Ltd. 1960) p. 88
98 *Chronicle Telegram* Elyria, Ohio 13 January 1923

displayed amazing footwork and boxing ability besides demonstrating that he has a real punch, and the ability to take punishment.'[99]

Off that Garden fight between the veteran Brennan and the Iowa youngster, Tex Rickard decided that the Chicago man would be the safest bet for Firpo's return to the Big Apple. He announced to the press that he regarded Firpo as 'the most promising of the young heavy-weight contenders and looked for him to emerge as a logical contender for the champion's crown. If he defeats Brennan, I may match him with the winner of the Floyd Johnson–Jess Willard contest scheduled at the Yankee Stadium on 12 May.'[100]

Trainer Jimmy De Forest was on hand to tell the press boys, 'Firpo has a terrific punch and possesses unusual possibilities as a champion contender, but he is slow and lacks defensive ability. He must correct these faults before he becomes a real challenger. I believe he can do so with the right sort of work.'[101]

De Forest wasted no time getting his protégé the right sort of work. Firpo did not go in for calisthenics, preferring to box with the big gloves and he would go from six to ten rounds every afternoon, his ring partners being compatriot Carlos Scaglia, a light-heavyweight, and Buddy Jackson, a black heavyweight from Newark who had fought Harry Wills. Visiting reporters were impressed with the big Argentine scrapper. 'Firpo,' wrote one, 'has made amazing improvement in his boxing. Firpo's fight with Brennan is only eight days distant and he is slugging away with the swiftest and most durable sparring partners that can be found for him. During the last few days he has developed almost incredibly in boxing science.'[102]

Maybe some of Jack Johnson's silky skills had rubbed off on Luis in the gym sessions they shared. The former world heavyweight champion was pushing 45 yet he handled Luis as though he were the hired help. Al Mayer figured it would be a good idea to hire Johnson and Jack was more than happy, since he was reportedly receiving $250 a day. 'Johnson played to the crowd and made Luis miss punches by a mile,' Mayer said later. 'Now and then he locked Firpo's arms in a vice-like grip and grinning, turned to the watching spectators and waited for the round of applause which he always received.'[103]

---

99   *Laurel Daily Leader* 13 January 1923
100 *Bradford Era* Penn. 23 February 1923
101 *Bridgeport Telegram* 23 February 1923
102 *Appleton Post Crescent* 7 March 1923
103 Al Mayer *Boxing & Wrestling* July 1957

In his column a few days before the Brennan fight, Henry L. Farrell wrote, 'Fighters preparing for a big bout invariably pick out soft sparring partners…Firpo picked a former champion of the world, Jack Johnson, old, but yet so good that Harry Wills will have nothing to do with him. He also picked Al Reich, who can knock out any fighter in the game.'[104]

Associated Press reported a few days before the fight, 'Up in Harlem, where Brennan did his work for this engagement, they are stringing along with Bill. The way they figure it up there is that Brennan with his superior knowledge of boxing will make Firpo look silly. Some of the Brennan followers think that Firpo will be an awful bust.'[105]

Yet Brennan's training, or lack of it, was called into question by at least two columnists in the lead-up to the battle. 'Firpo ought to win,' wrote Henry L. Farrell, 'not because age eventually falls for youth, but for a flock of reasons. Brennan is not in shape and he has not been training. Firpo is going someplace with a big project behind him, and Brennan hasn't any place to go, even if he beats Firpo.'[106]

'Brennan ought to take the Argentine behemoth without much trouble,' wrote Sparrow McGann. 'The impression has got abroad however, that Brennan is not going to win, that he will fall upon the ring floor sometime early in the bout and take the required ten-second snooze…Again there has been the feeling that Brennan hasn't been breaking his back training.'[107]

Support for Firpo came from veteran manager Dan (Dumb Dan) Morgan, who told United Press, 'He's a cinch to beat Brennan and when he learns how to box and get around a little there's no telling where's he's going.'[108]

A couple of days later, Morgan's old meal ticket Jack Britton announced that he was thinking of coming back to the ring and had indeed asked Morgan to get him some business. The former welterweight champion was one of the few prominent boxers who considered that Luis Firpo, the South American heavyweight, had any class. 'He looks good to me,' Britton said. 'He acts just like Jeffries used to, and what impresses him most with me is that he

---

104 Henry L. Farrell *Charleston Daily Mail* 11 March 1923
105 *Salt Lake Tribune* 12 March 1923
106 Henry L. Farrell *Wisconsin State Journal* 11 March 1923
107 Sparrow McGann *Salt Lake Tribune* 11 March 1923
108 *Sandusky State Journal* 8 March 1923

is not overanxious. As soon as he sharpens his punches he will be a good fighter.'[109]

The analogy with former world heavyweight champion Jim Jeffries was also used by Grantland Rice in his 'Sportlight' column.' Those who have been working with Firpo,' wrote Rice, 'look upon the South American as another young Jeffries, only a trifle stronger, heavier and a harder hitter. If Firpo picks the right people to handle his destiny, someone like De Forest, he may be the first man to take the championship south of the equator.'[110]

So on that Monday evening in March of 1923, an excited crowd of more than 12,000 paid $50,755 into the Madison Square Garden box office to see Luis Angel Firpo, the new sensation from South America, swap leather with Chicago veteran Bill Brennan over 15 rounds, or less. After watching Firpo work out, Runyon had warned, 'Bill Brennan is apt to have a tough time with Firpo when they meet.'

At the afternoon weigh-in, Firpo had scaled 220lb to 203 for Brennan. The referee appointed by the New York State Athletic Commission was Jack Appell. Coming out at the first bell, Firpo landed a left to the head but Brennan blocked the right hand. Then he was driven into a corner where Firpo landed left and right to the head before Bill fought his way out with a hard right to the body. Round two and Brennan shook Luis with a solid left to the head but the giant set up a two-fisted attack that drove the Chicago fighter into the ropes. Heavy blows to the head shook Brennan and the crowd was in an uproar at the bell.

Into round three and Brennan tried to drive Firpo back with lefts to the head but the Argentine ignored the blows and hammered heavy clubbing rights to the head, taking Bill to the ropes where he smashed home several body blows. Brennan was glad to hear the bell. As Firpo rushed from his corner for round four, Brennan halted him with two hard lefts to the head, only to be rocked to his toenails by a savage right uppercut. The South American had Brennan reeling with a series of lefts and rights to the head to take the round.

In the fifth Brennan fought back strongly, swapping rights with Luis before a right uppercut sent him back on his heels. Brennan recovered, blocking most of Firpo's swings and finding his face with strong left jabs, one of which opened a cut over Firpo's left eye. Round

109 *Waterloo Evening Courier* 10 March 1923
110 Grantland Rice *Ogden Standard Examiner* 10 March 1923

six was an action-packed three minutes as Brennan used his ring experience to have Luis swinging wildly and his punches brought the blood again from Firpo's eye. Firpo roared back with a terrific right and they stood toe to toe smashing punches from either hand at close quarters. Just before the bell a left uppercut staggered Firpo.

Observing Firpo's eye injury, Henry L. Farrell recorded, 'From the fifth on the blood poured down into his eye, down his chin and off onto his chest, making him a picture of savagery. Only a very game man could have borne up under the handicap.'[111]

In the seventh round, Firpo absorbed a hard right to the body and a thudding left to the head. He was swinging his punches now but when they landed Brennan knew about it. There was a lot of clinching as both men were feeling the pace. Jimmy De Forest sent Firpo out to finish it in the eighth round and he tried. He smashed a right to the ribs and swung lefts and rights in an effort to bring the Chicagoan down on his face.

As they backed from a clinch, Firpo sent a right to the jaw and the fans booed lustily as he went to his stool. Round nine and they slugged away at each other with the crowd going wild, Firpo's harder blows rocking Brennan's head side to side. A hard right to the jaw rocked Luis and a stiff left brought the blood flowing again from the cut over his left eye. Brennan was fired up coming out for work in round ten and solid jabs forced the South American back across the ring.

Luis missed with a couple of big swings but landed two to the body, Brennan firing back with a thudding right into the ribs and a right uppercut staggered the big fellow. Luis gesticulated in protesting Brennan's apparent butting but referee Appell waved them on. They opened round 11 at a fast pace, trading hard blows to the head before Brennan ducked a big left hook that threatened to take his head off his shoulders and buried his right hand in Firpo's ribcage. Firpo got home with a left swing but caught a hard right to the jaw at the bell.

Associated Press reported the dramatic finish in round 12, 'Firpo turned loose a battery of rights and lefts that sent Brennan staggering to the ropes. Brennan tried to duck but was caught by a right swing to the jaw. The South American leaped in like a tiger and sent Brennan crashing to the floor with another powerful right for the count.'[112]

---

111 Henry L. Farrell *Oakland Tribune* 13 March 1923
112 *Bradford Era* 13 March 1923

Brennan lay still after the round ended at the two minutes and 37 seconds mark and had to be assisted to his corner as the big South American received a terrific ovation from the crowd. Luis Angel Firpo had arrived in the Big Time!

At ringside for United Press, Henry L. Farrell observed, 'Firpo has great possibilities. He has a game heart, prodigious strength, mentality above the ordinary and everything but boxing skill. He can be taught to box when he possesses all those other qualifications. It may not be for another year or so and it may never be, but Señor Firpo is a potential champion.'[113]

Two days after the fight it was revealed that referee Jack Appell had tried to stop the bout in both the sixth and seventh rounds as Firpo struggled to hold off Brennan's attack due to the blood flowing from his damaged left eye. 'Vehement protests, however, from Jimmy De Forest, Firpo's trainer, against any such interference, and hasty instructions from William Muldoon, chairman of the State Athletic Commission, it was declared, kept Appell from ending the match.'[114]

Charges that the fight had been fixed for Firpo to win were published in two afternoon newspapers, but were blown away by the overwhelming majority of writers and critics who had watched the contest. Strong protest came from Brennan and manager Leo P. Flynn, who pointed to the fact that Brennan in 107 [sic] fights had never won or lost on a foul or had in any way been accused of throwing a contest.

'I gave the best I had,' said Brennan, 'but Firpo was too strong for me. He is a natural fighter and what he lacks in science he makes up in brute power.'[115]

That brute power saw the Chicago fighter admitted to New York's Jewish Memorial Hospital at 3am on 16 March suffering from a slight concussion. Brennan had walked around for a day and a half after the contest and visited Rickard's office to collect his purse. But when he later consulted his physician, Dr Travers, complaining of bumps above his neck and being unable to sleep because of pain, a second doctor was summoned and he ordered Bill into hospital at once.

Brennan lapsed into unconsciousness and was out for four hours. The diagnosis was concussion of the brain and an X-ray revealed no injury to the skull but there was a swelling in the region of the mastoid bone. The blow which knocked out Brennan was a right hand swing,

---

113 Henry L. Farrell *Cedar Rapids Republican* 13 March 1923
114 *The Arizona Republican* 14 March 1923
115 *The Bee,* Danville Va. 14 March 1923

landing just behind the left ear with the force of a sledgehammer. Brennan's left side was a mass of bruising and his left kidney also showed a large swelling. While in hospital, Brennan had two visits from Luis Firpo and his interpreter but they were not permitted to enter the patient's room.

The *Danville Bee* (Virginia) dated 17 March carried a headline, 'RABBIT PUNCH MAY BE OUTLAWED IN PRIZE FIGHTING'. The report from New York stated, 'Brennan was hit with what Robert Edgren christened as the occipital punch. Since then it has been successfully used by Jack Dempsey and styled the "rabbit punch". The blow is permissible, according to the present rules, but it is understood that the Boxing Commission will take steps to have it barred in this state.'

After the fight, Brennan went home with a headache. The Firpo fight should have been his last one but eight months later he travelled to Omaha to fight Billy Miske and was knocked out in four rounds. Eight months later, Bill Brennan, a week shy of his 31st birthday, was dead, gunned down in the Tia Juana Cabaret he owned at West 171st Street in the Washington Heights district of Manhattan. In those Prohibition times, it was assumed that Brennan had bought his beer from the wrong mob and paid the penalty. He left a wife and three-year-old daughter. His killer was caught, sentenced to 20 years in Sing Sing but was paroled in 1938, serving just 14 years.

After the fight, Luis Angel Firpo, with a score of friends, went from the Garden to a Greenwich Village cabaret where he tangoed and made merry until three in the morning. 'Firpo, exhibiting the famous dance as it is done in the Argentine, was the most carefree of the party. Except for a patch that covered the cut over his left eye, he showed no trace of the strenuous ring battle he had gone through.'[116]

Firpo's celebration was magnified a thousand times in Buenos Aires where it was reported, 'Firpo has become an even greater national hero with his victory over Bill Brennan Monday night. Vast crowds thronged the streets about the newspaper offices here watching the returns from the ring round by round. When the knockout was flashed the people went wild and staged a mighty parade lasting until the morning hours.'[117]

---

116 *Sioux City Journal* 23 March 1923
117 *Iowa City Press Citizen* 14 March 1923

The next day, the Argentine was in Tex Rickard's Garden office to talk future fights, with the promoter telling the press boys that Firpo would box the winner of the Jess Willard–Floyd Johnson fight scheduled for 12 May at Yankee Stadium. Firpo would also appear on the Stadium card against an opponent to be named, but the name that was put before the New York State Athletic Commission to go against the South American, Farmer Lodge, was instantly rejected by William Muldoon, the commission chairman.

Declaring that the Minneapolis heavyweight was not a suitable opponent for the South American, Muldoon ordered that either Jack Renault of Canada, Tiny Jim Herman of Omaha, or Jack McAuliffe II of Detroit be chosen to box Firpo. 'When Muldoon expressed the opinion that Renault was the logical match for Firpo, Frank Coultry, general manager of Madison Square Garden, acting in the absence of Tex Rickard, announced that he was negotiating only with McAuliffe and Herman and expected to close a match tomorrow with one of the two.'[118]

When tomorrow dawned, Jack McAuliffe II was the one to get the call, 15 rounds with Luis Angel Firpo at Yankee Stadium on 12 May, purse $7,500. The original Jack McAuliffe was called the Napoleon of the Ring and rightly so. He was one of the few fighters to retire undefeated, with a record of 42 fights, won 34, seven draws, one No Decision, and he reigned as world lightweight champion for eight years from 1886–1894.

The heavyweight McAuliffe was actually born Henry Bussineau on 9 August 1898 at Dunns Valley, Ontario. He left Algoma District aged 18 to get work in the Detroit steel mills and it was in the Motor City he was spotted by local promoter Mark Shaughnessy, who 'showed him how to hit, put the gloves on with him and soaked Jack with everything he had, and when McAuliffe took it, came back for more and then knocked his instructor out, Shaughnessy was satisfied with his nerve and his ability'.[119]

A stand-up boxer rather than a puncher, Jack nevertheless won seven of his first 12 fights by knockouts, with a decision win and four draws. An agency dispatch out of New York dated 16 April reported, 'A forfeit of $1,500 was deposited today with promoter Tex Rickard by Mark Shaughnessy, manager of Jack McAuliffe of

118 *The Findlay Morning Republican* Ohio 28 March 1923
119 *Sandusky Register* 3 March 1923

Detroit guaranteeing the boxer's appearance for his 15-round match with Luis Angel Firpo at the Yankee Stadium on 12 May. McAuliffe has been in training for some time.'[120]

When Firpo resumed training after the Brennan fight, there was a new face in the gym working alongside Jimmy De Forest. It was an old face actually, that of fistic legend Sam Langford, the renowned Boston 'Tar Baby', an uncrowned champion who Rickard chose to help the fighter he considered the future champion of the heavyweights, Luis Angel Firpo. It was said that another ring great in Tommy Ryan was also on Rickard's shortlist, but he finally chose Langford.

De Forest told the press that Firpo was one of those men who grasp new things with the utmost ease. 'Sam Langford is working out with the big fellow and everything the Tar Baby has to teach is speedily absorbed by the Argentinian. Firpo will be a real surprise to those who saw him fight Brennan when he appears in the ring 12 May.'[121]

In his syndicated column 'Sport-O-Graphs', Frank G. Menke quoted De Forest as saying that the Firpo who whipped Brennan was, in the strictest fighting sense, a crude bit of battling machinery who had nothing but a powerful physique, great strength and a swinging right hand to recommend him. 'I fully believe that if Firpo can be taught to punch straight, to deliver short hooks with his right hand and a jab hook with his left that no man in the world can stand up before him for six rounds.' Then Jimmy added, 'And that statement embraces even Dempsey himself.'[122]

Previewing the fight, Davis J. Walsh wrote, 'The Firpo–McAuliffe affair is believed to involve the moot question of whether the punch is faster than the feet, and right now the wise gamblers are trying to guess whether the Detroiter's pedic extremities are nimble enough to keep him away from Firpo's right hand punches for fifteen rounds.'[123]

On that Saturday morning in May 1923, when the ten heavyweight boxers tested the weighing machinery at Madison Square Garden, rain was falling in a heavy shower, not enough however to dampen the spirits of the fans standing in line for the one- and two-dollar seats. Rickard had already announced the advance sale had reached $250,000 and he anticipated a crowd of 70,000 filling the massive Yankee Stadium ballpark.

---

120 *New Castle News* Pa. 16 April 1923
121 *Marion Daily Star* 30 March 1923
122 Frank G. Menke *Steubenville Herald Star* 14 April 1923
123 Davis J. Walsh *New Castle News* 12 May 1923

Great interest was being shown in the return to the ring of former champion Jess Willard, aged 40 but said to be in better condition than when he lost the title to Dempsey in 1919. The giant Kansan would test the rising talent of Floyd Johnson, who had given Brennan a beating over 15 rounds. Willard and Firpo were made almost prohibitive favorites. Very little Johnson money was in sight and McAuliffe had even less. 'It was considered ominous by the sages when Mark Shaughnessy, the manager of McAuliffe, sold his contract yesterday for $10,000. Shaughnessy said McAuliffe would win but that he himself was not in the proper health to manage a heavyweight contender.'[124]

Shaughnessy sold the contract to Benny Friedman, a real estate operator in New York. The fighter was troubled by this, and according to Tom Keenan, sports editor of the *Sault Star,* 'The night he fought Firpo, he had a manager that knew nothing about boxing and a second who knew even less in his corner.'

By 3pm the morning rain had stopped and Rickard's luck was holding up...he had never lost a show to the weather. The first preliminary bout saw Englishman Harry Drake take a four-round decision over Joe McCann; Tiny Jim Herman of Omaha hammered Al Reich to a six-round knockout; Fred Fulton was disqualified in round four of a ten-round bout for fouling Jack Renault of Canada.

Firpo and McAuliffe entered the ring at 4.12pm. Referee was Jack O'Sullivan, judges Patsy Haley and Charles F Mathison. Ring announcer Joe Humphreys bawled out the weights, 212lb for Firpo against 200 exactly for McAuliffe, a heavyweight elimination contest over 15 three-minute rounds.

The clang of the timekeeper's bell broke the silence and a roar came from the crowd as the young man from Detroit carried the fight to the man from South America, a right to the body and a left hook to the jaw. Firpo smashed a right to the body and a left hook to the jaw, McAuliffe another right into the body, then a terrific right swing almost broke Jack in half. He gasped as Firpo charged in and another crushing body blow sent McAuliffe reeling back to the ropes.

Jack got on his bike and danced around Luis, tantalising left jabs finding his face, and the Argentinian was missing with many of his right swings. He clinched at close quarters but McAuliffe boxed him off with lefts to the face. Firpo was on target with a big right hand to

---

the head and McAuliffe was rocked to his heels, but he landed a hard left to the face as the round ended.

Round two and Firpo rushed from his corner and landed on McAuliffe, drawing blood from his mouth, but Jack came back with four jabs to the face to have Firpo looking bewildered, looking to his corner. McAuliffe missed a left swing and Firpo almost floored him with a heavy right to the chest. Jack was moving again and made Firpo miss with a tremendous right uppercut that threatened to take his head off.

McAuliffe had success with his jab again but a thunderous right to the body made him wish he was back in Detroit. Firpo was getting home with short rights at close range but when he opened up with left and right swings most of them hit the smoke-laden air drifting over the ring. Then a tremendous right to the jaw sent McAuliffe reeling to the canvas and Jack O'Sullivan counted to three before the bell ended the round. They got McAuliffe back to his corner but he still looked shaken coming out for round three.

'The Detroit youngster danced around the hairy-chested giant until Firpo caught him with a wild right swing in the second round and the gong saved him,' wrote Henry L. Farrell for United Press. 'Two right uppercuts, sent in with the force of a falling freight elevator dropped McAuliffe to the floor early in the third round.'[125]

The timekeeper stopped his watch at one minute and two seconds of the third round. 'Firpo stooped when the count was tolled and picked up his opponent. Gathering him in his arms like a child, he carried him to his corner and placed him, a limp mass, in his chair. Tex Rickard stopped by the press benches to say, "There's the next heavyweight champion sure as anything."'[126]

Ring Lardner, sports columnist and short-story writer best known for his satirical take on the sports world, was at ringside for Rickard's heavyweight carnival. On the Firpo–McAuliffe fight, Lardner wrote, 'Jack is too nice looking to be in the same ring with a guy like the so-called Wild Bull of the Pampas. The bull needed a shave, including his chest. Anyway when Jack woke up from his nap he wanted to know how Firpo's middle name happened to be Angel.'[127]

'Firpo's quick victory over McAuliffe was dramatic,' observed one agency reporter, 'but the triumph of the 40-year-old Willard over a

---

125 Henry L. Farrell *The Lima News* Ohio 13 May 1923
126 *Eau Claire Leader* 13 May 1923
127 Ring Lardner *Salt Lake Tribune* 13 May 1923

youngster half his age in a hammer-and-tongs struggle from start to finish was the high spot of the show.'[128]

Willard stopped Floyd Johnson at the end of round 11 after the Iowa fighter had taken the worst beating of any fighter since the days of Battling Nelson. Johnson fell on his face as the round ended and his seconds dragged him back to his stool. He could fight no more.

United Press had put Jack McAuliffe, the old undefeated lightweight champion, in a ringside seat to give his opinion on the contenders for Dempsey's crown. 'My choice is Luis Firpo,' wrote the veteran, 'the greatest natural fighter I have ever seen…I doubt very much that Dempsey with everything he has would be able to stop Firpo. Willard did make a comeback but he would last no longer with Dempsey than he did in 1919.'[129]

'Young Jack McAuliffe,' ran an item in the *Middletown Daily Herald* on 12 May, 'was picked by Jim Corbett as the next heavyweight champion. That perhaps was the jinx McAuliffe carried because Corbett never has picked a winner.'

Before the big crowd, later reported at 87,000, had left the arena, Rickard announced that Firpo and Willard would be matched in a 15-round bout to decide a championship opponent for Jack Dempsey. The fight, he said, probably would be held in Yankee Stadium on 30 June. Speaking to Associated Press, Rickard said that in his opinion Willard had staged a remarkable comeback considering the odds he was against, adding that Firpo had proved beyond a doubt that he is one of the greatest natural fighters uncovered in years.[130]

There was not a dissenting voice heard from the 9,890,000 inhabitants of Argentina. For most of them, Luis Angel Firpo was already the heavyweight champion of the world.

128 *The Galveston Daily News* 13 May 1923
129 Jack McAuliffe *The Charleston Daily Mail* 13 May 1923
130 *La Crosse Tribune & Leader-Press* 13 May 1923

6

Firpo The Giant-killer

A S a merciless sun beat down on the ring, pitched on the shores of Maumee Bay, just outside the city of Toledo, Ohio, Jess Willard sat in his corner at the end of round three as referee Ollie Pecord was informed that the world heavyweight champion could fight no more. Jack Dempsey was the winner and new champion.

Willard, the Pottawatomie Giant, had been brutally cut down by the man they called the Manassa Mauler. It was Independence Day, 4 July 1919, a day for celebration, and even as the blood dripped to the canvas from his facial injuries, Willard found an inner happiness. He never liked the fight game, now he knew he need fight no more. A broken man at the end of that savage fight, he was far from broke.

'When a journalist went to his corner in search of a fast quote, Willard was repeating over and again, softly to himself, "I have a farm in Kansas and $100,000...I have a farm in Kansas and $100,000."'[131]

A few days after the fight, the former champion was back in the bosom of his family, back home in Lawrence, Kansas, with his wife Hattie and their five children. They would stage no benefits for this ex-fighter. Jess had real estate in Los Angeles where he had an interest in the motion picture business, apartments in Chicago and oil in

---

131 Mee pp. 308–309

Texas. No longer in the fight business, his name was in the book for all time: heavyweight champion of the world from that April day in 1915 when he knocked out Jack Johnson in Havana to the Dempsey fight in July 1919. He may not have been the best but he certainly was the biggest of the heavyweight champions up to the time he met Johnson, a towering 6ft 6.25in and 238lb.

'Willard never was a great fighter,' said Jim Savage, former sparring partner of the Kansan. 'The best thing he had was size and bulk and the strength of a bullock.'[132]

In retirement, Willard immersed himself in business, becoming more and more involved in his real estate interests in California, eventually moving there with his family after selling his ranch house in Lawrence, Kansas in 1921. In 1922 he planned on opening the first ranch market in Hollywood, at the corner of Vine and Afton, and decided to finance the deal by making a comeback to the ring. That decision was arrived at after talking everything over with his beloved Hattie.

'Boxing is a man's game,' she told *The Elkhart Review*. 'I never go to a fight. When Jess fights I stay at home and I don't worry. I have perfect confidence in his strength and skill.'[133]

'Ever since that Toledo affair,' wrote Jack Keene, 'Jess has done a little light training off and on. This has kept him in good health and prevented him from becoming too fat to move, but that is all. It stands to reason that he cannot be better now than he was at Toledo.'[134]

Those who watched Willard in his workouts at Toledo saw that he was too old to train even then. He could not do much roadwork because his legs were unable to support the weight of his big body. He took long walks but running even a distance was too much for him. For that reason he could not get his bellows into shape. Willard seemed to think that there was a conspiracy to keep him from regaining his title and that sportswriters were treating him unfairly when they pointed out the folly of his attempt to come back.

That alleged conspiracy theory could have been planted in Willard's mind by manager Ray Archer, 'a peculiar sort of manager' according to one press story. 'He doesn't speak for publication and doesn't care a rap for all the sporting editors and sporting writers in the world...When he meets a newspaper man he shakes hands with

132   Frank G. Menke *Mansfield News* 2 March 1923
133   *The Elkhart Review* 21 June 1923
134   Jack Keene *Olean Evening Herald* NY 20 December 1922

him and smiles, but once the greeting is over he steps out of the picture and lets Willard or Gene Doyle do all the talking.'[135]

Willard stepped up his training grind and his weight began to come down. He had weighed in at 245lb against Dempsey in July of 1919, but had bulked up to around 280lb when he started thinking of a comeback in 1922. To relieve the tedium of training, which he never did like even as champion, Jess had taken up golf. Based in southern California, he visited the Chula Vista Country Club near San Diego where the professional, Jim Simpson, was only too happy to give the ex-champ some pointers. Bitten by the bug, Jess was on the links nearly every day to play 18 holes, but he did confess, 'It's tougher than Jack Dempsey.'

By November, Jess was feeling good enough to make his first public appearance as a fighter in three years, and he was billed as the feature event of a boxing card on 15 November at the Hollywood American Legion Stadium for the benefit of the assistance league for ex-servicemen. The former champion boxed two exhibition rounds each with Tom Kennedy and Joe Bonds, Los Angeles heavyweights. Among the large number of socially prominent people at ringside were W.G. McAdoo, former secretary of the treasury, and Mrs McAdoo, daughter of former President Wilson.

Under the heading 'BIG JESS WILLARD LOOKS GOOD' ran the story, 'Willard received a rousing reception. His two opponents, although large men, looked small beside him. Kennedy made the better showing, swinging four or five hard rights to the jaw. Willard was quick on his feet and his rapid sparring gave one the idea he was not far from being in fair fighting trim.'[136]

News of Willard's comeback sparked interest in New York where veteran Tom O'Rourke told the press he wanted to promote a return bout between champion Jack Dempsey and the former champ Jess Willard. Gene Doyle, one of Willard's representatives, said that Ray Archer, Willard's manager, had received a telegram from O'Rourke announcing he was mailing Willard a registered letter offering to stage a bout between him and Dempsey at the Polo Grounds in New York in May.

Archer arranged three dates in December for his big fellow, first stop Milwaukie, Oregon, where Jess 'let Scotty Messer and Ben

135 *Clinton Daily Republican* 21 February 1923
136 *The Herald Star* Steubenville Ohio 16 November 1922

Barnson, flatten themselves against him here last night. Barnson hit Willard repeatedly below the belt but did not damage the former champion. The crowd gave Willard a great ovation when he first appeared, but the house was half empty before the show was over.'[137]

A week later, at Yakima, Washington state, Willard 'milled clumsily' in two exhibition bouts. He stung Alden Schumacher, a local heavyweight, at the start, and later boxed Frank Farmer. Two days later, Jess was in Tacoma with a local reporter filing the following story. 'Jess Willard, 265 pounds, former heavyweight champion boxer, and Frank Farmer, 178 pounds, flayed each other for four short rounds with huge instructor's gloves in an exhibition here Thursday night. In the third round the ex-champion opened his arms and let Farmer pummel him in the midriff, with no visible effect.'[138]

While big Jess was getting the feel of the ring again, champion Jack Dempsey came home to Los Angeles and announced he was ready to meet anyone in the world right now or any time suitable if the right kind of promoter offered a good inducement. Asked about Jess Willard, Jack said he would like nothing better than to take him on, but where was the promoter who would stage it? Dempsey said he thought Willard would be the easiest of the bunch. Willard, also living in Los Angeles, countered with the declaration that he was 'ready to sign articles today, tomorrow or any time to meet Jack Dempsey in a return bout. I have wanted this match and have been promised it for over three years, but Dempsey and Jack Kearns, his manager, never have made good on their promise.'[139]

January of 1923 saw Willard arrive in New York City, ready to prove to the writers and the public that he was in earnest about his comeback. Tom Gibbons was in town, from St Paul, Minnesota, to confer with promoter Tex Rickard and set tongues wagging as to who would get the shot at Dempsey and the title, or whether Willard and Gibbons would be matched in an eliminator.

Willard and manager Archer were also in conference with the promoter at his office in Madison Square Garden, and although no official announcement was made it was understood that Tex had assured Jess that he was ready to arrange a return bout between himself and Dempsey, possibly for July, if the former champion could demonstrate his fitness to the satisfaction of the public.

---

137 *The Lima News* Ohio 20 December 1922
138 *Goshen Daily Democrat* 30 December 1922
139 *Ogden Standard Examiner* 8 December 1922

Willard planned to remain in the city and keep himself in condition with daily workouts at the Garden gym. He expressed a willingness to box two or three heavyweights before critics in order to prove his claim that he can get into fighting trim again. 'If I can't convince newspapermen that I'm in good shape now,' he said, 'and able to train down from 260 pounds to about 240, my best fighting poundage, I'll quit and go back to the farm. I want to fight Dempsey first, but if necessary I'll go out and fight any other contenders.'[140]

One heavyweight in the reckoning was young Floyd Johnson from Iowa who was to fight Bill Brennan at the Garden on 12 January, and on that Friday night Jess Willard was ringside to check out the opposition. Earlier that night, Jess had met Jack Johnson in a café at the Garden. It had been eight years since that fateful day in April 1915 when Willard proved himself the best of the 'White Hopes' by knocking Johnson out in round 26 'to regain the world heavyweight championship for the white race.'

Willard stuck out his big hand and said, 'Hello, Jack, how are you?' Johnson beamed his big gold-toothed smile and said, 'Oh, I am just lovely, Mister Willard. Just lovely.'[141]

Before the big fight, black heavyweight Harry Wills was introduced to mild applause. Then came Tom Gibbons, but his greeting was drowned out by demands for Willard, and when Jess eased his bulk through the ropes the big crowd erupted with what could only be termed an ovation.

That reception for the former champion brought a smile to Tex Rickard's face; it was confirmation that he was on the right track bringing Willard back into the business. After Johnson had soundly beaten Brennan over 15 rounds, Tex announced that Floyd Johnson would be matched with Jess Willard on the big show he was putting together for the Milk Fund on 12 May at the Polo Grounds. Luis Angel Firpo would fight Jack McAuliffe II in the other main event.

Willard set up his training camp at Excelsior Springs, Missouri, and began pushing his big body to the limit. Now aged 41, he was faced with an enormous task, but he surprised camp visitors with his enthusiasm, telling reporters that as soon as he beat Johnson he would be ready for the South American. He promised to go into the ring against Johnson in the best shape of his career.

140 *Ogden Standard Examiner* 11 January 1923
141 *Laurel Daily Leader* 13 January 1923

A tall order for the giant, but when he arrived back in New York a couple of weeks before the fight he had dropped 20 pounds and looked ready for a scrap. However, when the man from the *New York Times* watched Jess in the gym he said it seemed as if it was an effort for the big Kansan to move his arms and legs.

Covering the workout for INS, sports editor Davis J. Walsh observed, 'His eye is clear, the muscles of his face are firm, his skin has a healthy tinge and his abdomen, never sylph-like, is not an ex-brewer's. One observer even went so far as to say that Willard is 100% improved in condition over his first appearance in this locality four or five weeks ago.'[142]

Veteran manager Alex McLean thought that Willard was making a big mistake meeting young Johnson after almost four years of inactivity. 'As to the matter of endurance,' he said, 'the story is all Johnson. Willard is almost twice the age of young Floyd, and it will require a lot of strength to drag his ponderous bulk around the ring for 15 rounds.'[143]

The age of Jess Willard in January 1923 was a subject of controversy. William Muldoon, chairman of the New York State Athletic Commission, declared that Willard was too old to box in the state which had an age limit of 38. The former champion claimed that he was only 36, despite records to the contrary. From Topeka, Kansas, where Judge W.E. Grutzmacher of the Pottawatomie county probate court had checked the records, it was stated that he had found a petition for guardianship taken out in 1901 specifying that Jess M. Willard then was 19 years old. 'That was 21 years ago so Jess must be 40 now,' said the judge.

Myron L. Willard, brother of the former champion, told reporters, 'Jess will be 40 right soon now.' According to my research, Willard was born on 29 December 1881, so that would make him 41 years old by January 1923.

On that day in May 1923, when Jess Willard climbed into the ring at Yankee Stadium to face 22-year-old Floyd Johnson, the gamblers were making him favourite. He was a favourite with the crowd of 63,000 (*New York Times*) and promoter Rickard was happy to pay the boys $25,000 each. Jess had weighed in at 248lb, a whopping 53lb heavier than his young rival, and he enjoyed advantages in height and reach.

---

142 Davis J. Walsh *Indiana Evening Gazette* 20 February 1923
143 Alex McLean *Bridgeport Telegram* 19 February 1923

His long left hand soon had the blood flowing from Johnson's mouth as the Iowan tried to take the fight to close quarters. Floyd was going for Willard's body because he could hardly reach his jaw, but his punches failed to trouble the big fellow. It was a huge task for the smaller man and it would prove too much for him. In round two Willard attacked viciously and heavy rights and lefts staggered Johnson, who was bleeding from a cut on his left eye as the round ended.

Associated Press reported of round three, 'Johnson punched Willard's head with raging rights at close quarters. Willard launched several heavy rights which fell short, but the Kansan's wind did not appear any too good....Round seven, Johnson worked his arms like a windmill, but the big Kansan never budged. Johnson hit Willard every place, but apparently there was nothing hurtful in his punches.'[144]

That was the story of the fight. Willard was just too big and strong and Johnson's punches failed to trouble the former champion. In the ninth round, 'Willard pounded Johnson's head unmercifully with uppercuts, hooks and straight punches...Johnson went down from a right to the jaw, but was up immediately as the round ended.'[145]

The fight ended two rounds later. Round 11 as seen by the AP reporter, 'Johnson's head rocked from a right hook. He went down from a right uppercut. He was up at nine. Johnson fell to the floor from a right uppercut as the bell rang, and was carried to his corner by his seconds. It was doubtful if he would be able to continue.'[146]

He couldn't. Henry Farrell observed for United Press, 'The seconds lost their hold on him when they reached the corner, and he fell across the ropes, like a sheet on a clothes line. His chief second then called Referee Jack Appell and told him Johnson could not continue. Johnson didn't quit – like General Lee, he surrendered.'[147]

'Youth, take off your hat and bow low and respectfully to Age,' wrote Damon Runyon in the *New York American* on 13 May 1923. 'For days and days, the sole topic of conversation in the world of sport will be Willard's astonishing comeback.'

The boys were still talking about it when Rickard announced that Jess would be matched with Luis Angel Firpo at Yankee Stadium in July. But commissioner Muldoon was adamant this time, he would not

144 *The Galveston Daily News* 13 May 1923
145 *Nevada State Journal* 13 May 1923
146 *The Davenport Democrat & Leader* 13 May 1923
147 Henry L. Farrell *The Lima News* 13 May 1923

license Willard because he was too old to fight in New York State. So Tex Rickard picked up his marbles and took his game over to Jersey City, to Boyle's Thirty Acres, the arena he had built for the Dempsey–Carpentier championship fight in 1921. He was welcomed by city mayor Frank Hague, as he had been two years previously when New York Governor Nathan Miller chased the Carpentier fight out of New York.

The massive wooden bowl had held close to 95,000 for boxing's first million-dollar gate, and Rickard was confident Willard–Firpo would do big numbers in that summer of 1923. 'I am sold on Willard,' he told sportswriter 'Fair Play', 'and think he is the one white man in the world just now who stands at least an even chance of giving Dempsey a great battle.'[148]

The Wild Bull of the Pampas, Luis Angel Firpo, threatened to trample all over Rickard's theory as to Willard's immediate future. Support for the Argentinian came from United Press sports editor Henry Farrell when he wrote, 'Unless all signs fail, Firpo is headed for the title. It may take some time for him to get there, but he is almost sure to arrive...Dempsey will get no better as he goes along, and the transformation that is being worked in the Argentine giant is marvelous.'[149]

That transformation was due to the efforts of Jimmy De Forest, the guy who made Dempsey champion of the world. It took him two years. What he had done with Firpo in four months, teaching a fighter who didn't understand a word of what he was being told, De Forest had made almost as much progress as he made with the champion. Yet the experts still weren't convinced, saying things like, when he learns how to box and gets so he can move around, Luis Angel Firpo will be a great heavyweight. After they had seen the giant South American club Bill Brennan to the mat with wild swings, they were still shaking their heads. Let him get clever before he talks about Dempsey, they chorused.

Jimmy De Forest shook his head when talking to Henry Farrell. 'There's one thing I don't want him to do, and that's get clever. He doesn't need it. All he needs to learn is to hit straight and use his left hand and he'll be there. A man who can take a punch like he can and hit like he can doesn't need any cleverness.'[150]

148 'Fair Play' *Decatur Review* 11 January 1923
149 Henry L. Farrell *Oakland Tribune* 25 May 1923
150 Henry L. Farrell *Sheboygan Press Telegram* 5 April 1923

Although lacking cleverness in the ring, Firpo was 'FOOLISH LIKE A FOX ON FAST FINANCE' according to the heading on one story, 'For the real commercial skill in transforming a ponderous right hand into dollars, pesos, or other currency, Luis Firpo stands out over his American brothers-in-gloves as the old Haig was superior to the present bootleggers' mixture,' wrote sportswriter Max Case, adding, 'In fourteen months he has only made a paltry hundred thousand dollars.'[151]

Since returning to New York from Buenos Aires, where he had flattened Jim Tracey and fattened his bank balance by $58,000, Firpo had received $10,000 for beating Bill Brennan and $7,500 for knocking over Jack McAuliffe, and his coming fight against Willard would see his first crack at the big money. The advance sale was expected to exceed all expectations with a crowd of more than 60,000 anticipated, something that was not lost on Señor Firpo as he negotiated with Mr Rickard.

The promoter had been obliged to guarantee Willard 40 per cent of the gross receipts before he would sign for the Firpo fight. Luis was demanding 30 per cent and Rickard said he could only have 20 per cent, thus guaranteeing 60 per cent of the receipts to the principals when 50 per cent was the maximum as prescribed by law. Firpo's frugal side was coming more to the fore as he moved into the big money with invaluable trainer Jimmy De Forest in the firing line.

'Firpo should be forever in his trainer's debt,' commented Davis J. Walsh. 'Instead, it is said he offered him $1,000 after the bout with McAuliffe. For a time the fighter and the trainer seemed about to part company, particularly when De Forest was notified that he would be expected to pay his own expenses on Firpo's tour which starts tomorrow.'[152]

There was a furious verbal exchange, via interpreters, after which it appeared that Firpo had compromised by offering to pay De Forest's expenses if he would work without salary. With the Willard bout arranged for 12 July, Luis Angel had booked himself a couple of fights in Central America: Italian Jack Herman in Havana, Cuba, on Sunday 11 June, and a week later, in Mexico City, he would face American heavyweight Jim Hibberd.

---

151 Max Case *Coshocton Tribune* Ohio 1 June 1923
152 Davis J. Walsh *Logansport Pharos Tribune* 23 May 1923

Firpo had already dismantled Herman in four rounds a year previously and he figured to have even less bother this time around. More than 5,000 spectators sweltered under the glass roof of the Nuevo Fronton in Havana to see what was optimistically advertised as a 15-round contest.

Associated Press reported, 'The fight lasted three minutes and nineteen seconds. Firpo was thirty pounds the heavier...The contest resembled somewhat that of a terrier against a Great Dane...The blow that ended the bout apparently was not intended by Firpo to land on a vital spot, for Firpo looked amazed when Herman fell to the floor in a neutral corner.'[153]

The following day, Firpo embarked on the steamship *Mexico* with his manager and Al Mayer, the newsman, and sailed for the city of Mexico where he was billed to fight Jim Hibberd, a New York heavyweight who had won only one of his six bouts. Al Mayer described him as 'a Buffalo cop on vacation'. It was a rather bizarre promotion, staged by Andreas de Segurola, one of the world's great baritones who also operated a singing school in New York, starred in movies and taught privately, one of his pupils being Deanna Durbin. For whatever reasons, he had offered Firpo $25,000 to fight in Mexico City, $10,000 payable in New York and the balance of $15,000 48 hours before the fight.

On the day before the contest, Segurola presented Luis with a cheque for $15,000. Luis didn't want the cheque, he wanted cash. Then followed a slanging match in Italian and Spanish and sometimes a bit of both with Segurola's blood pressure hitting the high notes. When things settled down somewhat, Firpo said he would accept payment from the gate receipts or there would be no fight.

Segurola was furious, pointing out that the money would all be in silver, how could Luis carry all that money? Firpo said he would manage, and he did. He had the bags of money loaded into an open car, took them to his hotel, stacked them in his room and took them to the bank when it opened on Monday morning. He had a cheque made out to his order for $15,000.

The fight? It was June, the rainy season, and it poured. But when it was announced that there would be a postponement, there was almost a riot. Armed police and soldiers ringed the arena and the fighters were instructed to go ahead. It didn't last long. Hibberd was no match at all for the powerful Argentine battler and was crushed as soon as the second round opened.

The Mexican fans were sure they had seen the next heavyweight champion of the world. Old-time fighter Jim Flynn was at ringside and he told reporters, 'The Argentinian's right swing would fell an ox. Firpo will fight his way to the top. He will defeat every American heavy who opposes him.'[154]

There is little doubt that Firpo's Central American excursion was a financial and an artistic success, but it was seen for what it was back in New York. 'Luis Angel Firpo didn't add greatly to his popularity in this country by going to Havana and Mexico City to bowl over a couple of setups,' ran one agency report. 'His bout with Italian Jack Herman was purely a peso proposition.'[155]

With Firpo travelling back to New York and cabling instructions for six or seven husky sparring partners to be standing by when he arrived, Jess Willard was being prodded and probed by three doctors in a full medical examination ordered by New Jersey State comptroller Bugbee.

'I have no objection to Willard boxing in New Jersey,' the commissioner told the press, 'but so much has been said and written about his age and physical fitness to meet so rugged an opponent as Firpo that I regard it as my duty to throw about the match every possible safeguard.'[156]

Rickard's office anticipated no problems with the medical as the big fellow had just passed, with a remarkably high mark, an insurance examination by Lloyds. The three physicians engaged by the commission subjected the giant Kansan to a searching examination that lasted 45 minutes, after which they signed a statement declaring him to be free 'from any physical defects'. Willard was characterised as 'a remarkable physical specimen in every respect,' by Dr T.H. Lemmers at whose office the examination was conducted in the presence of newsmen and photographers.

'I expect a tough fight from Firpo,' declared Willard, when asked about his coming match, 'but I'm certain I can whip him. You know I've never seen him in the ring, but they tell me he's a rough and ready scrapper. If that's so, I'll be ready for him.'[157] Willard had been training

154 *Oakland Tribune* 18 June 1923
155 *The Altoona Mirror* 26 June 1923
156 *The Constitution* Atlanta 22 June 1923
157 *Bridgeport Telegram* 26 June 1923

daily for the past week in Yonkers, New York, where he conditioned himself for the Johnson fight. One of his sparring partners was Tiny Jim Herman of Omaha.

Firpo set up training camp at Long Branch, New Jersey, and would work out under the direction of veteran trainer Jimmy De Forest. His fighting weight was around 218lb and his sparring partners included Jack McAuliffe II and Bill Tate, a rugged black heavyweight who had been the primary sparring partner of Jack Dempsey. From Montgomery, Alabama, Big Bill Tate stood 6ft 6in and bounced the scales around 220–240lb. In his own right as a fighter, he had beaten men like Sam Langford, 'Gunboat' Smith and Harry Wills, and with a reach of 81 inches he was a dead ringer for Jess Willard whose wing span was 83 inches.

A visitor to Firpo's camp was old Jack McAuliffe, the former undefeated lightweight champion, who was writing a column for United Press. 'When I saw Luis Firpo topple over Jack Herman at Ebbets Field a year ago, he was a crude, ungainly fellow. He showed power and was willing but that was all…Now that I've seen him again I am amazed at the improvement he has made. I never dreamed he would develop so rapidly.'[158]

'Firpo's workouts belied reports that he had strained his back,' ran a story in the *Bridgeport Telegram*. 'The big South American followed a four mile jog on the road by boxing seven rounds with Bill Tate and Jack McAuliffe II, and then shadow boxing and punching the bag for three more.'[159]

De Forest claimed that he had Firpo in better shape than for any of his fights, weighing around 215lb, and that the fighter would surprise everybody with his ability. Equally impressed with his charge was Willard's trainer, ex-pug Jack Skelly, who told the press, 'He is boxing like a lightweight, is punching harder and judging distance better than ever before. They talk about Firpo's strength, but remember, Willard is no weakling. Any man he hits Willard will beat, and Firpo can be hit.'[160]

As the big day drew near, an army of workmen swarmed all over the huge wooden bowl at Boyle's Thirty Acres making the necessary repairs that would see the final permit issued by the New Jersey Boxing Commission after the building department of Jersey City reported

---

158 Jack McAuliffe *Oakland Tribune* 9 July 1923
159 *Bridgeport Telegram* 9 July 1923
160 Jack Skelly *New Castle News* 12 July 1923

favourably on the condition of the arena. It would have to support a record crowd of 100,000, some 10,000 more than had watched the first bout there between Dempsey and Carpentier two years previously. That fight drew boxing's first million-dollar gate with receipts of $1,789,238. Rickard was estimating the Firpo–Willard fight, with no world title on the line, would draw at least $400,000.

A couple of days before the fight, Rickard told a reporter that he had never seen such an advance sale for a fight; he said it was the biggest since the day of the Dempsey–Carpentier fight. What also intrigued Tex was the class of people buying the tickets.

The people buying tickets also drew the interest of columnist Damon Runyon. The writer stood for an hour watching the line in front of the box office window at Madison Square Garden. 'Half the men in the line were small, dark, voluble, talking to each other in Spanish,' observed Runyon. 'Nearly all asked for the expensive seats. They are the new species of "ring worm", manufactured by the prowess of Luis Angel Firpo – Latin Americans.'[161]

Great crowds of New Yorkers and fight fans from all over the world headed via ferry and subway under the Hudson river to the great stadium in Jersey City where 90,000 persons two years previously saw Jack Dempsey knock out Georges Carpentier.

'When Firpo climbs into the ring with Jess Willard this evening,' wrote Paul R. Mallon, 'it will be decided once and for all just exactly what happens when an irresistible force meets an immovable object.'[162]

The man in charge of the action when the bell rang was Henry Lewis, all 196lb of him. He was big enough to handle the giants coming from their corners; Willard 242lb to Firpo's 214lb, the Wild Bull of the Pampas at a towering 6ft 2.5in conceding almost four inches to the Pottawatomie Giant. This was a big fight.

At the bell for round one, Firpo came out with a rush and a right hand, but Willard blocked the punch and jabbed his long left to the face. Ignoring the jab, Firpo took Willard to the ropes with a body assault and cuffed him about the head, bringing blood from his left ear. Just before the bell the former champ drove a hard right to the head.

Coming out for round two, Willard carried the action to the South American but missed with a big right uppercut. Firpo landed to the

161 Damon Runyon *Davenport Democrat & Leader* 10 July 1923
162 Paul R. Mallon *Oakland Tribune* 12 July 1923

body but was short with a right to the head. The big Kansan was already showing red marks on his left side and he signed for a heavy right to the head from Luis Angel. He evaded Firpo's follow-up at the bell.

Having sampled Firpo's power, Willard seemed happy to use defensive tactics in the third round, keeping that long left in Firpo's face, but the Wild Bull would not be denied and he bored in relentlessly, hammering both fists at the Kansas giant in an effort to bring him down on his face. But Jess was still standing at the bell.

Round four and Willard jarred Firpo with a solid left to the head and then a right uppercut halted Firpo's advance. But not for long. Luis came off the ropes with a heavy right to the body and when he threw both hands to the head the former champion smiled. Willard missed a huge swing and Firpo charged in to land left and right to the head, but Jess drove him into a corner at the bell.

The first break came in the fourth round when it seemed Firpo was about to win with a knockout. 'The South American launched a vicious right hand attack that had Willard groggy on the ropes,' wrote UP sports editor Farrell, 'but the same courage that brought him up from the floor seven times in one round at Toledo, enabled Willard to weather his way through.'[163]

In the fifth round Willard rocked Firpo's head back with that telegraph pole of a left but the man from the Argentine hammered a thudding right to the jaw and they clinched. With Jess blocking Firpo's attacks the crowd was chanting his name, 'Come on, Jess!' drowning out the cries of the Latin supporters. The sixth round and a heavy clubbing right from Firpo caught Willard on the neck and the Kansan covered up as Firpo circled looking for an opening. He found one and rushed in with lefts and rights to the jaw and Willard was glad to hold, wrapping his long arms about his tormentor. He shook under a right hand just before the bell.

Round seven and Willard's opening shot, a long hard right, sent Luis into the ropes where Jess caught him with a rabbit punch to the back of the head. Willard landed twice with his jab and Firpo was bleeding from a small cut under his right eye. The South American appeared confused and seemed to be feeling the pace he had set himself. But he smashed home a savage right to the body before the bell sent them to their corners.

---

163 Henry L. Farrell *Chester Times* Pa. 13 July 1923

In the eighth round Willard was aggressive, jabbing twice to the head, but Firpo regrouped and set up a fierce attack that had Willard thinking survival. As his left dropped, vicious punches rained on his head and he tried to keep Firpo off. But Luis was tasting blood now and he threw his fists at the man in front of him, driving Jess across the ring until a booming right to the jaw sent him reeling into the ropes where he dropped to one knee, shaking his head as referee Henry Lewis tolled off the seconds, the final seconds of his time in the ring.

In his fight preview, Damon Runyon had expressed the doubt that Willard would be able to stand Firpo's body punches for more than a few rounds, and it was a seventh-round smash to the pit of the stomach that Runyon saw as the match winner. 'It was a sickening punch,' he recorded. 'Willard's great face contorted with pain, he half stumbled as he walked back to his corner. His face took on a greenish tint which was heightened by the glare of the lights above the ring… Jack Skelly and "Scotty" Montieth worked feverishly on his great legs, now flabby with fatigue.'[164]

Grantland Rice would write, 'Firpo, still crude but effective, carried the war into hostile territory over the most of the route, always with his big right used as a club, always with the smash of the battle axe and never with the skilful thrust of the rapier.'[165]

'Battered down by a furious right hand attack that had all the power of a mountain boulder tumbling down from the peaks,' wrote Farrell of the finish, 'Willard was counted out in the eighth round while the hairy-chested Luis Firpo, the South American caveman, stood back of him snorting for more.'[166]

As he left his ringside seat, former welterweight champion Jack Britton smiled to a friend in the press row and said, 'Why teach him to be clever? It would spoil him. He's a natural fighter, and a dangerous one.'[167]

Associated Press reported, 'And so, the sporting world has focused its attention on the dark-browed young man with the black, yellow and purple bath robe, who, coming north from the Pampas about 15 months ago, battered his way to the fore-ranks of heavyweights with tremendous sledgehammer blows of his right fist.'[168]

---

164 Damon Runyon *Davenport Democrat & Leader* 13 July 1923
165 Grantland Rice *Daily News Standard* Uniontown Pa. 13 July 1923
166 Henry L. Farrell *Wisconsin State Journal* 13 July 1923
167 Jack Britton *Sandusky Star Journal* 13 July 1923
168 *Portsmouth Daily Times* 13 July 1923

7

Wanna Be Champ, Luis? Fight Dempsey!

ASSOCIATED Press reported, 'Paid admissions to the Willard–Firpo fight totaled 75,712, official checks by revenue men at Jersey City revealed, but Rickard stuck to his Thursday night's statement that the entire crowd numbered at least 100,000.'[169]

The difference of about 25,000 between the paid attendance and Rickard's figure was accounted for, Rickard claimed, chiefly by the fact that gatekeepers were unable to hold back the storm of thousands at the last minute. In addition to those gate-crashers there were thousands of policemen, firemen, ushers and other officials whose presence did not register in the box office.

Luis Angel Firpo pulled down his biggest purse to date, $85,000, while Jess Willard's share of the gate receipts amounted to a dollar shy of $118,000 for what would be his last fight. The former champion's performance against the Wild Bull of the Pampas drew criticism from his handlers in the week following the fight.

'Jess Willard could have got up but he quit,' according to a published statement attributed to his manager Ray Archer, who says Willard concluded, 'What's the use?' Archer is said to have explained that Willard figured the battle was over when he was hammered down

---

169 *Bridgeport Telegram* 14 July 1923

in the eighth round.[170] More outspoken was Jack Skelly, the veteran ex-fighter who was in charge of Willard's training for the Firpo fight and the Floyd Johnson bout which preceded it. 'Seventy-five thousand sucker fans paid their good money to see Jess Willard take a soft flop in his fight with Firpo,' said Skelly in charging that the big Kansan was not knocked out and could have continued.[171]

Skelly also told reporters he never learned until after the fight that Willard did not put in the hours of training that he had been told were part of the daily grind.

Fred Keats, boxing writer for the *New York Sun*, reported, 'It is plain that Willard knew from the start that he could not beat Firpo... In training for Firpo his only idea was to conceal his true condition... Willard showed little, for his heart was not in his work. As a result, he entered the ring with Firpo and took the earliest opportunity to quit.'[172]

'When big Jess went down on his knees in the eighth,' recalled Skelly, 'it was right near me. I yelled at him and said, "You're all right, get up," and pleaded with him to rise, but he just looked at me as if to say, "Go to blazes."'[173] When he did get up after the count, Skelly rushed to him with the smelling salts, but Willard pushed him to one side and then posed for the photographers.

So as Willard dropped back into obscurity, Luis Firpo looked forward to every heavyweight's dream, a fight for the championship of the world. Tex Rickard announced that the South American would meet Jack Dempsey on Friday 14 September at the Polo Grounds in New York City. Tickets would be priced at $3 to $25, the lowest for a heavyweight title bout and half the price charged for the Dempsey–Carpentier fight. A crowd of 80,000 was expected after Rickard's men completed the construction of new stands around the ringside.

'Firpo has been brought up to the point where he is prime to meet the champion,' wrote Sparrow McGann. 'They say that Firpo should have more time in which to develop. In the opinion of the writer he has developed as far as he is going to.'[174]

News of the Dempsey fight did not sit well with Firpo's trainer, Jimmy De Forest. At the training camp at Allenhurst, New Jersey,

170 *Morning Herald* Uniontown Pa. 16 July 1923
171 *The Bee* Danville Va. 24 July 1923
172 Fred Keats *Oakland Tribune* 24 July 1923
173 *Indianapolis Star* 24 July 1923
174 Sparrow McGann *Oakland Tribune* 15 July 1923

De Forest told Associated Press, 'If Luis Angel Firpo enters the ring with Jack Dempsey in less than four months he will be stepping into a slaughter house.' The trainer declared his protégé was not yet a polished enough fighter to risk his chance for the world's title at this time.[175]

When news reached Tex Rickard, the promoter said he was mystified by the statement of Firpo's trainer. 'I cannot understand,' he said. 'Only yesterday, De Forest told me Firpo was ready and able to meet anyone in the world.' Asked whether another opponent was contemplated for Dempsey, Rickard asserted that Firpo had been the man designated.[176]

If Rickard was mystified by the words of Jimmy De Forest, he was even more concerned at the behaviour of the South American heavyweight champion. Tex had his big fight all signed and sealed; 14 September, Dempsey v Firpo at the Polo Grounds, but he had a headache. A big headache. A 215lb headache named Luis Angel Firpo.

Within a week of his triumph over Jess Willard, Firpo was busy chasing every dollar not nailed down. With his cousin, a 200lb heavyweight from the Argentine named Natalio Pera who strutted around in spats and with a walking cane, his long hair flowing, they engaged in exhibition bouts in Ogdenburg, New York, and Boston, where Firpo also boxed Pat McCarthy for five rounds.

Then Firpo embarked upon a tour of the Midwest where he and manager Hughie Gartland had arranged a series of fights for local promoters with anybody bouncing the scales around the 200lb mark. First up was Joe Burke, heavyweight champion of Michigan but a loser in nine of his 13 fights. Firpo arrived in Grand Rapids a few days before the fight and spent hours selecting furniture which he said he was to ship to relatives in Buenos Aires.

'Speaking through an interpreter to newspapermen who asked if he expected to defeat Jack Dempsey, Firpo said he does not anticipate any more difficulty in disposing of the champion than he had with Jess Willard or Bill Brennan. Representatives or more than 20 newspapers will report tonight's fight.'[177]

There wasn't much of a fight to report. It took place in Battle Creek, Michigan, some 80 miles from Grand Rapids, and the customers were on their way home before the second round had run

---

175 *Joplin Globe* 14 July 1923
176 *Ogden Standard Examiner* 15 July 1923'
177 *The News Palladium* Benton Harbor, Mich. 27 July 1923

its course. A rabbit punch in the first round put Burke flat on his face for a nine count. Joe saved himself from a knockout by hanging on to Firpo until the bell gave him a 60-second rest. Coming out for round two, Burke ran into a thumping right to the heart and was counted out. The Detroit heavyweight had to be assisted from the ring by his seconds.

Next stop Omaha, Nebraska, where promoter Francis (Pat) Boyle had lined up Homer Smith in the ten-round main event. According to a 1927 newspaper, Smith, from Kalamazoo, had travelled 300,000 miles in a 15-year career, boxing in France, Germany, Belgium, England, Hawaii, Cuba and Spain. His proudest boast was, 'I fought the three greatest heavyweight boxers of all time, Jack Dempsey, Jack Sharkey and Jack Johnson.'

And on the third day of August 1923 he fought Luis Angel Firpo. Much to the big man's annoyance and to the credit of Smith, he was still on his feet at the end of ten rounds when Firpo received the decision of referee Ed Dickerson. Although the South American knocked Smith down so many times it seemed Homer was part of the canvas, he was unable to keep him down and was forced to go the distance for the first time since starting his campaign in the United States 11 knockouts ago.

Covering for the *Sioux City Journal*, Sid Sutherland, with tongue firmly in cheek, wrote, 'If the west wind brings to your olfactory organ the displeasing odor of ripe gorgonzola left over long in the sun, it is the fragrance that hovered about the ring here tonight when Luis Angel Firpo, mislabeled the "wild bull of the pampas", met Homer Smith, the ambulatory punching bag from Kalamazoo, in a boxing contest.'[178]

Before leaving on a train for St Louis at 11.30pm, Firpo collected his purse of $4,000 plus 40 per cent of the gate, but he needn't have hurried. His proposed No Decision contest with the big Englishman Tom Cowler had been ordered to be called off in a telegram received in St Louis by Phillip H. Brockman, president of the board of police commissioners, from Governor Arthur M. Hyde of Missouri at Jefferson City. In his telegram Governor Hyde said the proposed bout was in violation of state law.

Cowler would have been a good match for Firpo. Nicknamed the Cumberland Giant, he was an inch taller and about the same weight.

---

178 Sid Sutherland *The Sioux City Journal* 4 August 1923

He had fought extensively all over the States as well as England, Germany, Italy, Panama and Canada in compiling a record of 50 wins against 21 defeats and two draws. Tom didn't get to fight Firpo in St Louis but he did get to shake his hand, and that brief encounter left the Englishman in no doubt that he would have beaten Firpo had their bout not been cancelled.

A report datelined New York 9 August stated, 'According to Tom Cowler, the big English heavyweight, who has just returned from St Louis, Luis Firpo is on the verge of a breakdown. "I never saw anyone so nervous," said Cowler. "When I shook hands with him he trembled like a leaf, he is so run down."'[179]

Tom's words were echoed by his manager, O'Keefe, who told reporters that he wasn't surprised Homer Smith had taken Firpo the distance, adding that Cowler, although no world beater, would have beaten Firpo 'because Luis is as weak as a kitten and worried'.

Meanwhile, the Firpo bandwagon rolled on, to Indianapolis where promoter Jack Druley had arranged a match with Joe Downey at the Hoosier Motor Speedway on 8 August. However, following the sudden death of President Warren G. Harding on 2 August, Governor McCray of Indiana ordered the Wednesday contest to be cancelled 'following strong protest against holding the fight before the funeral of President Harding at Marion on Friday. It would be a disgrace to the name of Indiana to have an affair like this happen while the body of our President lies unburied.' The sheriff was ordered to block any attempt to hold the scrap.[180]

With the Downey fight on hold, the South American made a flying visit to New York to appeal to promoter Rickard to release him from his contract to fight Dempsey on 14 September or to postpone the date. Rickard, however, was becoming tired of Señor Firpo and his barnstorming tour of the Midwest. Upon learning that Firpo was planning on returning to Indianapolis for the Downey fight, re-arranged for 17 August, Rickard told INS, 'I certainly will protest against Firpo extending his tour. His most important contract is for a meeting with Jack Dempsey September 14. I hold the contract and am living up to my end of it, besides throwing many thousands of dollars into Firpo's pocket. I shall insist that he get down to business immediately.'[181]

---

179 *Bridgeport Telegram* 10 August 1923
180 *Oakland Tribune* 9 August 1923
181 *Indianapolis Star* 10 August 1923

For Luis Firpo, the business requiring immediate attention was a fight in Philadelphia with Charley Weinert on 13 August and a trip to Indianapolis four days later for the rescheduled contest with Joe Downey. For Universal Services, Thomas L. Cummiskey wrote, 'Though he won't be 28 until October, Weinert is pretty well down the scale of pugilistic ranking. The mere fact he was picked as a "set-up" for the Argentinian, and by such a wise fellow as Billy McCarney, is further proof of the fact.'[182]

They used to call Weinert the 'Newark Adonis' – a beautiful physique, a punch in either hand, and his rapier left made the experts rave. But he didn't hold a punch very well and when Gene Tunney knocked him out in Madison Square Garden a few months before the Firpo fight, it was thought that Charley was through. 'He sobbed in his corner in evident realisation of the fact,' added Cummiskey in his preview.

Going against Firpo in Philadelphia's Shibe Park, Charley had won 32 of his 39 fights since becoming a money fighter in 1912, mixing it with such names as Fred Fulton, Battling Levinsky, Billy Miske, Harry Greb, Jack Dillon and Gene Tunney. Charley lost to those guys and he would lose this one with Luis Firpo.

He had the left in Firpo's face in the first round, bringing blood from his nose, but that was the end of his fight. A thudding right uppercut dropped Weinert to a knee in the second round and when he got to his feet, a right to the jaw sent him crashing for the full count at one minute and 49 seconds of the round. Collecting his purse money on the way out, Firpo headed for the train station. He had a date with Joe Downey in Indianapolis.

When Firpo had started on what Damon Runyon called his 'pop-over' tour, the columnist pointed out that Firpo would be lucky to clear $20,000 on the four fights scheduled and considered it a foolish gamble on the part of the South American against the proposed $215,000 jackpot he would be getting for the Dempsey fight.

'The pop-overs are presented mainly to give the ring worms out in the other boxing centers of the country a chance to see the Argentinian,' wrote Runyon, adding, 'however, if one single pop-over plays him false and fails to pop, Firpo's chance of getting the fight with Dempsey is badly damaged, if not wholly destroyed.'[183]

---

182 Thomas L. Cummiskey *Indianapolis Star* 12 August 1923
183 Damon Runyon *Davenport Democrat & Leader* 30 July 1923

Another vital aspect of Firpo's preparation, or lack of it, was the news that he had dispensed with the services of trainer Jimmy De Forest. There had been rumours for some time, mainly of financial differences between the fighter and De Forest, and now that Firpo's big purse was at hand he was apparently not willing to pay the man who had brought him to the position of challenger for the world's heavyweight championship.

One of Firpo's rich Argentine backers, Horatio Lavalle, was already on his way to New York to take charge of training. The news was announced by G.W. Widmer, secretary to the South American, at Indianapolis where Firpo was preparing to fight Joe Downey.

Sportswriter 'Fair Play' expressed the opinion that Luis Firpo's decision to sidetrack Jimmy De Forest and to employ an Argentine trainer 'has an undercurrent of meaning. Firpo can get the Argentine man cheaper than he can get De Forest, but that is not the real reason. To be frank, Firpo has the idea that De Forest, being an American, might find patriotism stronger than his loyalty to a foreigner.'[184]

Associated Press reported, 'Luis Angel Firpo, somber-visaged pugilist of the Argentine, came to Indianapolis yesterday and inadvertently stirred up more commotion than has been visited upon the sporting world of the Hoosier capital in some time.'[185]

Firpo was scheduled to meet Joe Downey of Columbus, Ohio, in a ten-round bout. The contest was held but the disorder, financial mix-ups and disappointment which attended it were likely to place a serious obstacle in the way of holding of future fights. Downey, whose brother Bryan fought all the top middleweights and was recognised as world champion in Ohio, was heavier than his brother but not so good, losing five of his 13 fights up to meeting Firpo.

The meeting with Downey was actually billed as an exhibition since prize fights were not legal in the state of Indiana. Governor McCray had decreed that the combatants wear 16oz gloves and Sheriff Snider of Marion County was ordered to station himself at the ringside with a corps of deputies to stop the contest if it became brutal.

Since arriving in the States, Firpo's shaggy, black-haired, scowling appearance had brought him various colourful names from the newspaper hacks, such as 'human grizzly!'

---

184 'Fair Play' *Decatur Daily Review* 9 August 1923
185 *The Herald Star* Steubenville Ohio 18 August 1923

On the morning of the Downey contest, the *Indianapolis Star* opened their preview with 'Luis Angel Firpo, the civilized gorilla, fresh from the pampas of Argentina, awaits the gong which sends his flaying fists in the direction of one Joe Downey at the Hoosier Speedway arena tonight, where the giant from the steppes country will be the dessert to an appetizing fistic menu served by the National Sporting Club.'[186]

Advance ticket sales even last night indicated, according to matchmaker Jack Druley, that the attendance would be greater than for the original date and the additional seating facilities were expected to be filled by the time the heavyweights entered the ring. And that was when the fun started. After the announcement that the bout was to be merely an exhibition, the crowd which jammed the arena roared its disapproval.

Then followed a delay of nearly two hours before Hughie Gartland, business manager for Firpo, announced from the ring that the Argentine fighter had received only a part of his guaranteed purse and that efforts to locate Jack Druley, promoter of the contest, who was said to be in possession of most of the gate receipts, had been unsuccessful.

As a result it was announced that the bout would be cut down to a four-round exhibition affair. This last statement aroused the angry fight fans to breaking point and they swarmed about the ring demanding their money back. A serious disturbance was averted by Mayor Lew Shank who jumped into the ring and restored order to the assemblage. He announced that the boxers would box ten rounds as originally scheduled or he would have all persons connected with the show, including boxers and promoters, placed in jail.

The contest does not appear in the records of either Firpo or Downey listed by the BoxRec.com website. It is listed variously as exhibition four rounds, ten rounds, or No Decision ten rounds by cyberboxingzone.com, depending on the source.

'At this time, however, Druley was located and after apparently satisfying the boxers they would receive their money, the bout was started near midnight. Firpo, after sparring tamely for the first three rounds, tore into his opponent. Downey stayed the limit but was given a terrific mauling.'[187] He collapsed after the bout and was taken to a local hospital in a semi-conscious condition where it was said he was suffering from injuries about the head.

---

186 *Indianapolis Star* 17 August 1923
187 *Ogden Standard Examiner* 18 August 1923

The first three rounds were exceedingly tame, neither boxer being able to inflict much damage with the larger gloves. Firpo used his left hand almost entirely except in the third round when he missed two vicious right hooks. Firpo began fighting more earnestly in the fourth round and spun Downey across the ring with a hard left jab. In the next two rounds he tore into his opponent and began clubbing him with his right. Downey was hanging on at the end of the sixth round. The exhibition bout had become a prize fight.

'Downey was in a bad way when the seventh round opened,' reported Associated Press, 'but fought back gamely and landed a stiff right to the South American's chin. Firpo resumed his attack and gave Downey a terrific battering. The Ohio fighter hung on during the last round and was in distress when the round ended.'[188]

'Joe Downey, who lost a ten round bout with Luis Firpo after an exciting and turbulent contest here last night, was resting in hospital today…Firpo was much concerned over Downey's condition and stayed at his bedside until early daylight. Downey would be discharged this afternoon, his manager, Harry Sully, said.'[189]

The day after the contest, promoter Druley re-appeared, claiming that had he stayed, Firpo and his manager would have continued the negotiations for the entire sum stipulated in the contract. After the gate receipts were counted, Firpo's manager Hughie Gartland said he had received $2,000 of the $4,000 for his boxer and part of the railroad transportation of his party. Joe Downey, for his pains, was paid $800 of the $1,000 he was due. Druley said he did not have enough money to pay for his room rent. He confirmed that the prelim boxers, attendants and other workmen had not been paid.

An Associated Press report from Indianapolis dated 18 August stated, 'Luis Angel Firpo left here this afternoon for New York without taking any legal steps to obtain $2,000 alleged to be due him for his contest last night with Joe Downey…Hughie Gartland, manager for Firpo, declared it was up to Mayor Stanley Lewis Shank to see that Firpo's contract was fulfilled to the letter.'[190]

Firpo was back in New York, much to the relief of Tex Rickard who saw his big fight threatened by the Argentinian's search for the Yankee dollar and the bad press coverage of his bouts with Homer Smith and Joe Downey. Now Firpo had to get ready for what would

188 *The Joplin Globe* Missouri 18 August 1923
189 *Cumberland Evening Times* Maryland 18 August 1923
190 *Eau Claire Leader* Wisconsin 19 August 1923

be the pinnacle of his ring career, and he didn't have that much time to do it.

United Press sports editor Henry L. Farrell wrote, 'Luis Angel Firpo is the most unique young man of the ring, and the more he does the more unique he becomes. The South American champion apparently thinks that he can get ready to fight Jack Dempsey in less than thirty days. Thirty months perhaps would be better for him.'[191]

International News Service sports editor Davis J. Walsh was another to question Firpo's title bout preparations. 'Firpo is making no serious attempt to prepare himself for his impending fight with Dempsey. It lacks just 18 days of the time when Firpo will be asked to face the crisis of his fistic career. Eighteen days of preparation is not considered enough for the champion. They are hardly enough for the challenger.'[192]

'Firpo has a whole lot to learn and there is only one man in the country who could teach him a small part of what he lacks in a short space of time,' wrote Farrell. 'That man is Jimmy De Forest.'[193]

But apparently Señor Firpo had decided that he no longer required the services of the trainer and announced that De Forest would not be handling him when he started his three weeks of training for Dempsey. Horatio Lavalle, a wealthy sportsman from Buenos Aires, had arrived and was to take charge of Firpo's training camp. When Damon Runyon asked the fighter if Lavalle was a professional trainer, Firpo shook his head, and through interpreter Carlos Vega, replied, 'No, but he has had some experience and Filip Bunge, my adviser in the Argentine, has told him what to do...Luis Firpo is the manager of Luis Firpo. Bunge is my friend, not my manager. He gives me good advice.'[194]

That advice was questioned in another column by Runyon when he wrote, 'If the announcement that Firpo is discarding the services of Jimmy De Forest is true, the writer thinks Firpo's danger to Dempsey is reduced 50 per cent...After a long period as the best advised fighter in the business, Firpo seems to have run into some very bad advice. He will live to be sorry.'[195]

---

191 Henry L. Farrell *Waterloo Evening Courier* 9 August 1923
192 Davis J. Walsh *Indiana Evening Gazette* 28 August 1923
193 Henry L. Farrell *Eau Claire Leader* Wisconsin 10 August 1923
194 Damon Runyon *Davenport Democrat & Leader* 16 August 1923
195 Damon Runyon *Davenport Democrat & Leader* 10 August 1923

8

Hail The New Champ! Boo!

T HE Independence Day celebrations were in full swing in the Ohio city of Toledo and on that 4 July night in 1919, one man had more reasons to celebrate than any of the people milling about him in the Secor Hotel. He was Jack Dempsey, and that afternoon in the big wooden bowl on the shores of Maumee Bay he had annihilated Jess Willard, the Pottawatomie Giant, to become heavyweight champion of the world. When he finally tumbled into bed around 2am, he still couldn't believe it.

'That night I dreamed I had been knocked out,' he recalled. 'I woke up, dressed and went out onto the street. Newsboys were still hollering their extras. I called to one of them, "Say, buddy, who won the fight?" He said, "Dempsey. Say, aren't you Dempsey?" I was so tickled I gave him a dollar.'[196]

Any remaining doubts the young champion had were quickly dispelled as he devoured the morning papers. 'Fight fans are in for a long stretch of joyful homage to a king of heavyweights unlike any other the world ever before saw,' wrote H.C. Hamilton for United Press. 'In Jack Dempsey pugilism has gained a boss who beams good-natured smiles at every one, is loyal to his friends, a gentleman at all times and a love of children.'[197]

---

196 Jack Dempsey with Myron M. Stearns *Round by Round* (New York: Whittlesey House 1940) p.185
197 H.C. Hamilton *Oakland Tribune* 6 July 1919

In his syndicated column, Runyon told his readers of 'Jack Dempsey, the young mountain lion in human form, from the Sangre del Christo hills of Colorado.'[198] Frank G. Menke wrote, 'Jack Dempsey sizes up as the greatest punching heavyweight of all time – the miracle man of the fistic world. And they are venturing the prediction now that Dempsey probably will hold the throne longer than any other king that ever reigned in pugilism.'[199]

Lightweight champion of the world Benny Leonard said, 'I wish to go on record as saying that Dempsey is a real champion. He has all the attributes that go to make a champion. He has youth. He has speed. He has stamina. He has strength and he is willing. He should be champion for some time to come.'[200]

Former holder of the title James J. Corbett called Dempsey 'the greatest heavyweight since Jim Jeffries was in his prime…he gave a man fifty pounds heavier the most terrific beating ever handed a heavyweight champion and there is no fighter in the limelight today who would stand a chance against him.'[201]

Heady praise indeed for a young fighter, a young fighter who didn't have a dime to his name. The day after the fight, Dempsey asked manager Jack 'Doc' Kearns why, now that he was the world's heavyweight champion, was he still broke. Jack knew that their end of the purse came to $27,500. What happened to it?

'Champ,' said Kearns, 'when I got you this fight, we didn't have no money of our own. I had to borrow all our movement money from Rickard. That came to eighty-five hundred. Rickard held on to that and gave us the rest, nineteen thousand. But then I had to cover the ten thousand dollars we lost on the bet, because you couldn't knock out the big bum in the first round. Anyways, Champ, that bet you lost for us cut us down to nine thousand dollars. Then I had to cover your training camp expenses and pay off your sparring partners and your trainer and that come to nine thousand easy. So I got nothing left.

'But look at it this way, Champ. At least we ain't in debt. And I just booked us into a theatre down in Cincinnati where they're gonna pay us five thousand dollars a week just for telling people how we knocked out big Jess Willard.'[202]

198 Damon Runyon *Syracuse Herald* 5 July 1919
199 Frank G Menke *Logansport Pharos Reporter* Ind. 5 July 1919
200 Benny Leonard *Washington Post* DC 5 July 1919
201 James J Corbett *San Antonio Evening News* 5 July 1919
202 Roger Kahn *A Flame of Pure Fire – Jack Dempsey and the Roaring Twenties* (New York: Harcourt Brace & Co. 1999) p.101

On Monday 7 July 1919, just three days after his brutal beating of Jess Willard, Jack Dempsey, boxing's brand new world heavyweight champion, opened at Chester Park and Vaudeville Theatre in Cincinnati, Ohio, and the crowds rolled up in their thousands, lured by the posters stuck up all over town that proclaimed 'JACK DEMPSEY ALL DAY AND ALL WEEK SPARRING EXHIBITIONS DAILY AT 5.00PM AND 10.00PM BETWEEN DEMPSEY AND BIG BILL TATE SHOWING THE PUNCH THAT TOOK THE PEP OUT OF BIG JESS: TICKETS $1.00, 75c AND 50c'.

Dempsey was self-conscious about his tenor voice, which got even higher when he got nervous, which he often did on stage. But the people liked him, and Jack liked the $1,000 a day they were paying him. It got better a couple of weeks later when he joined a vaudeville troupe called Jones, Lenich and Schaffer which promised a ten-week engagement at $10,000 a week. There was a chorus line, comedians and a band, and Jack Dempsey. Trainer Teddy Hayes acted as master of ceremonies. They opened in Chicago on 20 July and closed after seven weeks. Dempsey and Hayes were paid for three. Welcome to showbusiness!

Next stop, the circus. Teddy Hayes recalled, 'Otto Floto got us a deal with his Sells-Floto Circus at $2,500 a week. We carried two sparring partners and I acted as the advance man. There were other offers waiting out there, including one from Hollywood, which was more to Jack's taste. A circus for grown-ups. The good times were still rolling.'[203]

By December they were in Hollywood where Jack rented a house in the Silver Lake district of Los Angeles. With him were Doc Kearns, Hayes, Big Bill Tate and his wife. Tate acted as the butler with his wife in the kitchen looking after the pots and pans. Kearns had negotiated a deal with Fred C. Quimby, president of Pathe Studios, for Jack to star in an 18-episode serial called *Daredevil Jack*, $10,000 up front and $1,000 a week.

Off screen, Jack was soon rubbing shoulders with the big names. Douglas Fairbanks, Charlie Chaplin, and Rudolf Valentino were more than happy to be seen with the world heavyweight champion, as were the ladies of the silver screen. Jack was soon dating beauties like Bebe Daniels, Mabel Normand and Marion Davies who would become the great love of William Randolph Hearst. Like the weather

---

203 Teddy Hayes *With The Gloves Off* (Houston: Lancha Books 1977) p. 32

in California, it was sunshine and blue skies all the way. But there was a black cloud on the horizon that threatened to blot out the blossoming career of Jack Dempsey, champion boxer and budding screen star.

When the United States formally entered World War I on 6 April 1917, President Woodrow Wilson was unable to offer the Allies much immediate help in the form of troops; in fact the Army was only able to muster about 100,000 men. Wilson immediately adopted a policy of conscription, the Selective Service Act (the draft) became law on 16 May 1917, and by the time the war ended on 11 November 1918, more than two million American soldiers had served on the battlefields of Western Europe and some 50,000 of them had lost their lives.

When William Harrison (Jack) Dempsey filled in his draft questionnaire, he applied for exemption classification 4-A, claiming his father Hyrum, his mother Celia, his widowed sister Effie and her three children relied on him for support. He also claimed for his wife Maxine. Dempsey's deferment was granted and he was able to continue boxing.

Teddy Hayes would recall, 'How easy it is now to look back and see that this would be the last war with glamour and music and troop trains pulling out of stations, while young girls waved damp hankies. It was the war Irving Berlin set to music…I called Martin Delaney and told him I wanted to join the Navy…I kept telling Doc that he ought to enlist Jack in the Navy. Doc said, "Naw, he's doing exhibitions for the Red Cross and appearing in the shipyards. That's enough. Hell, I didn't start the war." I wrote Dempsey almost daily urging him to join the Navy. But Kearns would have none of it. I could not shake the feeling that Doc was leading Dempsey to grief.'[204]

Dempsey did fight on many benefit shows with money going to charities and servicemen's relief funds, but there was an ill-advised photo shoot in a shipyard in Chester, Pennsylvania, showing the heavyweight champion holding a riveter's gun, wearing shiny patent leather shoes. That was not one of Doc's better efforts, but he argued that Dempsey had indeed enlisted many hundreds of men to work in the shipyards.

'Kearns,' Paul Gallico would write, 'had not nursed and raised a million-dollar heavyweight championship prospect to be a target for something a boxer couldn't block – shot and shell. And so he put him into a shipyard and gave him a riveter's gun, instead of a

---

204 Ibid p. 24, 27

khaki uniform and a rifle…It was unforgivably stupid of the otherwise clever Kearns so to damage the image of his meal-ticket. For had he permitted Dempsey to enlist, his charge would probably have faced no danger, greater than that of becoming an athletic or boxing instructor in some soldier camp.'[205]

A couple of days after the Willard fight, top sportswriter Grantland Rice used his syndicated column in the *New York Herald* to hurt Dempsey more than anything Willard hit him with.

'If he had been a fighting man he would have been in khaki,' wrote Rice, 'when at twenty-two he had no other responsibilities except to protect his own hide. So let us have no illusions about our new heavyweight champion. He isn't the world's champion fighter. Not by a margin of 50,000,000 men who either stood or were ready to stand the test of cold steel and exploding shell for anything from six cents to a dollar a day. It would be an insult to every young American who sleeps today from Flanders to Lorraine, from the Somme to the Argonne, to crown Dempsey with any laurels of fighting courage.'[206]

Rice's column was used in an editorial in the Indiana *Kokomo Tribune* headed 'DEMPSEY NO CHAMPION'. 'Dempsey was a slacker when the world needed fighters. His so-called honor won in Toledo is not to be thought of in contrast with the record of Sergeant York, for instance. That championship belt bestowed upon him for dethroning the former champion should have engraved on it: "To Jack Dempsey, slacker".'[207]

Newspapers across the country picked up on the slacker story, a story that perked the interest of Maxine Cates, the champion's estranged wife, a prostitute who played the piano in western dance halls and saloons. Maxine sent off a letter to the *San Francisco Chronicle* in which she stated that Dempsey was a slacker and draft dodger, claiming she had 35 letters from Jack, some of which told of how he and Kearns had conspired to avoid the draft. As for him supporting her, she said, 'To tell the truth I had to support him.' An investigator stated that many of the letters were of a 'salacious nature'.

'Dempsey had met Maxine Cates in the spring of 1916 before he left for New York,' wrote Randy Roberts in his book *Jack Dempsey*,

205 Paul Gallico *The Golden People* (New York: Doubleday & Co. Inc. 1964) pp. 78, 80

206 Jack Dempsey *Dempsey with Barbara Piattelli Dempsey* (New York: Harper and Row 1977) pp. 122–123

207 *Kokomo Tribune* 7 July 1919

The Manassa Mauler. 'She was a common prostitute of the dancehall variety who worked in the red light district of Salt Lake City along Commercial Street. Before he left for New York he had displayed only minor interest in the woman who was at least fifteen years older than he was.

'However, he returned from New York a beaten man; his confidence had been severely shaken and he was now vulnerable to Maxine's well-worn charms...she suggested that they make the relationship more binding. Dempsey, thinking of no real objection, agreed, and on 9 October 1916, in Farmington, Utah, they were married by a justice of the peace. After a brief honeymoon in a cheap hotel, the couple returned to Salt Lake City.'[208]

It was not a marriage made in heaven. Jack would be on the road, taking fights where and when he could, taking odd jobs in between and sparring in gyms with better fighters. Maxine refused to travel with him and drifted back to her old ways. In early 1917, a promoter offered Dempsey a few fights around San Francisco and his wife agreed to go along. In May, a doctor was called to the Gibson Hotel where Maxine had suffered a dislocated jaw when tripping over the door sill. She would later claim that Jack had hit her with a right-hand punch.

Dempsey denied the charge and Maxine left a few days later to visit her mother in Yakima, Washington. She did not return. He later found that she was working as a prostitute in Cairo, Illinois. Jack always sent Maxine money whenever he could track her down but they never again lived as man and wife. But Maxine was not done with Jack Dempsey.

When Jack suffered his only knockout defeat on 13 February 1917 to Fireman Jim Flynn, he claimed that he had injured his right hand working in a bowling alley. Actually he was in no condition to fight the experienced veteran of 70 fights against the best in the business. In the first round, Flynn 'gave Dempsey's head a quick shove toward his right and sent a short right hand hook through Dempsey's guard and straight to the point of the chin. Dempsey was down ten seconds into the bout and he remained on his back for twenty seconds.'[209]

'Maxine told another story. She chattered in saloons in Utah and later in San Francisco about "what really happened". The truth, she said, was that Dempsey threw the fight. "They offered him more

---

208 Randy Roberts *Dempsey The Manassa Mauler* (Baton Rouge: Louisiana State University Press 1979) p. 83
209 *BoxRec.com*

money to lose than to win and he took it.'"[210] Dempsey denied it, just as he denied that Maxine's chattering had anything to do with her dislocated jaw.

The California State American Legion demanded a federal investigation into Dempsey's draft deferment and the federal district attorney in San Francisco took up the case. Recalled Teddy Hayes in his book, *With The Gloves Off,* 'The charges against him were serious. Serious enough not only to turn the public against him but to send him to prison. Jack was accused of being a draft dodger, a slacker. Dempsey was never drafted. His case hinged on whether he was entitled to the deferment he received. The newspaper headlines blazed out with the news 'DEMPSEY TO STAND TRIAL AS SLACKER'. At Pathe Studios, the work stopped immediately on the *Daredevil Jack* series.

'For the time, at least, Dempsey was through as a film star. I was troubled a great deal more by the thought that he might be through as a boxer. Maxine wrote a letter to the Justice Department, and was now to be their chief witness against him. A grand jury heard Maxine's testimony, and Jack was indicted. The rumor was that she had not only accused Jack and Kearns of fraud, but brought up his fight with Fireman Jim Flynn, when he took a dive for $500.'[211]

Pathe's Frank Spellman tracked Maxine down and talked things over with her. He had already stated that they had invested $300,000 in Dempsey's serial *Daredevil Jack* and if Dempsey was shown to be a slacker that investment would be lost. Whether or not Spellman gave or promised Maxine any money was never clear. What was clear was the statement she made to Charles W. Thomas, the assistant US attorney in charge of the case.

'Maxine told Thomas that everything she had said or written about her former husband was untrue. In truth, she said, Jack had been "a wonderful man and husband". He had supported her, as well as his mother, father, sister and brothers. As for the letters, she reported that there were none. Everything she had said was a lie. Her only hope was that the whole matter might be forgotten.'[212]

But the government had moved too far along to let things go. Dempsey and Kearns were arrested and charged and soon released on $1,000 bail. Doc knew one thing; they needed a lawyer, the best that money could buy. They got Gavin McNab, then working on Mary

---

210 Kahn p. 121
211 Hayes p. 35
212 Roberts p. 80

Pickford's divorce, who agreed to take the case for $75,000. Kearns made a hurried trip to Washington, calling in any political favours owed him. He felt happier when he returned to San Francisco where the trial was due to begin in April. Then it was postponed, eventually opening on 8 July 1920 with a new judge in office, a judge more in sympathy with Dempsey's situation.

Maxine was the government's first witness. She said she couldn't remember how much money Jack had forwarded to her in 1917. McNab reminded her, shoving $2,000 of receipts in her face. Maxine cracked. She was broke and Dempsey had always been a soft touch. She stepped down from the stand and McNab called his witnesses. They included Jack's mother, father, sister and brother, and Lt John F. Kennedy of the Great Lakes Naval Station.

He told how Jack had wanted to do his bit for the Navy and said that he'd been arranging a release from the San Francisco draft board when the Armistice was declared. Jack's mother declared under oath that her son had been and still was her sole support and that she and the rest of the family couldn't have survived without his assistance in 1917.

Dempsey recalled, 'On Tuesday, 15 June, 1920, at 10.30 am, the jury retired to deliberate my fate. They returned at 10.45 am. "We the jury find William H. Dempsey, the defendant at the bar, not guilty. John H. Clendenning, Foreman." I was ordered discharged. I was the happiest man in the world.'[213]

The lawyers' fees were met by Tex Rickard and his friend, John Ringling. In addition to the $75,000, they also picked up the press bill at the Continental Hotel in San Francisco. Later, Rickard told Jack that the total had amounted to approximately $150,000. That day was the last Dempsey ever saw Maxine. In 1924, in a fire which destroyed a dancehall in Juarez, Mexico, Maxine was burned to death, trapped as she slept in the room above.

---

213 Dempsey with Piattelli pp.130, 131

9

Miske – Capone – Brennan

'THE draft issue did not end in 1920,' wrote Randy Roberts. 'Throughout the rest of his career Dempsey heard the word slacker often attached to his name...So the pain remained so much scar tissue on his psyche. Otherwise, life went back to normal. Pathe released *Daredevil Jack* to an American public curious to see the champion on the silver screen.'[214]

Dempsey enjoyed his time in Hollywood and decided to look around before heading east. 'I was young, eligible, a champion... People wanted to introduce me to their daughters, their sisters, but not their wives. Then Doc started going to his parties and I started going to mine. I preferred not to see him at all.'[215]

Hollywood's big names liked having the world heavyweight champion around and Dempsey liked palling around with Chaplin and Valentino and Fairbanks. They soon roped him into a film, *All Good Marines,* with former champion 'Gentleman' Jim Corbett also on the cast list. Jack went straight into another picture, *Dead or Alive*, and when it was finished, Doc called time on playtime. The money was running out, and for Kearns that meant only one thing, back to business – the fight business. When Doc headed for New York, Dempsey and Hayes took a side trip to stay with an old friend who ran

---

214 Roberts p. 87
215 Dempsey with Piattelli pp. 131–132

a hotel down in Missouri. But after a few days, trainer Teddy knew it was time to get his champion back in the gym. Dempsey was about 35lb over his fighting weight and if Doc had managed to hustle up a fight for Jack, the sooner they got back to New York the better. Back in the Big Town, they hooked up with Kearns at the Belmont Hotel.

'It was there that we learned that Billy Miske, one of the bravest fighters I ever knew, was a victim of Bright's disease,' recalled Hayes. 'His days were numbered and he knew it, and he needed money badly to pay his doctors and provide for his family. He had retired from the ring in the spring of 1920 and gone into the automobile business. Within five months he had lost $55,000 and now there was only one way to get it back. He needed to fight again.'[216]

There are several versions of how that third fight between Dempsey and Miske came about. 'Kearns didn't like it,' recalled Hayes. 'But Jack and I insisted, and arrangements were made to stage the fight at Benton Harbor, Michigan, on Labor Day.'[217]

Dempsey wrote in his 1977 autobiography, 'Doc had had a falling out with Tex Rickard and was going to be his own promoter from now on. Another promoter, Floyd Fitzsimmons, had helped him arrange the whole thing pretty fast, since Miske badly needed the dough.'[218]

In his 1960 book, Dempsey recalled, 'My first defense of the title was on Labor Day 1920, against a dying friend of mine. I knocked him out because I loved the guy. Hell of a guy. Billy Miske…He was dying of Bright's disease.'[219]

Kearns said in his 1966 book, 'We had boxed him twice in 1918… Floyd Fitzsimmons called me and said he wanted to promote the fight in Benton Harbor, Michigan. I owed Fitzsimmons a favor. Back when we arrived in Chicago, in January 1918, hungrily looking for a bout which would lead to recognition, it was Floyd who gave me our big break. He was managing Homer Smith, but Floyd got us that shot in which Dempsey knocked out Smith and started us on our way. "It'll be a big favor, Jack, if you'll give us the shot." So on 6 September 1920 we made our first defense of the title as an 11/5 favorite against Miske.'[220]

---

216 Hayes p. 48
217 Ibid p. 48
218 Dempsey with Piattelli p. 135
219 Dempsey with Considine & Slocum pp. 126–127
220 Jack (Doc) Kearns with Oscar Fraley *The Million Dollar Gate* (New York: The Macmillan Co. 1966) p. 126

Recalling the third Dempsey–Miske fight in his 1999 book, author Roger Kahn wrote, 'In 1919 Miske felt flushed, feverish and bloated. His back hurt as though he had been knifed. Doctors at a hospital diagnosed Bright's disease and told Miske he had better give up boxing. His kidneys were failing...He called Dempsey and pleaded for a fight. Dempsey never forgot Miske's words. "I can't pay my doctors. I can't feed my wife or my kids. Champ, give me a shot. I need a payday. Please."'[221]

When Dempsey made it clear to Kearns that he would fight Miske next, Miske and nobody else, Doc embraced the idea as his own. He told Dempsey he would promote the fight and they would get a better deal than they could get from Rickard. Dempsey didn't argue. If Kearns wanted to run without Rickard, Jack didn't mind, just so long as Billy Miske got his payday. Doc worked a deal with Fitzsimmons, giving $55,000 for Dempsey and $25,000 for Miske. The fight would go on in a baseball yard in Benton Harbor, Michigan.

In July, when the fight was officially signed, Miske's manager, Jack Reddy, told reporters that when he called Billy long distance to give him the news, Miske smiled so loud Reddy heard it on the other end of the line. Billy started his training in Chicago and impressed people who watched him, people who had heard various things about his condition.

'Reddy proclaimed Billy a "new man", saying he had rid himself of the curvature of the spine through chiropractic care, a condition he had suffered since he was 16. Reddy proudly proclaimed Billy's one-inch height increase and weight gain of 15lb had resulted from the near miraculous treatments.'[222]

When Miske moved to Benton Harbor, Dempsey had already been in training there a week and was hard at work. Kearns, as he usually did, had arranged excellent sparring partners for his tiger and in camp were Bill Tate, Panama Joe Gans, Marty Farrell and Harry Greb. They called Greb the Pittsburgh Windmill, a middleweight on his way to becoming world champion and one of the ring's greatest fighters. He would hand Gene Tunney the only defeat of his career, a fearful beating over 15 bloody rounds, and he gave Jack Dempsey all the heavyweight champ could handle in that Benton Harbor training camp as he prepared to fight Billy Miske.

---

221 Kahn pp. 206–207
222 Clay Moyle *Billy Miske St Paul Thunderbolt* (Iowa City: Win by KO Publications 2011) p. 106

Among the visitors to Dempsey's camp was a man he didn't immediately recognise. It was Tex Rickard, wearing spectacles and a false beard. The promoter knew that Kearns wasn't around and he wanted to talk to Jack privately. Tex was insulted that Doc felt he could do better without him, and he warned Jack against Doc. He talked to Dempsey for a couple of hours and set him straight on Doc's shrewd handling of money and expenses. 'I understood what Tex said, but I couldn't bring myself to cross Doc in any way. I was grateful to Doc for everything.'[223]

An unexpected observer of Dempsey's workouts was Al Capone. The Chicago crime boss was a great fight fan and admirer of the heavyweight champion. Walking into Jack's dressing room after his training session, Capone made an offer which Jack had the good sense to refuse. Al was impressed with Dempsey and offered him money, any amount he named if he would stage an exhibition at his private club. Jack refused, but it was tempting, especially when Capone thumbed through his wad of bills and asked if Jack had ever seen so much money before. 'Capone was the kind of guy you either liked or hated. He was a rough customer who wanted to be accepted as a man, not a racketeer.'[224]

As the day of the fight drew closer, there were fears that there may not be a fight at all. Doc Kearns was insisting that his choice of referee was Jim Dougherty, a fight promoter from Leiperville, Pennsylvania, and a good friend of Doc's. But chairman Thomas Bigger of the Michigan State Athletic Commission refused to license Dougherty, appointing Al Day of Detroit as referee. Kearns blew his top and threatened to call the fight off. Al Day even offered to stand down in favour of Dougherty. On the eve of the fight, Bigger relented and agreed to issue a license to Dougherty. The fight was back on!

A night of heavy rain eased off to a drizzle by morning as the fans began arriving at the arena. To keep order, squads of soldiers from nearby Camp Custer served as ushers. Around the ringside section, fences of barbed wire had been erected as a precaution against what had happened at Toledo when Dempsey beat Willard for the title the previous year, when hundreds of fans stormed the ringside seats and refused to be moved. By three in the afternoon, time for the first

---

223 Dempsey with Piattelli p.135
224 Ibid p. 136

preliminary bout, a crowd officially recorded as 11,346 were in their seats having paid a gross gate of $134,904.

At the morning weigh-in, Miske had scaled 189lb, two heavier than the champion. Dempsey was 25 years old and stood 6ft 1.25in, Miske a year older and 6ft 1in. Their physical measurements were almost identical. In their two fights in 1918, the St Paul man had defied Dempsey over ten and six rounds with the Manassa Mauler unable to even knock his man down. That was the proud record Miske carried into the ring that day at Benton Harbor, never knocked down and never knocked out in 78 professional fights.

'From a historical sporting aspect, the Dempsey–Miske fight was going to be significant regardless of the outcome because it would be the first radio broadcast of a prize fight. That August, a Detroit station named 8MK, later WWJ, had claimed to be the first radio station in the world to broadcast regularly scheduled programs. The broadcast of 20 watts, from the second floor of the *Detroit News* building, was only received in an estimated 30 Detroit homes. The championship fight in September provided the first ringside radio broadcast over a year before the first broadcast of a baseball world series.[225]

The contest was scheduled for ten rounds with no decision being rendered should the distance be completed. The only way in which Miske could win the title was if he was able to stop or knock out the champion. Billy and manager Jack Reddy had asked the state commission to make an exception and allow an official decision to be made but their request was refused. The champion and his handlers were in no doubt as to the result – Dempsey by knockout.

Knowing what he knew about his opponent's medical history, Jack's only problem was how to handle Miske – carry him or knock him out as soon as he was able. He was busy making his mind up when the bell rang for round one.

Billy Miske had made his mind up before he entered the ring. He was going to take the fight to the champion just as long as he had strength in his body. He had no fear of Dempsey, having fought him twice before and gone the distance each time. This time Billy was going for a knockout.

He tried. Miske went straight for Dempsey and landed a light left hook to the champion's face, then hooked a right to the neck. Dempsey landed two left hooks to the chin but they weren't loaded. The referee

---

225 Moyle p. 118

broke them out of a couple of clinches and Billy took the champ's left hook on his elbow. He took two rights to the body that made him gasp and a following left hook rattled his jaw. Dempsey crowded Miske, landed a left hook and got the better of a close exchange. The champion unleashed three left hooks to the head so fast they looked like one punch. There was already a red spot on Miske's body, just under his heart, left there by a thudding right hand. Dempsey missed a wicked left but got home a hook to the jaw and Billy was glad to clinch. At the bell it was Dempsey's round.

'In the first round,' wrote Nat Fleischer in his 1929 book, 'Dempsey set himself and drove one of his famous pile-driving straight rights deep into Miske's body. The blow landed just under the heart. It looked then as if the end had come, but Miske weathered the storm and managed to last out the round. He went to his corner a badly hurt man…He never fully recovered from the effects of that blow.'[226]

Coming out for round two, Dempsey was on his toes, circling his man before going in with a right to the body. It hurt Billy and he clinched. He grabbed again when the champion threw a hard right to the side of his head and Dougherty was having his work cut out tugging them apart.

'As they came out of a clinch,' recorded Fleischer, 'Dempsey stepped quickly forward and sank a right into Miske's bruised ribs under the heart. The challenger dropped in his tracks. His legs crumpled beneath him and he sprawled on the canvas. It seemed as he was temporarily paralyzed from the waist down, and might be compelled to take the count while he was still perfectly conscious but unable to rise to his feet.'[227]

It was the first time Billy had been knocked down in eight years as a professional fighter and he was determined his fight would not end there. Billy somehow got to his feet and started fighting gamely, but his punches were wild. Dempsey threw a right but it was too high on Miske's head. He missed a right to the jaw, but got home with a couple of solid punches to the body which shook Miske. Dempsey's body shots were taking their toll of the St Paul puncher but he got a left hook to the champion's face before the bell ended another round for Dempsey.

---

226 Nat Fleischer *Jack Dempsey the Idol of Fistiana* (New York: The Ring Publishing Co. 1929) p. 93
227 Ibid pp. 93–94

Refreshed by the minute's rest, Billy came out punching and hammered a right to the jaw, but took a punch under the heart in return. Dempsey sent two lefts to the jaw and brushed off Miske's left to the face. The champion smashed a right to the body then whipped a terrific left hook to the chin. Billy reeled back to his own corner before dropping full length on the canvas. Referee Dougherty's count could barely be heard above the noise of the crowd as they sensed the end was near. At seven, Billy stirred and his fighting heart dragged him to his feet as nine was called off.

Dempsey was standing near the ropes on one side of the ring. The champion was intently watching his rival, a businessman studying a situation. He waited patiently for Miske to rise and then set himself to finish his job. Miske regained his feet and gazed out over the throng. He did not realise where he was.

The report in the *Sheboygan Press* detailed the end of Billy Miske's dream of becoming heavyweight champion of the world, 'He did not know that stepping lightly but determinedly toward him was Jack Dempsey, with right fist clenched within his five-ounce glove, poising himself to deliver the blow that would end it all. The punch crashed over Miske's left shoulder...It landed and Miske dropped to the floor.'[228]

As referee Dougherty called ten and out, the crowd went crazy, throwing hats in the air and rushing towards the ring to hail their hero. Their hero was busy helping his victim back to his feet and over to where his seconds had shoved the stool into the ring for him.

'I carried Billy to his stool and nearly got sick to my stomach while the two seconds worked on him bringing him to,' recalled Dempsey in his 1960 autobiography. 'Suddenly, and for the first time in my fight life, I hated those guys who were cheering for me. Billy Miske, my friend, was still out. It was the only time in my life I was ashamed of being a fighter.'[229]

Doc Kearns objected to snide comments that Dempsey had fought a 'dead man', pointing out that, although Bright's disease finally killed Miske, he didn't die until three years, four months after his fight with Dempsey.

Between the time he fought Dempsey for the title and the day he died, 1 January 1924, Billy Miske had another 24 fights and won them

---

228 *Sheboygan Press* 7 September 1920
229 Dempsey with Considine & Slocum p. 129

all, beating such guys as Homer Smith, Willie Meehan, Fred Fulton, Bill Brennan and Tommy Gibbons. The best day he ever had, Billy Miske would never have beaten Jack Dempsey and become champion of the heavyweights. But he got his chance, for which he was eternally grateful, reportedly saying on his death bed, 'Tell Jack thanks. Tell him thanks from Billy.'

The day after the fight in Benton Harbor, Miske told reporters, 'It is my thought today that there is not a man alive who can stand up before Jack Dempsey – the Jack Dempsey I met yesterday – for ten full rounds...I was beaten by a great fighter – certainly the greatest of this day – and probably the greatest of all time.'[230]

Billy's words were echoed by top sportswriter Frank G. Menke, who wrote, 'And now with Miske's name added to the list of Dempsey victims, what man fights today who can test Dempsey to the utmost of his powers? What man can force him to lash out with all the might that is in his hands and arms, power which so far has never been fully tapped?'[231]

A Chicago bartender named Bill Brennan was sure that he was the man sportswriter Menke was looking for, a two-fisted fighting man who could hammer Jack Dempsey loose from his coveted championship. Promoter Tex Rickard was ready and willing to give him the chance and throw in a diamond-studded championship belt for the winner.

Kearns recalled, 'Boxing now was legal in New York again and, wanting to show Dempsey in the big town, I quickly agreed to meet Bill Brennan at the old Madison Square Garden on 14 December. After all, we had flattened him in Milwaukee early in 1918.'[232]

Dempsey, on his first visit to New York looking for fights, had been happy to spar with Brennan for 50 cents a day. Now, as heavyweight champion of the world, he was guaranteed $100,000 to fight Brennan in the Garden on 26th Street. Jack trained in New York for this fight; gym chores on the old USS *Granite State*, a naval ship tied up at the Hudson River dock, roadwork in Central Park. 'Jack did not train well for the fight,' recalled Teddy Hayes. 'Jack worked out on 57th Street where Doc Van Kelton had an open air handball court. Admission was a buck and we drew almost no crowds, but one of our regulars was Al Jolson who was appearing on Broadway...Jolson was a ham,

230 *New Castle News* 7 September 1920
231 Frank G. Menke *San Antonio Evening News* 7 September 1920
232 Kearns with Fraley p. 128

but he couldn't lick his lips. It was harmless, but I wanted Jack's mind a little more on his work.'[233]

If Dempsey's mind was on his work during the day, his nights were spent on the town. Kahn, in his biography of Dempsey, stated, 'Capone then dispatched a beautiful mob lady to visit New York City. She was to seek out Dempsey and do everything a smart and stunning woman could do to prevent the champion from training properly.'[234]

'I finally learned that Dempsey had been doing the town each night with a sleek, sophisticated divorcee,' recalled Kearns. 'When Dempsey climbed through the ropes on the night of the fight, it was obvious that he was in the poorest condition of his career. Brennan, on the other hand, was in the best condition of his life. There was no question in my mind that he had trained as if somebody held a gun to his back.'[235]

The Garden was jammed to the doors that December night and the 11,956 seats overflowed to a thousand bleacher seats with about 2,000 fans willing to pay for standing room. 'Wild cheers penetrated the thick smoke haze when the handsome Irishman from Chicago entered the ring, clad in green tights and a red sweater,' wrote Roberts in his 1979 book. 'With a look of complete bewilderment, Brennan grinned nervously at the celebrities in the ring…Dempsey's entrance was another matter. Booed from the twenty-five dollar seats to the two-fifty seats, the champion stepped through the ropes at ten-thirty. He scowled at Brennan, sneered at the audience, and moved about like a pent-up tiger in long white boxing trunks.'[236]

Coming out for round one, Dempsey chopped a right to the head. They exchanged lefts and rights to the body and Brennan got his left hook working to the head. Dempsey fired two rights to the head, one just missing Bill's jaw. A left hook from Dempsey scraped Brennan's right eye and at the bell it was Dempsey's round. Both led off with the right as round two opened, then Dempsey missed a left hook. Brennan got in a solid left to the body and they swapped blows inside. The champion was short with a right to the head and Brennan whipped in two half-arm uppercuts just over the heart that made Dempsey gasp. Most ringsiders had Brennan a shade ahead at the bell.

233 Hayes p. 49
234 Kahn p. 215
235 Kearns with Fraley p. 130
236 Roberts p. 97

Into round three and both landed short right uppercuts. The champ ducked into a right hook and caught a left and right to the head as the crowd cheered. Then Dempsey forced Brennan across the ring with left and right hooks but they weren't fully loaded and the Chicago fighter fought his way inside. Dempsey crashed over a right to Brennan's left ear, the hardest blow so far in the fight. Just before the bell the champion brought blood from Brennan's mouth with a thudding left hook. It was Jack's round.

As the fourth opened, both landed to the body. Brennan sent his right twice to the head, Dempsey came back with a jarring left to the face and a right cross to the ear, then he opened up with a sizzling left hook and two vicious rights to the head. There was more steam in his punches and Brennan was feeling the heat. At the bell his mouth was bleeding again. Round five and they exchanged short-arm punches before clinching. Referee Johnny Haukop cautioned the champion for touching Brennan's face lightly as they broke, then Jack hammered three hard rights into the body.

He forced Bill into a neutral corner and hooked the right twice to the stomach, and as they broke into the centre of the ring Dempsey blasted the right deep into Bill's body, making him wish he was somewhere else. Brennan came back with two rights to the body just as the bell sounded the end of the round, which was a good one for the champion. Dempsey carried on the good work in round six, scoring heavily to the body with trip-hammer rights, and he was able to block a lot of Brennan's best punches. The seventh saw Dempsey using his left to good advantage, jabbing and hooking, and Brennan's blows were having little effect on the champion. Jack hammered a hard right into the body and caught Bill's right ear with a left hook. Then a hard right jab flattened Brennan's nose and he signed for two sizzling rights to the head as the round ended.

'Just as the bell rang at the start of the eighth round,' recalled Fleischer, 'one of the two largest of the six lights that hung over the ring went out, and from far up in the distant regions of the top gallery a voice called out, "Goodnight, Brennan." Dempsey came out of his corner with something akin to a rush and quickly drove a right uppercut to Brennan's body. He followed this with a straight right to his rival's ribs and to those at the ringside it seemed that the champion was preparing the challenger for the finish. Brennan rocked under the force of the blow but he was far from being on the verge of a knockout...When the bell sounded, the light that had been out during the round suddenly burst forth again in all its brightness.'[237]

The challenger picked up the pace in the ninth round and after an action-packed three minutes many ringsiders gave him the round. Dempsey circled his man, jabbing the left into Bill's face. Brennan missed with a left hook and Dempsey made him pay with a driving right to the body that brought a grunt from the Chicago fighter. Forcing his way inside, Dempsey used a short right to great effect and, making room for himself, smashed a terrific right cross to the jaw that rocked Bill to his toenails. Brennan looked in trouble and Dempsey hammered in a left and right to the head and Bill was glad to hang on. He went slowly to his corner as the bell brought a 60-second relief.

It was in the ninth round that Dempsey recalled, 'Bill reached down and hit me with a chopping right that cut me all along where my ear joined my head…Suddenly the whole side of my head was warm with my blood. I touched my ear and it felt like it was hanging off, like a busted awning. I was afraid that if Bill hit me a solid punch, or even a grazing one, he might knock the ear off.'[238]

Fleischer recalled, 'It was in the tenth round…As they went into a clinch, Brennan swung his right to Dempsey's left ear. Whether this cut the champion's ear lobe or whether Brennan's head collided with the spot could not be definitely decided, but the blood was gushing down the side of Dempsey's jaw and under the ear…He rushed Brennan and drove in a series of short rights and lefts to the body. Brennan's knees sagged but he pitched forward into the clinch and was able to last out the round.'[239]

According to the Associated Press round-by-round report, carried in newspapers across the country, in the 11th round, 'Brennan came out in fairly good shape and they exchanged lefts and rights to the head, one of which cut Dempsey's ear. Dempsey bled considerably from the mouth and ear while in his corner.'[240] The injury to the champion's left ear, whether it occurred in round nine, ten or 11, was horrific and would be graphically described by sportswriter Grantland Rice as looking 'like a cross between a breaded veal cutlet and a sponge dipped in gore'.[241]

---

237 Fleischer pp. 99–100
238 Dempsey with Considine & Slocum p. 130
239 Fleischer p. 100
240 *Janesville Daily Gazette* 15 December 1920
241 Grantland Rice *New York Herald* 15 December 1920

The corner did a good job patching Jack up while Kearns read the riot act to his tiger. He screamed into Jack's good ear, 'You've thrown it all away because of a cheap broad. If you got any guts left at all you'll pull up your socks and go out there and belt this bum out.'[242]

The end came in round 12 as reported by Associated Press, 'Dempsey drove a hard right over the heart and hooked his left to the stomach. Brennan crumbled and almost doubled from the effect of these blows, and as he tottered toward the floor Dempsey sent him sprawling on the ropes with a right smash on the head.'[243]

As referee Haukop began to toll off the fatal ten seconds, Brennan writhed in agony and strove gamely to regain his feet. At the count of seven it looked like Bill might make it but he slipped back again to a squatting position. He did get to his feet, just as the referee was counting ten. Dempsey moved as if to deliver another punch but he was restrained by Haukop as he stepped between the men and waved Jack back to his corner, grabbing Brennan by the arm to lead him to his stool as his seconds came into the ring. It was all over at one minute and 57 seconds of round 12 and Jack Dempsey was still the heavyweight champion of the world. But as trainer Teddy Hayes recalled, 'Early in the 12th Jack sank a terrific left into Brennan's belly, and when Bill clutched himself in pain, Jack hit him behind the ear with a savage right, a rabbit punch. From that day on the rabbit punch was illegal, but it saved Dempsey's title that day in 1920, no mistake.'[244]

---

242 Kearns with Fraley p. 131
243 *Janesville Daily Gazette* 15 December 1920
244 Hayes p. 49

10

Carpentier 'The Wonder Man'

S EVERAL gentlemen of the pugilistic profession breathed a heavy sigh of relief when Jack Dempsey emerged triumphant from that exciting battle with Bill Brennan at Madison Square Garden on 14 December 1920. For some five weeks previously, these gentlemen had gathered in the great hall of Claridge's Hotel in New York City to put their collective names to a contract matching world heavyweight champion Jack Dempsey in a contest with Georges Carpentier, the French holder of the European title and the newly crowned world light-heavyweight champion. Present at the signing were promoter Tex Rickard, his partners in the deal William A. Brady, the Broadway producer, and London theatrical producer C.B. Cochran, Dempsey and manager Jack Kearns, Georges Carpentier and his manager Francois Descamps. Leading sportswriter Bob Edgren was there to act as stakeholder.

This contract stated that Dempsey would be paid $300,000, Georges $200,000. The agreement also stated that on or before 20 November the three promoters must post $100,000 and the managers $50,000 each in forfeit money, at the Central Trust Company of New York. However, of the promoters, only Cochran was able to post his share by the due date, and the managers also failed to honour their agreements. Instead of posting Dempsey's $50,000 with the Central Trust Company, Kearns had put the money into a safety deposit box, gone back to California, and could not be contacted. Meanwhile,

Descamps was told in no uncertain terms by French government sources that he could not send $50,000 out of the country to New York or anywhere else for that matter. Paris decided they couldn't afford it.

Rickard and Brady had failed to raise their shares of the $100,000 because of threats governor-elect Nathan L. Miller had made to repeal the Walker Law. And Miller, a Republican, who had been elected that month in the 1920 landslide that swept Warren G. Harding into the White House, was assuming office on 1 January. The promoters had counted heavily on putting the fight on at one of the big New York ballparks, thus eliminating the cost of an arena. The idea of building one, after gambling $500,000 on the purses, scared off the backers Tex and Bill Brady had approached. Brady withdrew, using the excuse that the fighters' forfeit money had not been delivered on time, and Cochran also pulled out of the deal shortly afterwards.

Charles Samuels, in his 1957 biography of Rickard, wrote, 'Tex, however, insisted he would go through with the match. "I'll put this fight on alone if I have to," he told the sportswriters. "I feel duty-bound to do that. And this one will be the best and biggest fight I ever promoted."'[245]

On 14 January 1921, world lightweight champion Benny Leonard defended his title against Ritchie Mitchell in a thriller at Madison Square Garden for Miss Anne Morgan's favourite charity, the American Friends of France. Miss Morgan co-promoted the bout with Rickard and it drew the 'high-hat-and-ermine' crowd Tex had always dreamed of attending his shows. Three weeks after the fight, Rickard posted the $100,000 promoter's bond for the Dempsey–Carpentier bout and announced officially that he had taken over Brady's and Cochran's interest in the championship contest.

'With two such unprecedented guarantees before a ticket was sold,' wrote Budd Schulberg in his book *Ringside*, 'there wasn't a house big enough for the kind of business he needed to get off his half-million dollar hook. So the enormous bubble grew and grew. He would build an arena especially for the occasion, with the largest seating capacity in the world, 100,000 seats. 'When Rickard broke ground for this at Boyle's Thirty Acres outside of Jersey City, Brady and Cochran were convinced they had involved themselves with a madman. No match in boxing history had drawn over half a million dollars, but Rickard was sleep-walking into one that would need nearly a million to break

245 Charles Samuels *The Magnificent Rube* (New York: McGraw Hill Book Co. 1957) pp. 231–232

even. His backers were sensible showmen, not wide-eyed gamblers. They picked up their marbles and went home.'[246]

Rickard was once again the lone wolf gambler from the Yukon and the cards were running against him. Over in Jersey City, the lumber mill was calling for its money, the contractor threatening to pull his men out. Then Fate dealt Tex a winning hand in the unlikely shape of Mike Jacobs, then a Broadway ticket speculator, looking to do some business. Rickard wasn't in the mood, telling Mike the building contractor wanted $20,000 by that afternoon or Tex had no arena.

'Mike reached into his pocket and pulled out twenty thousand-dollar bills. "Go pay the son of a bitch," he growled. "An advance on the first five rows of ringside." Tex began to look more like his usually ebullient self. "I'll need two hundred grand to open the show. The rest can come out of the receipts...Mike, you're saving my life," Rickard added. "I'll never forget you for this." Then Mike went out to do a selling job among his fellow speculators...He convinced eight brokers to put up $25,000 apiece in return for choice sections of the house (after Mike got his, of course), and Rickard was saved.'[247]

Jack Dempsey versus Georges Carpentier didn't figure to be a great fight. 'I'm leveling when I tell you that it was probably the worst mismatch in the history of the heavyweight division,' recalled Dempsey in his 1959 autobiography.[248]

After seeing the champion crush Billy Miske at Benton Harbor, Frank G. Menke wrote, 'They've talked Carpentier, the French boxer, as a Dempsey foeman. And they are talking the Frenchman into being slaughtered. For, great as Carpentier may be, he cannot be classed with Dempsey. Those who espouse the Parisian's cause insist that his superior boxing ability and greater agility will enable him to keep out of Dempsey's way until Dempsey tires himself. What a fallacy: for, first of all, Dempsey is tireless beyond almost human conception in his endurance powers. As for speed, well, Dempsey made Miske, long regarded as one of the speediest hoofers in the game, look like a wooden-legged circus fat man. Throughout the entire fight on Monday, Dempsey whizzed Miske with the speed of a panther – and whenever Miske tried to spring away from attack Dempsey overhauled him without real effort.'[249]

246 Budd Schulberg *Ringside* (Chicago: Ivan R. Dee 2006) pp. 300–301
247 Ibid pp. 301–302
248 Dempsey with Considine & Slocum p.132
249 Frank G. Menke *Oakland Tribune* 7 September 1920

The *New York World's* fight expert Hype Igoe, who had seen every world championship fight since the days of John L. Sullivan, warned readers, 'Have your eyes open every second after the bell rings, for, dear innocents, you are going to have a hair-raising run for your money. Dempsey is going to smash the Orchid Man to canvas inside of one minute and thirty seconds! That's my honest-to-goodness guess after going over every detail of the men's past and present as ring warriors. Georges may escape annihilation within the time limit of one minute and a half that I have set by scooting like an eel suddenly dropped on a mossy bank. If he does escape in my time limit, he may leg it lickety-split into the third round, but that period will mark the end of his quest for the golden crown. His end in one minute and a half, with the possibility that he may struggle hopelessly on until the third round. No further.'[250]

Old-time champ Battling Nelson declared, 'I look for the battle to end before either Dempsey or Carpentier gets warmed up…Of course, I am sticking to Dempsey. He looks better to me than when he fought Willard; he's got more class, knows more stuff, and is a better and more polished boxer. You'll recall that I told the boys at Toledo that Willard would get the punching of his life. Well, the same goes for Carpentier. Dempsey looks like a cinch. If he gets a fair shot at his body with his right hand, Carpentier will be slowed for a left hook that will knock him into somebody's lap.'[251]

Some writers predicted that the spirit of Lafayette would inspire Gorgeous Georges in the ring at Boyle's Thirty Acres. Others said he could win only if Dempsey was hit by lightning during the fight. But if the boxing experts couldn't see Dempsey–Carpentier as a great fight, it was certainly viewed as a great attraction. In his biography of Rickard, Samuels stated, 'It has long been Paul Gallico's pet theory that a good deal of Rickard's success as a promoter was the result of his ability to make the public see one fighter as a hero and the other as a villain. In the impending imbroglio that had already been done for him. In Carpentier he had his custom-made hero.'[252]

On the other hand, factions in the newly established American Legion and other patriotic groups had painted Dempsey a villain of blackest hue. They branded him a slacker, and some of them even urged that the fight be barred on that ground.

---

250 Hype Igoe *The Boston Globe* 30 June 1921
251 Battling Nelson *Syracuse Herald* 1 July 1921
252 Samuels p. 235

Dempsey biographer Randy Roberts used the same analogy as Gallico, writing, 'Give the masses of people some rosy-cheeked, clear-complexioned Lancelot to cheer and some thick-bearded, scowling Simon Legree to boo and jeer, and the money would roll in in waves and people of both sexes and all classes would perk up and take notice...Never would a Rickard hero be so white and a villain so black. Carpentier, from his French accent to his frail, almost ethereal features, was the ideal Lancelot for Rickard's medieval morality play promotional formula... Next to Carpentier, Dempsey appeared to be deficient in both charm and valor. In every way he was Carpentier's opposite. Carpentier was the light-skinned cosmopolitan, ever-smiling war hero. Dempsey was dark-complexioned; his beard was coarse, his eyebrows were thick, and his face seemed to be cast in a permanent iron scowl.'[253]

But to millions of Americans, Lancelot was nothing more than a mythical figure from ancient folklore. Rickard's Lancelot was going to need a high-powered publicity campaign if he was to convince those millions of Americans that he was the real deal. It started in 1920.

'The trouble was that the American public did not know me well enough,' Carpentier recalled in his 1955 autobiography, 'and it was therefore doubtful whether a match with me would bring in sufficient to make it worth Dempsey's while. In these circumstances a group of New York promoters suggested that I should make a preliminary trip to the States to meet certain less prominent men.

'Neither Descamps nor I were much in favor of this proposal. We wanted Dempsey, or, if we couldn't have Dempsey, then Battling Levinsky...We agreed to go to the United States without a fight with either of them. I accepted the offer of a film company to go to New York to star in a film and the American promoter Jack Curley agreed to organise an exhibition tour for me throughout the country.'[254]

Before the tour got under way, Carpentier had to work on the film, which to his delight was entitled *The Wonder Man* with Georges in the starring role. It was shot in New Jersey, across the river from New York, and a car collected the Frenchman and took him to the studio every morning. Movies were still silent in those days but Georges still had to learn his lines and speak them on camera. The whole business didn't appeal to the boxer very much but he was a lot happier when

---

253 Roberts pp. 109, 111
254 Georges Carpentier *Carpentier by Himself* (London: Hutchinson 1955) p. 123

filming was finished and he received a cheque for $45,000 for 25 days of work.

For the next two months, Carpentier and his entourage criss-crossed America on the tour organised by Jack Curley. Curley's real name was Jacques Armand Schuel and he was born in San Francisco in July 1876 after his parents fled France following the Franco-Prussian war. The family returned to Europe and young Jacques spent his time between Strasbourg and Paris before moving back to the States as a teenager. 'He was a true cosmopolite and a far more versatile showman than Tex,' wrote Samuels. 'In his time Curley managed the tours of wrestling troupes, the Vatican Choir, Mrs Lydia Pankhurst, the militant British suffragette leader, and Annette Kellerman, the swimmer. Curley, a thick-lipped, round-faced lovable man, designed the one-piece bathing suit that made Miss Kellerman's figure the most talked about feminine torso of the day.'[255]

Curley also promoted the Jack Johnson–Jess Willard fight in Havana and the heavyweight championship wrestling match between Frank Gotch and George Hackenschmidt which drew $94,000, which for years remained a record gate for the grunt-and-groan boys.

'Curley was a big, fattish fellow with a warm and enthusiastic manner,' remembered Carpentier. 'I had most to do with Curley and our relationship was always excellent. The tour lasted almost two months and during that period I boxed in about forty towns. I would box my four rounds with Lenaers as the chief attraction of a boxing tournament specially organised for the purpose…Often I would go to bed at night in some station or other and wake up the next morning hundreds of miles away with the yawning question, 'Where the devil are we now?' We returned to New York at the beginning of July after three months that brought me in – with film and tour together – almost a hundred thousand dollars.'[256]

It had been a brilliant public relations exercise, but the press boys were not yet sold on Carpentier's suitability as the man to take away Dempsey's title, calling him 'smiler' and a 'screen boxer'. So Georges was delighted when, on 5 July, manager Descamps signed for him to challenge Battling Levinsky for his world light-heavyweight title sometime in October. After a few weeks back home in Paris, and a holiday in Dieppe with his wife Georgette, a wire was received from

---

255 Samuels p. 238
256 Carpentier pp. 127, 129

Jack Curley with the news that the Levinsky fight was set for 12 October in Jersey City.

Levinsky's real name was Barney Lebrowitz and he was born in Philadelphia. He boxed as Barney Williams until 1913 when teaming up with fabled manager 'Dumb' Dan Morgan who promptly named him Battling Levinsky. Morgan kept him busy and when the Battler retired in 1930 his record added up to 289 bouts. 'I used to give him Wednesday off,' Morgan said dryly. Levinsky won his claim to the light-heavyweight title in 1916 by beating Jack Dillon, the 'Hoosier Bearcat'. Dillon had picked up the title after the retirement of Philadelphia Jack O'Brien and embarked upon a nine-fight series with Levinsky. Their ninth meeting, in Boston, saw the Battler outwit the critics and Dillon, using his left jab and left hook to punch his way to the decision over 12 rounds to become champion. Morgan kept him busy fighting guys like Billy Miske, Harry Greb, Tommy Gibbons and Jack Dempsey who knocked him out in three rounds. That was in November 1918, six months before Dempsey annihilated Willard to win the heavyweight title.

Now it was October 1920 and Levinsky was chosen for Carpentier's American ring debut to see how the Frenchman would shape up as a challenger for Dempsey. Reporting from Jersey City on 12 October, the man from Associated Press wrote, 'Georges Carpentier, French war hero and European heavyweight boxing champion, will engage tonight in a 12-round bout with Battling Levinksy, American light-heavyweight title holder. Under New Jersey law no decision is permitted. The contest will be held in the open air in Jersey City baseball park. Fair mild weather is forecast.

'Both men are clever boxers, but the Frenchman is credited with possessing the stronger punch, having scored spectacular one-round knockouts over two English champions, Bombardier Billy Wells and Joe Beckett. Equal in height, the two boxers are also expected to weigh about the same, probably slightly under 175 pounds. The American has a slight advantage in reach.'[257]

That, and four-and-a-half pounds in weight, were the only advantages Levinksy had that night as Carpentier stormed his way to a fourth-round knockout, adding Levinksy's American title to his European belt and cementing his claim to the world championship.

---

257 *Olean Evening Herald* 12 October 1920

From ringside, syndicated columnist Westbrook Pegler wrote, 'Georges Carpentier has made good, and the country's fight promoters will now probably be taking pen and pencil in hand to figure new fancy prices to offer for a fight between the French champion and Jack Dempsey for the world's heavyweight title. In knocking out Battling Levinsky in the fourth round of a scheduled 12-rounds bout here last night, Carpentier showed everything as advertised...Levinsky never had a chance. He looked like a cheap imitation when he shaped up against Carpentier for the first round...The Frenchman was attacking all the time, high on his toes and whenever he landed a punch he considered that an invitation to rush in and toss over at least two more.

'The best punch he showed was that overhand chop with the right which travelled about eighteen inches and hit like the kick of a mule... Carpentier made a mark of Levinsky's jaw and he played for that mark from the time the fight began until he finally put over the haymaker smack on the point. Referee Ertle said after the fight that he had never seen a man that could hit as hard as Carpentier hit Levinsky. He said the blow that really put Levinsky out was a right which caught the Battler in the neck just below the jaw. "After this experience I am convinced that Carpentier can knock out Dempsey almost as easily as he knocked out Bat," said Dan Morgan, manager of Levinsky, after the fight. "He is such a natural fighter with such a wonderful punch that he doesn't have to box...I tell you those terrible punches to the jaw will knock out Jack Dempsey. He will knock him cold."

'Long after the fight was over, Levinsky was led out under the grandstand of the ballpark, staggering on the arms of his handlers. He was still punch drunk and his eyes were shut. Carpentier remained in his dressing room for almost an hour and when he came out there were thousands of fans waiting in the darkness and standing ankle-deep in the mud to cheer him as an idol who had made good.' [258]

Newspapers carrying the reports of the fight on the sports pages, also carried on the entertainments page a glowing advert for the film *The Wonder Man,* then showing in movie houses across the country.

'GEORGES CARPENTIER In the Million Dollar Picture – An All Powerful Absorbing Drama 'THE WONDER MAN' The Idol of Two Continents – He Won Fame in the War – He Won Honors in the Ring – See How He Won a Girl in a Million Dollar Attraction

---

258 Westbrook Pegler *Kansas City Star* 13 October 1920

GEORGES CARPENTIER – The Most Talked of Man in the World – Therefore the Most Popular.'[259]

Typical of the nation's press was the announcement in the *Billings Gazette* of Montana on Sunday 10 October. 'Georges Carpentier, idol of France, whose notable record in the ring has won him fame and fortune and whose fascinating personality has made him the idol of two continents, will be the chief attraction at the Strand Theatre in *The Wonder Man*, a Robertson-Cole production, for a three-day showing, beginning today. The picture promises an entertainment unique in the realm of the cinema art. Unlike the previous efforts of producers to bring champions of the prize ring before the public on the screen in the roles of daredevil heroes or in hair-raising serials, Georges Carpentier is given as a vehicle an intriguing romance of American society, with himself in the role of a smart well-dressed man about town.

'*The Wonder Man* gives the public its first opportunity to really know this favorite son of France – in fact it gives the first opportunity for his many admirers to see him. The great demand to see Carpentier in the ring was proved beyond a doubt by the crowd that flocked to the studio to see him when a great fight scene for the picture was staged. More than 2,000 persons braved the muddy roads of New Jersey to see him in his fighting togs for the first time in America.'

However there was a somewhat mixed reaction from the New York boxing writers who saw Carpentier in his fighting togs for the first time in an American ring, against Levinsky in Jersey City. W.N. Jones wrote in *The Globe*, 'He knocked out Battling Levinsky in the fourth round…Yet last night's bout is no true indication of the ability of the Frenchman. While the battler appeared to be in excellent physical condition, his mental processes were badly out of gear, not functioning properly.'[260]

In the *Evening Post*, Herbert Reed observed, 'Compared with Dempsey at the moment, he left the impression of being just a remarkable amateur.'[261]

In *The Globe*, Alfred W. McCann didn't give the Frenchman much credit, writing, 'It was no contest. It was a setup. Levinsky went into the ring to get the money.'[262]

---

259 *Billings Gazette* Montana 10 October 1920
260 W.N. Jones *The Globe* New York 13 October 1920
261 Herbert Reed *Evening Post* New York 13 October 1920
262 Alfred W. McCann *The Globe* New York 13 October 1920

Thomas Aloysius Dorgan, veteran sportswriter and cartoonist who signed himself TAD, didn't mince words in his report for the *New York Journal*. Dorgan wrote, 'As Georgie Cohen says, "P.T. Barnum had the right idea. The more you trim a sucker the better he likes it." New York and New Jersey saps paid more than $300,000 to see Carpentier, the French wonder man, tip over an old, foundered boxer like Levinsky, in four rounds. Any guy who knows his left shoe from his right could figure that Carpentier would win in a punch or two. The Frenchman did. He had nothing in front of him to fear. He could do as he pleased. The punching bag before the Frenchman wasn't even lifelike. It did not bounce back worth a darn. Levinsky went in to get the short end, and that's just what he got. He knew he was in for a licking, and he got that, too.'[263]

Yet on paper, Battling Levinsky was a credible opponent for Carpentier's American ring debut. Aged 29, he had been recognised as world light-heavyweight champion for four years, and the only knockout on his record was to a guy named Jack Dempsey. After the fight, Levinsky told reporters that Carpentier was a much better puncher.

'I've tested the hitting ability of the two men,' said Levinsky as his seconds tried to soothe his wounded feelings, 'and I know what I am talking about. Why, when that Frenchman hit me with that right wallop in the second round that knocked me down, I thought a building had fallen on me. That was the punch that sent me on my way, and I never was right after that.'[264]

The betting on the fight was interesting, to say the least. 'Both Broadway and Wall Street apparently were in on things, for men went so far as to name the round the afternoon before the mill,' claimed one report out of New York. 'George T. Vickers, assistant prosecutor of New Jersey had this to say. "I know that Wall Street was betting Levinsky would be knocked out in the fourth round and that probably started the frame-up talk." The prosecutor was there and he seemed to think everything was all right, however.'[265]

'Descamps had no end of a mad-on because people weren't giving his boy credit for a tremendous feat of fisticuffs in beating the patriarchal bat,' wrote Pegler. "Georges, he do not have to be on guard against Levinsky," the keen-eyed manager sputtered. "Against

---

263 'TAD' *The New York Journal* 14 October 1920
264 *Kansas City Times* 14 October 1920
265 *New Castle News* 15 October 1920

Dempsey he fight a different way. He will knock out Dempsey in four rounds." Descamps wants half of the gate money and says he will not let the lad step into the ring with Dempsey for a cent less.'[266]

A couple of weeks after the Levinsky fight, manager Descamps was in the Hotel Claridge in New York City to put his name to a contract giving his boy his biggest ever purse, $200,000, with the champion of the heavyweights getting $300,000. Tex Rickard and his associates announced that the fight would be staged in or near New York on 4 July, and the French party sailed for home a few days later, where Madame Carpentier was telling reporters, 'I hope the next fight with Mr Dempsey will be his last, win or lose, so that he may come back to me.'[267]

---

266 Westbrook Pegler *Kansas City Times* 15 October 1920
267 *Madison Capital Times* 14 October 1920

11

The Million-Dollar Gate

'NOW that it's sure I'm to meet Carpentier,' Dempsey said to Robert Edgren of the *New York World*, 'there's just one little thing I want to say about it. Seems to me everybody thinks the Frenchman hasn't a chance. I wish I was half as sure as a lot of my friends say they are. I never went into a fight yet feeling sure that I would win…Another thing, you can throw that fight with Levinsky out. Levinsky was all in when I knocked him out a couple of years before, and any fair heavyweight or good middleweight could whip him now. He couldn't fight, and Carpentier never had a chance to show what he could do.'

Edgren would write, 'Dempsey is a sportsman. He didn't go to see Carpentier fight Levinsky.' 'Carpentier never saw me fight, and I didn't think it was fair to take the advantage of going to see him,' said Dempsey. 'Just one more thing,' added the writer. 'I've heard Carpentier described as a creature of keen intelligence, able to outwit any more ponderous antagonist – Dempsey, for instance. But Dempsey is no slow thinker himself. In all the Dempsey fights that have come under my observation I've been impressed by Dempsey's mental alertness even more than by his physical speed and power. Carpentier may be swift of thought, but our own Jack Dempsey is no 'brother to the ox'.'[268]

---

268 Robert Edgren *Boston Evening Globe* 30 October 1920

Jack Curley, Carpentier's American manager, was in no doubt as to the Frenchman's fighting ability. Pointing out that the eyes of the critics were on the Carpentier–Levinsky contest, their minds were on a Carpentier–Dempsey match, 'and no fight expert can draw on his imagination to do justice to Carpentier by comparison, mainly because it was Battling Levinsky facing the Frenchman and not Jack Dempsey…I came away from the ringside absolutely satisfied with the Frenchman's performance, and more convinced than ever that he has more than an even chance to defeat Jack Dempsey.'[269]

Once the signing of the contracts hit the headlines, the Dempsey–Carpentier fight became global. Every move the fighters and Tex Rickard made was front-page news. Rickard had chosen Boyle's Thirty Acres in Jersey City as the battle site and originally ordered a 50,000 seat stadium. But as orders for tickets flooded in with every post, Tex increased the capacity, first to 70,000 then again to 91,613. He was confidently predicting a million-dollar gate, the first in boxing history. Even the tickets made news.

'When the first batch of tickets went out they created a sensation,' wrote Samuels. 'They were oversized, beautifully engraved, and had embossed gold backs. Rickard's hunch was that they'd be shown around by everyone who bought them, giving the fight that much more free word-of-mouth advertising. He also knew that many fans who paid up to fifty dollars for a ticket might like them for souvenirs.'[270]

'Viewing the two boxers, the American public was faced with a perplexing dilemma,' wrote Roberts. 'Carpentier was a war hero but also a foreigner; the American, Dempsey, was labeled as a draft dodger. Obviously, this was no easy choice to make. Intellectuals on both sides of the Atlantic overwhelmingly favored the dapper Frenchman. If the intellectuals were astute enough to realise that Carpentier stood no chance against the champion, this dismal knowledge only served to further endear the Frenchman to them…Here was no common pugilist with a broken nose and cauliflowered ears. On the other hand, Dempsey's followers earned their living with their hands. In the champion they recognised something familiar. As one commentator observed, "Why, if he weren't a prizefighter, he'd be a teamster."

'Heywood Broun, who visited Dempsey before the fight, found the champion to be a timid gentleman who enjoyed romantic literature

---

269 Jack Curley *Trenton Evening Times* 20 October 1920
270 Samuels p. 234

and was highly sensitive to the controversy over his draft record. The Veterans of Foreign Wars of Atlantic City sounded a sympathetic chord when they pledged their support for him: "We look on Dempsey as the American champion going into the ring to uphold America's title of supremacy in a game in which it has excelled for generations." Thus both Carpentier and Dempsey were converted into cultural heroes.'[271]

They weren't heroes in the eyes of James A. (Jimmy) Gallivan, the Democratic representative from Massachusetts. Denouncing Jack Dempsey as a 'big bum' who dodged the draft, Gallivan introduced a resolution in the house to stop the world's championship prize fight until Congress granted a bonus to the veterans of the world war. 'It is a notorious fact that Dempsey showed himself to be a big "bum" in that war when he dodged the draft, and, unless I mistake, France was in distress and had been for months before Carpentier joined the colours of his country. After he did get into a uniform, it is alleged he did good service, but my mind goes back to the early days of the war when he was engaged in fighting, as a prizefighter, for money.'[272]

Newspapers the following day quickly accused Gallivan of not knowing what he was talking about. 'The records from the French war ministry show that Georges was in the thick of the war from the very first day or even before the official declarations were given out. He served 18 months in actual flying at the front for which he received the decorations Croix de Guerre and Medaille Militaire…As for Gallivan's resolution to stop the fight it looks like the Massachusetts man was looking for some free publicity, but he stepped on the wrong pedal when he started to talk about Carpentier's war record.'[273] Gallivan's resolution was sent to the Committee on Ways and Means, and promptly forgotten.

Dempsey liked being heavyweight champion of the world. He was determined he would be in top condition for Carpentier, after his mediocre showing against Brennan, and moved into camp even before the Frenchman left home. Jack started his training at Summit, New Jersey, before taking over an abandoned airfield near Atlantic City.

The challenger, rested after a European tour, embarked on the SS *Savoie* on 20 May, accompanied by manager Francois Descamps; trainer-masseur Gus Wilson; heavyweight sparring partner Paul

271 Roberts pp. 112–113
272 *The Decatur Daily Review* Illinois 9 June 1921
273 *The Decatur Daily Review* 10 June 1921

Journee; Charles Ledoux, bantamweight champion of Europe; Marco, former fighter turned cook; and Carpentier's pet dog, Flip. There was a minor problem when the ship docked in New York on 16 May. The port authorities wanted to place Flip in quarantine as was the usual practice with dogs entering the country, but some smooth talking sorted things out and when the French party left in a fleet of cars for Manhasset, Georges and his canine pal were happily on board.

Jack Curley had rented the Matthews farm in Manhasset, Long Island, near the Payne Whitney estate and privacy was the order of the day. The public, and even members of the press, were not welcome. To emphasise the point, barbed wire was strewn around the farm and barn where the challenger would train. The grounds were patrolled by a deputy sheriff accompanied by a large Belgian police dog. The American sportswriters weren't used to such conditions and were further outraged when society figures including Vincent Astor and William H. Vanderbilt were welcomed into the camp.

Some of the press boys, determined to see Carpentier at his training drills, resorted to various subterfuges to keep their editors happy. They climbed trees to get a vantage point, and Sid Mercer of the Hearst papers wrote of having disguised himself as a gardener to gain entry to the camp. Old-time lightweight champion Jack McAuliffe, covering for one of the news agencies, wrote that he had observed the Frenchman's workouts from a small hill adjoining the property, mingling in a small herd of cows.

Former heavyweight champion James J. Corbett had shown he was as adept with a pencil as he had been with his fists and he covered a lot of fights for the International News Service. He was favoured with entry to Carpentier's camp and backed the Frenchman's desire for privacy, writing, 'Georges Carpentier's system of training has come in for a lot of adverse criticism. Because he has shown little in the way of ability as a boxer or puncher and has excluded the general public from his camp, he has become a target for a veritable barrage of unfavorable comment. But why? To my mind, Carpentier's training system is far superior to that of Jack Dempsey, because he enjoys a certain amount of privacy that is surely welcome to a fighter of his temperament. Dempsey may not mind the daily inpouring of fans at Airport. Carpentier is different. He wants quiet. In my fighting days, I was that way, too, and, perhaps that is why I sympathise with his views.'[274]

---

274 James J. Corbett *Syracuse Herald* 9 June 1921

The difference in the training methods of the two fighters was something top boxing writer Robert Edgren observed in his column in *The Syracuse Herald* on 10 June 1921. 'It is a difference I have noticed in all of my daily visits to the camps,' he wrote. 'When Dempsey boxes he always tears in, encouraging his sparring partners to hit as hard and as often as they can. It isn't part of his idea to maul them without letting them maul him. In his actual fights Dempsey never receives any injury, for he attacks so furiously that his opponents have always been too busy on the defense to do much accurate hitting.

'In training, Carpentier uses all his skill to find openings and hit without being hit. If he is as elusive in a real fight as he is in practice bouts, even Dempsey is going to have trouble finding him. Not that Carpentier runs away. He doesn't. His footwork is very much like Benny Leonard's…He moves straight in and straight back, only a few inches or a foot or two, in quick steps, balanced well on his toes and so lightly that his feet make no sound and seem hardly to touch the floor. He is always just near enough to deliver a blow if he sees an opening, and far enough away to duck out of danger.'

The champion's training camp at Atlantic City was an altogether different story. It was wide open and there was always an assorted bunch of characters hanging around; fighters, ex-fighters, managers, trainers, hoodlums and harlots. Jack didn't mind as long as they didn't get in the way. 'When they weren't watching me sparring, shadow-boxing and pulling weights in the ring at two bits a head, they'd be playing gin or pinochle – if they weren't trying to smuggle dames into camp.'[275]

At Atlantic City, Doc Kearns always welcomed the press with open arms and a full bottle, but there was one exception. 'The first newspaper writer to be denied admittance to the camp since Dempsey started training here was turned down at the gate Thursday afternoon after he presented a pass issued by the personal representative of Jack Kearns, manager of Dempsey. He had written stories which Dempsey's handlers had considered offensive, and when he presented the pass, it was promptly torn up. He was told that he would not be admitted, even if he paid a dollar, which is all spectators are charged.'[276]

In the sparring ring, Dempsey was his usual anti-social self. 'Larry Williams stood up nicely under two or three drives,' he recalled, 'and

---

275 Dempsey with Piattelli p.140
276 *The Decatur Daily Review* 11 June 1921

assuming he was in shape to take 'em as fast as I could shoot them over, I planted a right to the chin and followed with a left. Larry went down. He got up and we wrestled around awhile. Then Larry said he was ready for some more mixing. But it didn't last long. I didn't mean to hurt Larry. But Larry came in at me with a wild rush. I saw his jaw exposed and I let fly. He went down in a heap and Teddy Hayes and I helped him to the corner. Larry was not badly hurt but that ended him for the day. Jack Renault worked out the final round with me. Jack's orders were to try to smash me with a right hander for the jaw... Jack made about 30 swings for my chin but I don't recall that a single one of them landed.

'Battling Ghee, [sic] the Memphis Negro, has severed connections with my camp. The Negro came from the south with the promise of giving me the best workouts that any man ever had. He invited me to let loose in our first work. I did – and he went down three times. When we worked Monday I wanted him to tear in but the battler wouldn't. He said that he was a little too smart, that once had been quite enough and today he served notice that he thought he could get a job elsewhere that would pay him just about as much without half the trouble.'[277]

For the International News Service, Sid Mercer recorded an interview with William Gahee, the Battler's real name. 'Following his first experience as a sparring partner of the champion Friday afternoon, the Battler propped himself weakly in front of a mirror in the cottage of Dempsey's sparring partners and ruefully contemplated a recent extension of the right side of his mouth – a cut of about three-quarters of an inch long – tugged at a loose front tooth and gingerly fingered his puffed brunette features. "Kid Norfolk told me Mister Dempsey couldn't hit me," said the Battler. "But I knows better. Man, I knows better!" Mr Ghee [sic] may get over his experience with Dempsey but he will never be the same. He has been hanging around for eight days waiting for the chance he got yesterday and now he is satisfied. It was rumored, however, that a big dark man was seen moving off in the gloom back of Airport last night muttering to himself, "That Kid Norfolk ain't no friend of mine."'[278]

'Dan McKetrick, who had seen Gorgeous Georges in some of his most inglorious moments in the ring,' wrote Samuels, 'was quoted

277 Jack Dempsey *Lima News* Ohio 22 June 1921
278 Sid Mercer *Logansport Pharos Tribune* 18 June 1921

as grimly warning Dempsey not to underestimate the lightning-like striking power of Carpentier's right.'[279]

The *New York World* ran a story written by a scientist who declared that Carpentier had a great advantage over Jack because his muscles were long, not spherical like the champion's. The scientist's point was that long muscles possessed far greater punching power. On 23 June, as though to confirm this, Carpentier knocked out all three of his sparring partners.

As promoter Rickard looked forward to what was shaping up as a record gate, not everyone was so bewitched by the forthcoming battle. In Washington, the board of temperance and public morals of the Methodist Episcopal Church issued a statement condemning the Dempsey–Carpentier fight to be held at Jersey City on 2 July. Declaring that it was astonishing that 'any state in the American Union would tolerate an exhibition not only bloody and brutal in itself, but intended to appeal to all that is abysmal in the average man. All right thinking Americans,' the statement continued, 'ought to see to it that this is the last prize fight fought on American soil…Men who habitually see such things inevitably become not only brutal, but cowardly, and lose every sense of sportsmanship. Women who see these frequently in the end become things that are certainly not women.'[280]

The Methodist Episcopal Church notwithstanding, it was later estimated that from 10,000 to 25,000 women attended the big fight, the majority drawn by the charismatic Frenchman Georges Carpentier. And to give further thought for the church elders, it was considered in some press reports 'that the presence of the women in such large numbers probably was responsible for the fact that the crowd, despite its great size, was the most orderly seen at a fistic event in this country'.[281]

'Jersey City is ready now to open her gates to 90,000 fight fans,' wrote Farrell three days before the fight. 'Tex Rickard's big pine arena is not quite completed but the city is prepared. "All of our plans are ready. We will take care of the crowds," Mayor Frank Hague said today. The ring is to be built today. More than a thousand police will be inside and outside the arena. One thousand firemen will have posts to guard just outside the arena. The stadium will be surrounded by a dead line of four blocks away from the arena through which no

279 Samuels pp. 241–242
280 *Bridgeport Telegram* 11 June 1921
281 *Ogden Standard Examiner* 3 July 1921

one can pass without a ticket. Mounted cops will keep the "curious" moving. To take care of the boys who want to see the fight for $5.50 general admission tickets, Tex Rickard will provide ticket wagons of the circus variety all around the stadium. The tickets will be passed out by experts trained in the school of John Ringling.'[282]

'Some days before the fight,' wrote Samuels, 'the New York police raided a cellar and discovered there a printing press and other paraphernalia being used to manufacture counterfeit tickets for the fight. This inspired Rickard to arrange with the plant that printed his tickets to send over to the fight twenty veteran lithographers and engravers. These men would be stationed near the various entrances and would pass judgment on any pasteboards the ticket takers suspected were phonies.'[283]

For the fight, Rickard had purchased a portable steel ring which measured 18 feet inside the ropes. Oak boards, strongly reinforced, made the floor, which was covered with a fine grade of heavy felt more than an inch in thickness. Over the padding was a tightly stretched canvas, and backless and legless stools swung on long steel arms attached to each boxer's corner.

The size of the ring was the subject of a column by old-time champ Jack McAuliffe, who wrote, 'The Frenchmen have just awakened to the fact that Dempsey will be hard to run away from in an 18-foot ring. They are not registering a protest about it, but they are saying in a rather diplomatic fashion that the Queensberry rules call for a 24-foot ring. Descamps is too smart a manager not to know that the original agreement called for an 18-foot ring. This size ring is not unusual. Many championship battles have been fought within those confines. It looks to me that the Frenchmen have finally learned that they were misinformed about the speed of the champion. It also looks positive to me that Carpentier is going to fight a running battle.

'Descamps evidently thought when he signed the agreement that Carpentier was good enough to mix it with the champion in a small ring or that Dempsey was so slow that the fleet-footed Georges could get away from him.'[284]

The ring was actually 20 feet square, according to an item in *The Bridgeport Telegram* of 1 July. 'It was at first reported the ring would be only 18 feet square, and this brought a howl from manager Descamps

---

282 Henry L. Farrell *Freeport Standard Journal* 29 June 1921
283 Samuels p. 243
284 Jack McAuliffe *Wisconsin State Journal* 29 June 1921

10-Round Boxing Contest
ALHAMBRA Theatre

Ogden, Utah **Wed., May 3** **Ogden, Utah**

Claimant of the World's Light Heavyweight Championship

TERRY KELLER *vs.* Jack Dempsey

OF BALTIMORE, FORMERLY OF OGDEN   OF SALT LAKE CITY, UTAH.

Greatest Sporting Events Ever Given in the Intermountain Country—Big Preliminaries.

PRICES: $1.00, $1.50, $2.00, $2.50, $3.00   GET YOUR RESERVATIONS EARLY—DON'T WAIT
EXCURSION RATES ON ALL RAILROADS.   PHONE ALHAMBRA, 207.   H. E. SKINNER, Manager.

In May 1916 Dempsey, then a young light-heavyweight, won a ten-round decision over Terry Keller at the Alhambra Theatre, Ogden, Utah

Rising heavyweight contender Dempsey with his promoter, Tex Rickard. Together they brought the million dollar gate to boxing

Jack Dempsey, the Manassa Mauler

The heavyweight champion of the world Jess Willard, ready to face his challenger Dempsey in 1919

Dempsey and Willard in the ring at Toledo, July 1919, waiting for the bell

Promoter Tex Rickard, the man with the Midas touch

First title defence as Dempsey knocks out Billy Miske in three rounds, Benton Harbour, Michigan, September 1920

Tough contender Bill Brennan, ready for his title shot at Dempsey in December 1920 at the old Madison Square Garden, New York City

Brennan's manager Leo P Flynn (l), Brennan, Referee Billy Haukup, Dempsey, Jack (Doc) Kearns, Dempsey's manager, famed announcer Joe Humphreys. Seconds out…

Champion Dempsey loved Hollywood and made serial thriller Daredevil Jack

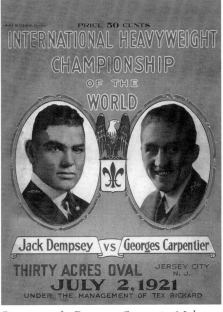

Programme for Dempsey–Carpentier 2 July 1921, boxing's first million dollar gate

Relaxing after the Carpentier fight Dempsey enjoys a day at the racetrack, here talking to 16-year-old jockey Ivan Parke

Rising Argentine heavyweight Luis Angel Firpo on the cover of El Grafico *magazine*

In America, Firpo works under famed trainer Jimmy De Forest

The heavy bag takes a beating from Firpo's iron fists

Young Bob Fitzsimmons Jnr, son of the former champion, was a regular sparring partner of Firpo, seen picking Bob up after knocking him down

After knocking out Bill Brennan, Firpo faced Jack McAuliffe II in May 1923. Firpo kayoed his man in three rounds

Idle for two years, Dempsey has to go 15 rounds to defeat Tommy Gibbons in a battle called The Rape of Shelby. Jack has Gibbons, dark trunks, on the ropes

Another shot of Dempsey retaining the heavyweight title against Gibbons, 4 July 1923

Firpo (on right) earns Dempsey fight with savage knockout of former champion Jess Willard in eight rounds

Firpo, now a contender, ready for a gym workout for the Dempsey fight

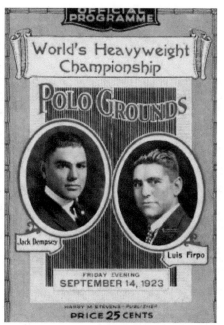

Programme for Dempsey-Firpo heavyweight championship 14 September 1923

Calm before the storm. Firpo (in robe) shakes hands with champion Dempsey as Referee Johnny Gallagher looks on

First round action with Firpo taking one of seven first round knockdowns

First round sensation as Dempsey is knocked clean out of the ring by Firpo

Firpo floored in round two. The end is in sight

It's all over, Firpo is knocked out after 57 seconds of round two

Artist George Bellows captured Dempsey's dramatic tumble into the press row

King of the Ring – world heavyweight champion Jack Dempsey

LOUIS FIRPO HARRY WILLS
AGE 28 yrs.   AGE 32 yrs.

17 in.	NECK	17 in.
16 in.	BICEPS	16 in.
13½ in.	FOREARM	14 in.
8 in.	WRIST	8 in.
41 in.	CHEST Normal	44 in.
44 in.	CHEST Expanded	49 in.
36½ in.	WAIST	33 in.
23¾ in.	THIGH	24½ in.
15 in.	CALF	17 in.
9½ in.	ANKLE	9 in.
6 ft. 2½ in.	HEIGHT	6 ft. 2 in.
223 lbs.	WEIGHT	215 lbs.
79 in.	REACH	84 in.

HEAVYWEIGHT CONTENDER   HEAVYWEIGHT CONTENDER

Returning to America in 1924, Firpo is outboxed by Dempsey's nemesis Harry Wills

Three years' ring rust and Gene Tunney took Dempsey's title in 1926. A year later, Tunney survived the famous Battle of the Long Count to again defeat Dempsey in what was Jack's last fight

More popular than ever, ex-champ Dempsey shows his fists on a visit to London

Argentine millionaire Luis Angel Firpo spars with champion-to-be Rocky Marciano in New York City in 1950

who thought the small size would interfere with Carpentier's footwork. Rickard had the ring measured and when it was found to be of the twenty-feet variety, Descamps was satisfied.'

In the last week before the fight, advance ticket sales were fast approaching one million dollars. It was the right time for Tex Rickard, the old Yukon gambler, to show his hand. On 29 June, Tex handed Jack Kearns and Descamps the shock of their lives by announcing that he would pay their fighters the straight $500,000 purse, instead of the 36 per cent for Dempsey and 24 per cent for Carpentier deal which was his alternative.

'After the fight,' wrote Samuels, 'when the last nickel was counted, it became clear that each fighter would have been paid almost twice as much if Kearns and Descamps had accepted the original straight 60 per cent offer. Kearns has never been able to live down this costly mistake, nor forgive Rickard for profiting by it.'[285]

Saturday 2 July 1921, big fight day – 'The human tidal wave that began rolling over Jersey dikes last night,' wrote Grantland Rice, 'will pick up impetus this morning as the vanguard starts its big offense toward Mr Boyle's thirty eminent acres that will be for Carpentier a Waterloo or a Marne.'[286]

That morning, Georges Carpentier, along with manager Descamps, trainer Wilson, Ledoux and Journee motored to Port Washington on Manhasset Bay where they boarded the 65-foot power yacht *Lone Star* which was to take them to a Jersey City dock.

There they were met by a closed car with a special guard of six motorcycle policemen to take them to the arena. In the challenger's bag was a brand new pair of white trunks with blue stripes down each leg. Pushing through the crowd of reporters, Descamps said 'I confidently expect Georges to win the world's heavyweight championship from Jack Dempsey inside of five rounds.'

Rickard had asked the police chief to bring Jack to the arena early on the excuse that rain threatened. 'Dempsey found Tex waiting for him at the top of the stairs near the dressing rooms. "Yes, sir," Rickard said, "this is the first million-dollar crowd. And now let me tell you something. This Carpentier is a nice fellow, but he can't fight. I could lick him myself. So I want you to be careful and not kill him. I mean that, Jack. If you kill him all this will be ruined. Boxing will be dead.

---

285 Samuels p. 242
286 Kahn p. 258

For my sake, would you take it easy for the first few rounds? You won't have any trouble knocking him out. All I ask is that you shouldn't be in too much of a hurry about it. If you do what I say, son, there will be many more million-dollar gates and you and I will make a lot of money, working together like this."

'Dempsey nodded, then shrugged, without actually committing himself. Afterward Tex said that not knowing what Jack would do added to the thrill of watching the fight.'[287]

Ring announcer Joe Humphreys gave the fighters' weights as 188lb for Dempsey to 172lb for Carpentier, referee was Harry Ertle. At the opening bell Carpentier walked forward and threw a left to the head. They fell into a clinch and Dempsey hammered lefts and rights to the body. The champion missed a left for the head but landed a right that staggered the Frenchman. First blood to Dempsey when a vicious left skimmed across the challenger's nose, and Carpentier backed away. A thudding left from Dempsey caused the Frenchman's knees to sag. They fought at close range, Dempsey's territory, and Carpentier fell through the ropes. Crawling back, Georges gamely flew at the champion and they clinched.

Just before the bell Carpentier landed a left and was punching the body when the round ended, a round for Dempsey.

Round two and Carpentier missed a left then fired a terrific right to the head that sent the champion to the ropes and brought a tremendous roar from the crowd. Jack got his own right to the jaw and in the corner Descamps looked worried. His boy came out of a clinch and threw a volley of lefts and rights to the head, but he paid for it when a Dempsey right hook split the flesh below his right eye. Both missed with swings and they were exchanging blows to the body when the bell ended a round most observers gave to the challenger. One each.

'In the middle of the second round,' wrote Farrell, 'Carpentier got in a staggering right flush to Dempsey's jaw. It rocked the champion up against the ropes and the crowd yelled like maniacs when Carpentier followed his advantage with right and left to Dempsey's jaw. The Frenchman perhaps lost the fight at this point. It was plain to see that he lost heart when he found himself lacking the punch to put the champion out when he was groggy.'[288]

---

287 Samuels p. 247
288 Henry L. Farrell *Appleton Post-Crescent* 3 July 1921

Chicago heavyweight Bill Brennan, Dempsey's last challenger, was at ringside for Universal Services. Brennan wrote, 'It was a case of too much Jack Dempsey. In the second round Carpentier certainly showed that he could shoot over that famous right hand of his with wonderful speed and power. But he was hitting Jack Dempsey's jaw, and that's a different sort of jaw than Joe Beckett's or Battling Levinsky's or Bombardier Wells's. I suppose Dempsey's jaw is made of bone like any other human's. But I hit the jaw just like the Frenchman did and I've got a suspicion that he wears a few slabs of iron there instead of bone. Dempsey got two socks on the chin. Everything that Carpentier had was in those blows. They didn't drop Jack, just jiggled him a little. And right then I saw an expression on Jack's face that seemed to say, "This bird can't knock me out. Nothing more to worry about. Now, I'll go out and get him." And that's when Jack got under way.'[289]

Doc Kearns gave his champion an ear-bashing before sending him in for round three, and Dempsey responded by forcing Carpentier to the ropes with a two-fisted barrage that made his supporters happy. Carpentier landed two right uppercuts to the body but almost fell down after missing a big right swing. Coming out of a clinch, Dempsey clubbed the Frenchman on the neck with a rabbit punch. Whenever they clinched it was seen that Dempsey was the stronger of the two. Georges circled looking for an opening for his vaunted right hand, but the body blows from the champion had weakened him. He fell back to the ropes as Jack came in with heavy punches from left and right and he looked in trouble at the bell. Dempsey's round.

'In the third round,' Farrell reported, 'Dempsey, with ever so slight a motion of his head would turn to the right and left and the blows of the Frenchman slid off the champion's wet head. Carpentier landed two rights flush to Dempsey's jaw and the champion laughed. Dempsey retaliated with another cruel body punch. The Frenchman was bleeding from the eyes, his mouth was open and the blood was running from his cut lips. His left eye was closing rapidly. It was strikingly apparent then that he could not last much longer. Starting the fourth round, Jack Kearns yelled from Dempsey's corner, "Go after him now, Jack, boy, you've got him."'[290]

As round four opened, it was seen that the size and strength of the champion was taking a toll of the lighter man. A thudding barrage

289 Bill Brennan *Oakland Tribune* 3 July 1921
290 Henry L. Farrell *Freeport Standard Journal* 3 July 1921

of lefts and rights to the body hurt Carpentier and his knees sagged before he sank to the canvas after about 55 seconds of the round. The challenger was not unconscious but looked in sore distress, lying curled on his side. Referee Ertle picked up the count from the timekeeper and he reached nine before Carpentier forced himself off the canvas, gamely facing the champion again, but he was out of ammunition. Dempsey's big guns were still firing and a crushing left to the body followed by a terrific right to the jaw hurled Carpentier to the floor and it was all over bar the shouting, and there was plenty of that.

'At 1.16 of the round, Ertle swung his arms across his body as his count reached ten, and Dempsey promptly stooped over Carpentier to help him to his feet, a reprise of the Frenchman's gesture toward the fallen Beckett two years before. Carpentier's corner men quickly interceded to fully lift their fighter and drag him to safety, as a dozen policemen encircled Dempsey, a man seemingly in no need of protection. He raised his arms to acknowledge the robust cheers now coming his way – winning was the antidote to suspicions and untruths. The newly converted all but clinging to him, Dempsey strode from the ring.'[291]

Irvin S. Cobb was America's reigning journalistic star as well as being a novelist, screenwriter, actor and radio commentator, and on that muggy afternoon in Jersey City Cobb was a fight reporter for *The New York Times*. He wrote, in part, 'Carpentier, an alien, a man who does not speak our language, was the favorite of the crowd before the fight started and while it progressed, and, if I am one to judge, was still its favorite when he came out of it summarily defeated though he was…three things stand out in my memory as the high points of the big fight, so far as I personally am concerned.

'The first is that Carpentier never had a chance. In the one round which properly belonged to him he fought himself out. He trusted to his strength when his refuge should have been his speed. The second is that vision of him, doubled up on his side, like a frightened hurt boy, and yet striving to heave himself up and take added punishment from a foe against whom he had no shadow of hope.

'The third – and most outstanding – will be my recollection of that look in Dempsey's lowering front when realisation came to him that a majority of the tremendous audience were partisans of the foreigner.'[292]

291 Jim Waltzer *The Battle of the Century* (Santa Barbara: Praeger 2011) p. 195
292 Irwin S. Cobb *At the Fights* (New York: The Library of America 2011) pp. 10, 19

12

Wrestlers And Showgirls

THE Battle of the Century was over, now just a line of type in boxing's history book. But it was always going to be more than that. Samuels called it Tex Rickard's masterpiece. It was a million-dollar masterpiece, with gate receipts hitting a record $1,789,238 paid by that great crowd numbered at anywhere from 75,328 to 93,000, and Uncle Sam, who never pulled on a glove, pulled down more than Dempsey and Carpentier.

America's champion had crushed Europe's finest in front of the greatest sporting crowd ever assembled. In that matinee performance in Jersey City, Daredevil Jack had vanquished The Wonder Man. But to many in that huge gathering of humanity, the local bully had just beaten up the nicest kid in town.

In his syndicated column, Ring Lardner wrote, 'Well, friends, I don't pretend to be like Bernard Shaw and always know what I am writing about, but now that the big fiasco is history, I guess it's OK and go ahead and make one prediction in regards to the outcome, namely that Dempsey won't get no credit for doing what he done, and the fight writers will get even less for telling you in advance that he was going to do it.'[293]

Lardner was right on the money regarding his fellow members of the Fourth Estate. A couple of days after his fight with Dempsey,

---

293 Ring Lardner *Boston Globe* 3 July 1921

Georges Carpentier had a fistful of press clippings that would have delighted a winner, never mind a loser.

Datelined 3 July, the *New York Times* wrote, 'Carpentier was quite rightly the more popular of the two men...Carpentier was the spirit of the fight; Dempsey was its body. Carpentier lost like a gentleman.'

New York Tribune – 'By the way in which he accepted his defeat, as a sportsman and a gentleman, the Frenchman has increased his popularity in America.'

Evening Telegram – 'Carpentier, a hero in defeat, was acclaimed by 120,000 spectators for his courage...He has won the esteem and affection of the whole of America.'

Morning Telegraph – 'The more powerful but not the better man won. All in all Carpentier is more popular in America today than he was even before the fight.'

The heavyweight champion was unmarked after the fight, but his ego suffered a terrific blow after reading those press reports. He could have cried 'foul' after reading an item that made the front page of the *Bakersfield Morning Echo* on 3 July 1921. Datelined Tulare, California 2 July – 'Urging an American Legion purse of $250,000 for any ex-serviceman of any of the allied armies who can defeat Jack Dempsey for the world's heavyweight championship, Tulare Post of the American Legion today telegraphed State Commander Burn R. Fitts, asking him to forward such a recommendation to National Commander Emery. Tulare Post urges you to take a poll of the American Legion regarding raising of a bonus purse of a quarter of a million dollars to the member or former member of any allied or associated armies who whips Jack Dempsey in the ring next year.'

Even former champion Jack Johnson got into the act. 'Hailing himself as the next world's champion prizefighter, Jack Johnson, in his first public appearance in Chicago since his release from the penitentiary at Leavenworth, threw an audience of 5,000 negro admirers into a frenzy at the Eighth Regiment Armory when he declared that Dempsey would fall before him just as Jeffries did years ago. "The public wants Dempsey whipped," he said, "and everybody knows I am the man to do it."'[294]

The American Legion would love Dempsey to fight Bob Martin, the heavyweight champion of the Allied Expeditionary Force in France 1919, now a professional and recent knockout winner over

---

294 *Lowell Sun* Mass. 15 July 1921

veteran Frank Moran, but manager Jimmy Bronson shook his wise old head.

Give Martin a couple of years…

Late on 5 July, Dempsey quietly left his hotel and was soon settled comfortably on a train speeding westwards, to Salt Lake City, Utah. There he would see his mother, Celia Dempsey, before going on to California. With the champion were trainer Teddy Hayes and his bodyguard, Detective Sergeant Mike Trant of the Chicago police.

'Trouble shot from two directions toward the champion during the day. His valuable ($10,000) limousine was seized by a deputy sheriff acting on a writ issued last Friday in Batavia, New York, in a $100,000 suit brought by Frank Spellman in connection with a motion picture enterprise. In Jersey City, counsel for the International Reform Bureau endeavored to have him hauled into court on a complaint charging him with assaulting Carpentier.'[295]

Trouble had also gone looking for manager Jack Kearns. Atlantic City 13 July – 'Mayor Edward L. Bader has received a cheque for $300 from Jack Kearns, manager of Jack Dempsey, to be turned over to Mrs Carrie Barrett, who acted as housekeeper for the champion while he was in training here for his match with Georges Carpentier. The cheque is in payment for wages which Mrs Barrett alleged in a suit recently started against Kearns was due her.'[296]

Arriving in Ogden, Utah, Dempsey and Hayes managed to elude a crowd of more than 300 people waiting to greet them, escape from the rail depot and, by switching taxicabs, arrived at the Bamberger electric road for the journey to Salt Lake City where his mother eagerly awaited the arrival of her champion son. Also waiting patiently for their champion was a large crowd, including state, county and city officials and members of the chamber of commerce. A band played 'When Johnny Comes Marching Home'. But this particular Johnny had jumped from the train one block from the depot, boarded a street car and proceeded to the home of his mother.

After the train had pulled into the depot and it was seen that Dempsey was not among the passengers, several admirers and reporters jumped into their cars and sped to the Dempsey home. Having embraced his mother, Jack was escorted back uptown where he spent an hour shaking hands and answering questions.

For the *Ogden Standard Examiner,* columnist Al Warden reported, 'The Utah mauler appears to be in the best condition of his career. He was brimming over with exuberance yesterday and stated that he was out to meet 'em all. "I am now ready to defend my title against all comers," said Dempsey. "My manager, Jack Kearns, will join me at Oakland within a few days, after which we will start to arrange our plans for the future." "How about a match with Jack Johnson?" I asked. "Johnson in my opinion is through as far as the American public is concerned. The public will not demand a match with the coloured boxer and for that reason it will never be staged." "What about a return go with Carpentier?" "A return contest will never be arranged between Carpentier and myself. There are several logical opponents in various parts of the United States who are clamoring for contests. My matches will be entirely arranged by Jack Kearns." Dempsey denied that he and his manager had severed relations.'[297]

In his suite in New York City's Belmont Hotel, Jack Kearns held a press conference, telling reporters, 'I've been battling rumors for two months. First, they had me run out of Atlantic City with the champion and now they have the champion and me on the outs. We're not on the outs and we never have been. I couldn't go west with the champion, because I had to stay here and settle up a lot of business, so he went alone. He's coming back in two weeks. About those bills in Atlantic City, I paid every one of them before we left. The cheque that I gave Mrs Carrie Barrett for her services was a bonus of $100. I paid her in addition for her services during the training period. I also gave several others who worked at the camp a bonus of from $50 to $100 in addition to the agreed salary. I gave a cheque of $3,000 for the rental of the training camp.

'Everything that happened in Atlantic City while we were there was blamed on me by the same crowd that is now starting the stories that we have split. They tried to say that we had a lot of gunmen with us, but we proved that they went there every year and that two of them had been thrown out of the training camp the first day they tried to get in…After we had won we still got the knocks. It was said that Carpentier was too easy and it was criminal to match him with the champion.

'They said that Carpentier broke his hand and would have won if it hadn't been for an accident. If Carpentier broke his hand in the

---

297 Al Warden *Ogden Standard Examiner* 10 July 1921

second round I'm all wrong. No one could hit like he did all through that round with a broken bone.

'The best one, though, was the story that the heavy gloves kept the Frenchman from winning. If there was any handicap in the weight of the gloves, it meant just as much to the champion. If Dempsey had been fighting with light gloves, Carpentier never would have lasted through the first round.' Kearns said he had nothing definite in mind for the champion. They had numerous theatrical offers, 'but Dempsey wants to fight,' he said.[298]

Kearns also added that Dempsey was ready and willing to sign for a match with Jess Willard any time that the fight could be made. One man looking for a match with the champion was Tommy Gibbons and he was prepared to bide his time until he was good and ready to face Dempsey. According to sportswriter Norman E. Brown, 'The sport public in general is looking to Tommy Gibbons of St Paul as the man who will eventually succeed Jack Dempsey as heavyweight champion of the world...Gibbons himself believes he is the man to turn the trick. His manager, Eddie Kane, believes it also. So Gibbons, with Kane to direct his movements, has gone into the woods near Osakis, Minnesota, to begin a year's training to prepare himself for a title bout with Dempsey.

'Gibbons plans to stay in the woods the rest of the summer and into the fall, with but one end in view – to gain a few pounds of weight and build up his powers of endurance – toughen himself. When Gibbons comes out of the woods he hopes to obtain fights with the best men in the heavyweight game outside of Dempsey. These bouts, Gibbons hopes, will come often enough to keep him in perfect trim and give him proper conditioning for a battle with Dempsey on July Fourth 1922.'[299]

Tommy was a year out in his plan for a Dempsey match; it wouldn't happen until 1923. In the meantime, manager Eddie Kane was in New York to talk business with Tex Rickard who had a match in mind between Gibbons and Carpentier for the Frenchman's light-heavyweight title. But that one wouldn't take place until 1924 by which time Carpentier was no longer the champion. Gibbons came out of the woods after a couple of months and racked up another knockout streak, but Rickard was still thinking of putting Dempsey

---

298 *Kansas City Star* 10 July 1921
299 Norman E. Brown *Madison Capital Times* Wisconsin 16 July 1921

back with Willard on Labor Day at his big arena at Boyle's Thirty Acres which was still standing despite the fears of many that it would collapse during the Carpentier fight. As the massive crowd took their places and the action in the ring got them excited, the wooden saucer began to sway back and forth, causing fear in the cheaper seats at the rear of the arena. The day after the fight, the builders said that the fact that the arena had swayed without falling apart only proved how well it had been put together. In August 1921 Rickard renewed his lease on the arena for another year, stating that 'a world heavyweight championship bout would be staged there next year'.[300]

Asked about a return fight against Willard, manager Jack Kearns told the press, 'Personally, I do not believe Jess Willard will attempt a comeback against Dempsey. If he wants to do it, well and good.' Ray Archer, Willard's erstwhile business representative, who still looks after the interests of the big Kansan in the east at odd times, says Willard is serious. 'You know that the big fellow's personal pride was hurt deeply by the defeat he received at Toledo. He'll take Dempsey under satisfactory conditions any time and I feel sure he will surprise everybody by the condition he will be in if they meet again.'[301]

In his syndicated column for the International News Service, TAD wrote of another Dempsey proposition, 'Do you think there is a wrestler alive who would have a chance with Jack Dempsey in a rough and tumble fight? Strangler Lewis was interviewed by someone out west recently and here is what he let go: "I believe I could go into a back room with Jack Dempsey, where everything went, and I would make him quit...Of course, in regular boxing neither I nor any other wrestler would have much of a chance. Dempsey would lick us easily. But in a rough and tumble Dempsey or any other heavyweight boxer would have a fine time reaching my jaw or any other vulnerable point. I would go into him all doubled up like a bowknot, and once I got my hands on him he would be at my mercy."

'We remember one night at Madison Square Garden when Zbyszko butted Lewis with his head and the latter went to the floor and stayed there for fully two minutes. He didn't look as though he would ever get up. It wasn't such a tough bump either. Game guys in print these wrestlers. Wonder what he'd do if Dempsey ever hit him on the chin with a right?'[302]

---

300 *Cedar Rapids Evening Gazette* 11 August 1921
301 Jack Veiock *Oakland Tribune* 2 August 1921
302 'TAD' *New Castle News* 30 September 1921

While the press boys played with the possibilities of Dempsey meeting Jess Willard, Luis Firpo, Tommy Gibbons or even Strangler Lewis, there was another guy in New York more than anxious to take a poke at the heavyweight champion. Al Siegel, well known along Broadway as a songwriter and piano player, was getting hot under the collar telling everybody that his wife had run off with the champ. In November of 1921, Siegel figured he would do better in a courtroom with Mr Dempsey than in a boxing ring.

The *Washington Post* of 11 November 1921 reported, 'New York 10 November – Jack Dempsey, whose name outside the prize ring is William Harrison Dempsey, was sued today in the supreme court for $250,000 damages by Albert Siegel on the allegation that he had alienated the affections of Mrs Bee Palmer Siegel, wife of the plaintiff and a performer in vaudeville.'

The tabloid press gleefully jumped all over this story, giving it full-page treatment with photos of the alleged lovebirds together with cartoon illustrations. 'It's just a business arrangement, declares Jack. But husband Siegel, back in New York, tells a different story. If what he says is true, then Bee Palmer is another illustration of the strange lure of gladiators, bullfighters, boxers, males of the cave man strain – for women of utmost beauty and exquisiteness. For Bee Palmer is one of them – a flower that sprang from a weed patch to blossom finally in the world's richest garden of beauty.

'A few years ago in Chicago, Bee Palmer was nobody. She had one asset – a pair of shoulders which the Venus de Milo would have been proud to own. Bee, who danced naturally like a wood nymph, learned that it isn't all in the feet. She perfected a new terpsichorean art – how to dance with the shoulders. She was performing then in one of the cheapest and wildest cabarets "back of the yards", a dive reeking with whiskey fumes, tobacco smoke and the mingled odor of sawdust, steers' blood and unwashed humanity. One night, when the dizzy dance halls were in brazen blast, a man muffled in a heavy Ulster entered the cabaret where Bee Palmer danced. He wriggled through the throng of roisterers and took his seat at an inconspicuous table in a far corner.

'None recognised in the slight form the greatest beauty picker in the world. Had they known him they surely would have wondered what mission brought Flo Ziegfeld to this garish haunt of hoboes, hoodlums, thugs and wantons. Over in his corner the stranger watched – first the dancer and then the effect of her extraordinary gyrations on the spectators. When the dance ended with a final wild shiver of the whole body, he rose and, swinging his Malacca stick, made his way to the table where Bee Palmer sat, flushed and panting. "What may I ask, do you call your dance?" he asked. "Oh, anything you like old dear – shaking the shimmy I guess!" And so Bee Palmer brought the shimmy to Broadway.

'Flo Ziegfeld, who discovered her that night in a tom-tom cabaret in Chicago, lifted her to stardom in the twinkling of a spotlight. She was 'rushed' by millionaires galore, but she chose to marry Al Siegel, the songwriter and pianist. He played her accompaniment and Bee continued to draw down the ducats shimmying in the Follies, the Palais Royal and other golden palaces. And then, so says husband Siegel, the magic of brawny shoulders, bull neck, and knockout punch tempted Bee Palmer where some of the handsomest and most debonair Beau Brummels on Broadway had failed. Bee met Jack Dempsey, fresh from his bloody slaughter of Carpentier, idolized by the American sporting public, six champion feet of glowing physical strength.

'The next thing Broadway knew, Dempsey and Miss Palmer had caught a train for Chicago on the first leg of a theatrical tour, and Bee's husband, in New York, had filed a $250,000 alienation suit against the prize fighter. "I have sufficient grounds, and I am red hot mad," said Siegel. "Nothing to it," declared Dempsey. "My manager simply engaged Miss Palmer as a headliner for my show. Besides, take a look at me. Do I look like a heartbreaker or a love thief?"'[303]

'Just before I brought my suit,' said Siegel, 'I was at the Belmont Hotel when Jack Kearns tried to induce me to drop my case against Dempsey. Kearns admitted that he had heard gossip connecting Dempsey with my wife. He suggested that I have a conference with his lawyer. That I refused to do. Miss Palmer only recently received an offer of $2,000 a week for twenty weeks. This she refused to accept to go into the Dempsey show for $600 a week. That shows what influence he has been exerting over her.'[304]

Chicago, December 20 – 'Bee Palmer, originator of the shimmy, stopped wiggling her shoulders long enough to take some digs at her husband, Al Siegel, and Jack Dempsey, heavyweight champion. Siegel is suing Dempsey for $250,000 for alienation of his wife's affections. Said Bee of her husband, "Al Siegel is a cheap piano player whom I

---

303 *The Register* Sandusky, Ohio 4 December 1921
304 *Fort Wayne Journal Gazette* 27 November 1921

picked out of the gutter and married." Concerning Jack Dempsey, who characterised the suit as the "scheme of two cheap vaudeville performers for publicity", the blonde Bee said, "It is true I appeared on the stage with Dempsey but our relations were purely professional. It was not complimentary for me to appear with a prize fighter. They all look alike to me.'"[305]

Early in 1922, Dempsey was relieved to read a news item out of New York headed 'BEE PALMER IS BACK WITH HER OLD LOVE AGAIN'. 'Bee Palmer, originator of the shimmy, and her husband, Al Siegel, popular songwriter who filed suit recently against Jack Dempsey for alienation of affections, have buried the hatchet, it is whispered on the Rialto. A little difference between Sophie Tucker and Mr Siegel is said to have brought the reconciliation to light. Mr Siegel, who has been acting as pianist for Miss Tucker, sent word to her one day last week that he was ill and would not be able to appear with her that evening. Sophie quibbled at the excuse but refused to swallow it.

'Miss Tucker lives at the Claridge, as do Mr Siegel and Miss Palmer. Sophie decided to find out how ill Al was, and it wasn't long before bellboys brought her the information that he was calling on Miss Palmer in her room. Miss Tucker, according to the story, immediately excluded Mr Siegel from her act and engaged another pianist. But it is not this fact that is amusing the jokesmiths of the Rialto. They remember how, when the suit was filed against Jack Dempsey, they told each other Al and Bee couldn't keep apart.'[306]

Tex Rickard and Jack Kearns figured it was time their champion meal ticket was back on the sports pages. The promoter still had hopes of a Dempsey–Jess Willard match for 1 July 1922 at Boyle's Thirty Acres, but Tex was annoyed at the former champ's reluctance in returning his contract. There was a rumour that Jess had made a strike in one of his oil investments, making it unlikely he was ready to throw himself into serious training. Dempsey was due to end his theatrical engagement the last week in December and head for New York where Rickard was talking up a rematch with Fred Fulton, the lanky plasterer Dempsey had destroyed in 23 seconds on his way to the title.

---

305 *Attica Ledger Tribune* Indiana 20 December 1921
306 *Davenport Democrat & Leader* 20 February 1922

'As for Fulton, he is crazy to get another crack at Dempsey,' wrote Sparrow McGann in the *Oakland Tribune* on 25 December 1921. 'There will be no trouble about signing him up. The average fan will be tempted to laugh his head off when he hears of Fulton as an opponent for the heavyweight champion, but the wise guys all tell you that with a little more heart Fulton would be a real contender. Maybe he has injected himself with the sort of stuff that made the mouse stand on his hind legs and ask, "Where is that cat now?" Or again, he may have figured out a way to beat Dempsey and will enter the ring full of confidence.

'There is no question that the fight would draw, if only for the reason that at any time Dempsey goes against a man in defense of his title the attraction is bound to pay. He and Benny Leonard are the only scrappers in the world of whom this may be said.'

For United Press, Henry L. Farrell wasn't impressed by the latest challenger to speak up, writing, 'Bob Martin has joined the little group outside the cage looking in at the mankiller. The soldier champion wants to fight Jack Dempsey. Hard Broadway fans look at the challenge with a "well, he'd last about as long as anyone". Unless Martin has to meet some kind of a huge mortgage on the old homestead or something like that, it is hard to understand why he wants any of Dempsey's game. He had a good racket playing to soldier houses around in the suburbs and he's still a good card, but he won't be so good if he gets polished off like the Frenchman. Jimmy Bronson's challenge hurled at Dempsey on behalf of his boy brought the heavyweight situation back to notice. It looks like another lean year for Dempsey.'[307]

---

307 *Henry L. Farrell Oakland Tribune 25 December 1921*

13

Rickard In Court – Dempsey in Europe

AS the year 1922 got under way, Dempsey's name in the headlines was sensationally replaced by that of his promoter. 'TEX RICKARD INDICTED IN GIRL CASES Geo. L. (Tex) Rickard, famous boxing promoter, was indicted by the grand jury today on charges made by young girls. Two indictments were voted against Rickard. Each contains three counts. They were based on the testimony of Alice Ruck and Sarah Schoenfeld, 15-year-old girls. These girls say Rickard lured them to his office in the tower of Madison Square Garden, which was formerly the studio of Stanford White, in which parties, described in the famous Thaw trial, occurred. They also allege he took them to an apartment house on 40th Street. Rickard's attorneys were notified to have him appear in the Supreme Court at once to plead to the charges. He is already out on $10,000 bail, which he supplied when first arrested.'[308]

A few days after the hearing, Rickard was approached by three men who demanded $50,000 to 'get him off the hook'. The promoter steadfastly refused their threats, saying he was willing to have his day in court.

Rickard's trial began on 20 March in the Criminal Branch of the New York State Supreme Court before Justice Isidore Wasservogel. Chief assistant district attorney Ferdinand A. Pecora insisted that

---

308 *Woodland Daily Democrat* Ca. 16 February 1922

Tex be held without bail, meaning the promoter had to spend nights in The Tombs, New York City's gloomy old prison. This so upset friends of Rickard's that they authorized his lawyer, Max D. Steuer, to offer bail in any amount up to half a million dollars. The offers were refused by the prosecution. With four indictments against Rickard, it was decided to take up first the one charging assault upon 15-year-old Sarah Schoenfeld.

'A remarkable feature of the case,' wrote Samuels, 'was the staunch loyalty of Tex's wealthy and influential friends. Some of them wired from Alaska, South America, Nevada, and other places that they would travel around the earth, if necessary, to testify to his good character.'[309]

Rickard's ordeal lasted eight days. On 29 March, Associated Press reported, 'Seldom has there been such a demonstration in the court house as that staged when the jury brought in its verdict freeing Rickard. Hundreds had lingered about the big building, thinking the jury would not deliberate long before reaching an agreement. When the first syllable of the verdict fell from the lips of the jury's foreman, the word was shouted through the corridors and passed along to the throng waiting in the street outside. Rickard was almost overwhelmed by his friends, but made his way through the crowd to a telephone, where he called his apartment and informed Mrs Rickard of his acquittal.'[310]

Before leaving the courtroom, Tex addressed the assembled reporters, saying, 'Thank you all. God bless you. You have all been very nice to me. I've never been happier in my life. Boys, I have shot craps for $35,000 a roll and I was never in any greater suspense than when the jury returned to the courtroom. Did you see the poker faces they had on?'[311]

When Tex left the sheriff's office, police reserves and court attendants were summoned to keep the crowd in check. He was given three cheers by the crowd as he stepped into his car to be taken home. Henry L. Farrell wrote, 'Rickard is the latest and most prominent on the list of New Yorkers said to have been selected as victims of a big blackmailing ring. Rickard declared he was asked for $50,000. He refused and spent $150,000 beating the fate with which they threatened him. The gang selected the "two little girls" game as the weapon. Several months before the same game had been worked on a

---

309 Samuels p. 254
310 *San Antonio Evening News* 30 March 1922
311 *Nevada State Journal* 29 March 1922

young New York banker and he turned over one payment of $75,000.... Rickard says he has the names of the men and he has the affidavit of one who got 'cold feet' and was willing to turn State's evidence.'[312]

'To many of his acquaintances,' wrote Samuels, 'Tex appeared a man who had forgotten the trial the moment it was over. But Rex Beach did not think so. The popular novelist felt that Tex was a marked and changed man from then on. Westbrook Pegler, who was seeing a good deal of Tex at the time, thought that Rickard brooded over the ugly and humiliating experience for a while, then shook it off as he had every other tough time he had survived.'[313]

With a somewhat relieved Rickard back in the Garden, Doc and Dempsey considered their options. Kearns decided to lay Jack off fighting for a while and dedicate their energies to business. "Tex felt that I should only fight about once a year," he recalled. "Overexposure or the wrong opponent, he feared, would lead to a small gate. I guess all of us had been spoiled by the million-dollar one."[314]

The two Jacks were fine in the fight business, not so good in the business world. A coal property in Utah cost them $75,000. So they hit the road again, New York, Denver, Washington DC, exhibition stuff with Packey O'Gatty, Eddie Eagan and Terry Keller. Eagan, who boxed Dempsey in Denver, had captained Yale's boxing team, won the 1919 AAU heavyweight title on his way to Olympic gold at Antwerp in 1920 and made Olympic history in 1924 winning a gold medal on the bobsleigh team. In the 1940s Eddie Eagan would serve as chairman of the New York State Athletic Commission.

Besides the exhibition stuff there was always the Pantages Vaudeville Circuit. Alexander Pantages was a crusty old Greek con artist, a former saloon porter who had struck it rich in the Klondyke. Virtually illiterate, he rubber-stamped his signature for years, but he was no fool. He had a fantastic memory and could tell you who played when, where and how, as well as why, if necessary. He had originally opened his vaudeville theatres on the west coast and eventually built up an entire cross-country circuit. 'We worked hard in vaudeville and loved every minute of it,' recalled Dempsey. 'I remember splintery stages and draughty, dilapidated dressing rooms which frequently smelled of sweepings from a gymnasium floor.'[315]

---

312 Henry L. Farrell *Kansas City Star* 30 March 1922
313 Samuels pp. 262–263
314 Dempsey with Piattelli p. 147
315 Ibid p. 137

When on the circuit, Doc would always tell Dempsey, 'Remember, Jack, as long as I keep you on the stage, there ain't no way you're going to lose your championship.'[316]

'When the vaudeville tour ultimately ended,' recalled Kearns, 'I decided it was time for us to make a trip abroad…I thought we should do it up in style.'[317]

Doing it up in style for Jack 'Doc' Kearns meant first class all the way. It meant the best suite on the Cunard liner *Aquitania* and destinations booked for London, Paris and Berlin. It meant Kearns, Dempsey, Joe Benjamin, Teddy Hayes and Damon Runyon who would chronicle the entire journey for the Hearst papers. It meant a big lavish send-off party with lots of showgirls, among them dancer Florence Walton, Mary Lewis of the Follies, and movie actress Mary Sherman. Poor Jack had to kiss them all several times for the newspaper photographers. And a large, shaggy-haired man pushed his way through the crowd on the dock to give Dempsey a kiss on each cheek. Beauty and the Beast.

It was Luis Angel Firpo, the giant Argentine heavyweight who had just knocked out Sailor Maxted in his American debut. 'I had no idea who the hell he was,' said Dempsey. They would meet again.

Jack Dempsey's big adventure began that April day in 1922 as the *Aquitania* moved out from the dock and headed for the open sea. This was a new world for the 26-year-old kid from Colorado. Growing up there he could never have dreamed of this day, leaving the New World on a mighty ocean-going liner, heading for the Old World. And like a kid in a candy store, Dempsey explored every inch of his new environment, this hotel on the high seas. He fascinated Runyon, who likened him to 'a big animal investigating a new cage. He went bounding about nosing into every nook and corner. He has never reminded us more of a mountain lion.'[318]

The champion never forgot who he was on that trip across the Atlantic. Every morning he donned his working gear and jogged five miles around the deck. Later, he made full use of the ship's well-appointed gymnasium; lifting weights, skipping, shadow boxing, then speed-sparring for three rounds with Joe Benjamin. Few passengers were admitted to the workouts, no women, much to their disappointment. Did the champion have a fight in his near future?

---

316 Kahn p. 297
317 Kearns p. 157
318 Kahn p. 282

Jack said, 'One of these Europeans might turn up with an opponent and a pot of gold, and I want to be ready.'[319] Jack Dempsey would always be ready for a fight.

London lionised the world heavyweight champion. Crowds followed his every move as he was feted, wined and dined. The big highlight of the trip, for Jack, was a lunch given him by Lord Northcliffe, the British publisher, at his town house. He found himself mingling with generals, lords and dukes. 'I don't think any fighter was ever treated better than I was that day by Englishmen who probably had trouble understanding the way I used their language.'[320] Halfway through the luncheon, Damon Runyon called at the house and handed in his card, stating that he was covering Dempsey's European trip and would like to attend the event. Runyon was politely informed that this would not be possible as this was a private party for Mr Dempsey. Damon never got over it, Jack would recall. 'He had known me when I was a bum.'

The boys liked Paris better. More girls, more action, parties, receptions. They gave Dempsey a medal, which surprised him after what he had done to their beloved Georges. There was some talk in the newspapers about a return match with Carpentier in Paris, but it was just reporters blowing smoke. They wouldn't fight again.

Berlin was another experience Dempsey wouldn't forget. The boxing fans mobbed him on the first day and almost stripped him of his clothing. Then Jack mentioned to reporters that he was crazy about dogs, his favourite. being the German shepherd, and he would like to buy one while he was in town. The story hit the papers and next day hundreds of German shepherds were paraded at the Hotel Adlon by their owners, anxious to sell to the world's champion. It was time to leave Berlin!

On their way back to the ship, they had to pass through Paris. The City of Light made an indelible impression on Dempsey. 'You should've seen it, and its girls, in 1922 – especially if you could have been my age and heavyweight champion of the world.'[321]

'They were all young in those days,' recalled Runyon in a 1936 column, 'and were like a family of rollicking youngsters. The times they had! They lived together and laughed together and loved together and fought together. There never was a pugilistic combination like it in the history of the game.'[322]

---

319 Ibid p. 284
320 Dempsey with Considine & Slocum pp. 140–141
321 Ibid p. 143
322 Damon Runyon *Chester Times* Pa. 26 June 1936

In May 1922, the boys were home and Doc and Dempsey were looking to generate some income. There was no big fight in the offing and Rickard was busy with other things. There was always a promoter somewhere ready to stick the heavyweight champ on one of his fight cards against some local duffer, exhibition stuff. Kearns made a few phone calls and soon Dempsey was stripping off in places like Portland, Bangor and Fairfield in Maine. Moving on to Montreal, Jack knocked out Elzear Rioux in the first round and eased up on Jack Renault and Paul Lahaye. A day later he was in Ottawa to punch Renault around for three rounds and then they shuffled off to Buffalo where he was slated to meet three more opponents at the Broadway Auditorium.

Just before entering the ring that night, Kearns received a telegram from the local office of the New York State Boxing Commission stating that Dempsey would be permitted to box only one opponent and that the bout must go to a decision. 'Yes,' said commission secretary Harry Burchell, 'it was a championship bout although it was not to have been. But we see to it that the laws are upheld in this state.' Dempsey, according to the posters on the billboards of Buffalo, was to have met three sparring partners in one-round exhibitions.

'Buffaloians paid a comparatively small admission fee to see the champion exhibit unaware that for a pittance they were to see a world boxing title hang in the balance. Just before the exhibitions were due to start, Jimmy Darcy, a light-heavyweight, was selected and Dempsey performed a bit livelier perhaps than he had intended. The champion received the decision. As a result, Darcy enjoys the distinction of being the only pugilist to stay the limit with Dempsey since he won the title, and of having lasted longer against the champion than Georges Carpentier, Fred Fulton, Jess Willard, Gunboat Smith or Carl Morris. And Dempsey had a good workout.'[323]

Harry Wills would have been somewhat upset reading that item in his morning paper, for he was generally accepted by the writers and their readers as Dempsey's top contender. In a poll conducted by more than 500 newspapers, Wills was picked as the boxer the public most wanted to see Dempsey fight. Wills received 131,073 votes with Tommy Gibbons the second choice, trailing by about 6,000 votes.

Known as the Black Panther, Harry Wills was born in New Orleans and started fighting in 1911. He stood 6ft 2in and weighed

---

323 *Thomasville Daily Times Enterprise* Georgia 26 July 1922

a solid 220lb. But once in every year, heavyweight Harry became a middleweight by fasting for a month, usually February, by putting nothing in his mouth but water, 'for the good of his health and his immortal soul'. When he wasn't fasting, Harry was a good fighter. When he retired in 1932, his record showed 107 contests with 68 wins, 54 by knockout, nine defeats, three draws, 24 no decision bouts and three no contests. And he did get to be the heavyweight champion, even if he had to settle for the colored heavyweight title. The top black fighters of Harry's era were forced to fight each other, as many white fighters drew the colour line.

When Jack Dempsey annihilated Jess Willard in the broiling sun of Independence Day 1919, the new champion, no doubt prompted by promoter Tex Rickard and manager Jack Kearns, 'announced that he would draw the colour line. He will pay no attention to negro challengers, but will defend his title against any white opponent as the occasion demands.'[324]

Since winning the title, Dempsey had used many negro fighters in his training camp; Bill Tate, Panama Joe Gans, The Jamaica Kid, Battling Jim Johnson. He had no fear of meeting Wills and would have been favoured in such a match. Trainer Ray Arcel, commenting on Wills, said, 'He didn't hit anywhere near as hard as Dempsey, and he didn't move anywhere near as smoothly as Carpentier. I would rate Wills as a very good journeyman.'[325]

'I suggested to Rickard that we take on Harry Wills,' recalled Kearns. 'Rickard told me to sit down. "Kearns," he said, "I thought, too, that Wills might make us a good opponent. The word came to me right straight from the governor's mansion that we can't fight Wills. We can't fight him simply because of the fact that he's a negro. Sounds silly, but that's the way they want it." I got a little mad. "Me and Dempsey got nothing against any guy just because of the colour of his skin. By God, we'll fight Wills just because of them, whoever they are."'[326]

Kearns tried, or so he would recall later. He contacted a promoter he knew, Floyd Fitzsimmons, and told him to make the match anywhere he could in the Midwest. About a week later, Fitzsimmons called Kearns and said he was having unexpected difficulty putting the fight together. When Kearns told Rickard, the promoter just nodded

324 *New York Times* 6 July 1919
325 Kahn pp. 300–301
326 Kearns pp.160

and said, 'I told you it wouldn't work. Those politicians don't want it and they've got a pretty strong outfit, whether you're in New York or Kokomo.'[327]

On 11 July 1922, Kearns and Paddy Mullins, manager of Wills, signed a contract in New York for the heavyweights to meet within 60 days after the acceptance of a satisfactory bid extended by a reliable promoter. That was Doc's way out of a sticky corner. The fight was doomed from the start. No one would touch it.

Four years later there was a serious bid to put the fight together, as reported by my friend Clay Moyle on the v2 Forum website on 14 August 2011. He quoted an article by Dempsey in a 1963 issue of *Ebony* magazine, which said, in part, 'The facts clearly show that in 1926 I tried desperately to arrange a fight with Harry Wills but the deal collapsed when my guarantee was not forthcoming. Wills and I had signed to fight with a promoter named Floyd Fitzsimmons of Benton Harbor, Michigan. Wills, I understand, received fifty thousand dollars as his guarantee for signing the contract. I was to have received one hundred and twenty-five thousand dollars in advance of the fight.

'As the date of the fight drew nearer and my money did not appear, I became anxious and asked Fitzsimmons what was the matter. He wired me to meet him in Dayton, Ohio, assuring me that he would have the money for me there. I met Fitzsimmons in Dayton who handed me a certified cheque for twenty-five thousand dollars and a promise to let me have the balance almost immediately. I balked at that, demanding the full amount right away. Fitzsimmons tried to placate me by calling the bank where he said he had deposited the money. The bank, unfortunately for Fitzsimmons, informed him that it did not have that much money on hand, that there wasn't enough to cover the twenty-five thousand dollar cheque he had given me. Furious, I returned the cheque to Fitzsimmons and told him the fight was off. Later, the Fitzsimmons syndicate financing the fight sued me for failure to honor a contract. I won the case…I am sorry Wills and I never got a chance to square off in the ring. I am sure it would have been one beautiful scrap.'

Dempsey at that time was no longer with Doc Kearns. Harry Wills at least got to keep his $50,000 guarantee, enabling him to invest in several properties in Harlem which ensured Dempsey's nemesis of a comfortable retirement.

---

327 Ibid p. 161

14

Lean Times For Million-Dollar Fighter

'JACK DEMPSEY WINS BATTLE WITH MOOSE – St John, N. B. 27 September 1922 – Jack Dempsey has won his first battle with a Canadian moose. A message reaching here today from the forests of Kings County reported the meeting between the king of the squared circle and the monarch of the north woods last Tuesday. The moose is dead. Dempsey escaped with a torn pair of breeches. Dempsey met his quarry in the early morning when the animal responded to the guide's call. At the first shot the moose fell, and Dempsey, disregarding the warning of his mentor, rushed up and seized it by the antlers. The next moment as the moose tossed his great head in a last agony, the champion was sent flying through the air, landing fifteen feet away. He was unhurt, but was in much need of a new pair of trousers. The moose had an antler spread of 48 inches with 14 points and weighed 700 pounds.

'Word came through from Havelock, N.B. this evening that Jack and his party had broken camp late today and would reach this city tomorrow on their way to New York. Dempsey learned today for the first time of the defeat of Carpentier by the Senegalese Siki. "I am sorry to hear it and very much surprised," he said. "This Siki must be a good man."'[328]

---

328 *Ogden Standard Examiner* 28 September 1922

Carpentier was very much surprised, but he wouldn't agree that Siki was a good man.

'Beaten almost beyond recognition, Georges Carpentier, former ring idol of France, tossed all night on his bed in a delirious frenzy, yelling for revenge and another chance against Battling Siki, the giant Senegalese heavyweight, who knocked him out yesterday in the sixth round of a fight scheduled for twenty rounds,' reported United Press from Paris. 'Ministrations of his doctors, his heart-broken wife and his faithful manager Descamps, availed nothing. He wept and pleaded that arrangements be made immediately for another meet with the black.

'No outsiders were permitted near Carpentier, but Dr Martel, his physician, said that both his eyes were completely closed, his lips were swollen immensely, his nose was broken, a long gash cut in his cheek, his right hand was fractured in two places and his left hand in one place. 'I made the mistake of trying to study Siki in the early rounds,' he told reporters. 'He got over a lucky punch and took all my strength away. I hit him with everything I had. His race is not made like mine.'[329]

The 'giant Senegalese heavyweight' referred to in the press was actually a light-heavyweight who weighed 174lb when he crushed Carpentier and stood 5ft 10.5in in his socks. No heavyweight by any standards, he was nevertheless officially recognised as heavyweight champion of France and Europe.

'The boxing federation tonight declared Battling Siki the light-heavyweight champion of the world and the heavyweight champion of France. It announced that it intended sending to the American boxing authorities a regular challenge for him to meet all comers. "You had better cable Mr Rickard tonight that I am willing to fight Dempsey right away," said the Senegalese to the Associated Press correspondent.'[330]

The same paper reported that an offer of $100,000 was cabled from New York for Siki to fight Harry Wills by the matchmaker for Ebbets Field in Brooklyn, with a suggested date of 12 October.

Henry Farrell wrote, 'When that Battling Siki flattened Carpentier in Paris yesterday he took an indirect poke of a serious nature at one of Jack Dempsey's vitals – his pocketbook. The

329 *Sandusky Star Journal* 24 September 1922
330 *Helena Independent* Montana 25 September 1922

champion's carefully nurtured designs to pack the Buffalo stadium for another fight with Georges this winter undoubtedly were smashed flatter than Carpentier. Jack Kearns, the champion's manager, could not be reached this morning, but one of his friends suggested that the passage the Dempsey party had booked for November would be cancelled.'[331]

Meanwhile, Battling Siki was the new darling of the boulevards and he was having a ball, one bar and café after another. His manager, Monsieur Hellers, was busy fielding offers from Tex Rickard and Tom O'Rourke in New York and Jeff Wilson in London, but he was playing hard to get, setting his stall out as follows: 1,100,000 francs net, exclusive of income tax, to meet either Harry Wills or Harry Greb in the United States, or 1,600,000 francs for a fight with Jack Dempsey, on 26 October or any date thereafter. Hellers stated that if he could not obtain his demands he would not go to the United States that winter, but would remain in Europe and fight England's best glovemen.

Despite press references to 'the giant black' it was a fact that Siki was smaller and lighter than heavyweight champion Dempsey, but a group of 'scientists and anthropologists at the University of Chicago took out their charts and reference books and looked over an assortment of Negroid skulls today after they read of the Siki– Carpentier affair in Paris. The consensus was that if and when the Siki person meets up with Jack Dempsey, the aforesaid Dempsey stands an excellent chance of being clouted for a row of dog houses. The lofty-brained and bespectacled scientists did not put it in just these words but that is just what they meant.

'Battling Siki, it appears from all the records, comes of a hard-boiled tribe. The anthropologists point out that Senegal produces a minimum of civilisation and a maximum of hardship. One does not survive there without having to overcome a list of things that would put a white man out in the first round. Battling Siki, they say, looks like the fittest of survivals. He has arms and shoulders and chest of his comparatively recent ape ancestors. Above the shoulders they admit he has not much except a parking place for his hat, but what brain he possesses functions amazingly on what to do in a rumpus. There is not a poet or a cake-eater or a statesman in his pedigree and he has not been softened by the luxuries of so-called civilisation. Hitting

---

331 Henry L. Farrell *Sandusky Star Journal* 25 September 1922

him on the head with a maul gets no farther than to put the maul out of business.'[332]

If Jack Dempsey fancied meeting Siki should the Battler make it to New York, the champion would have to get in line. 'Kid Norfolk of New York, negro light-heavyweight boxer, has deposited a forfeit of $2,500 binding a challenge to Battling Siki and will be entitled to first consideration as an opponent for the Senegalese in New York, according to announcement tonight by the New York State Athletic Commission. The challenge is for the world's light-heavyweight championship, now held by Siki...Tex Rickard announced he would comply with the order of the state boxing commission and start Battling Siki against Kid Norfolk at Madison Square Garden 30 November.'[333]

It would actually be one year later when Siki had his Garden date with the Kid, 20 November 1923, by which time Siki was no longer world light-heavyweight champion. He'd had the temerity to defend his title against an Irishman in Dublin on St Patrick's Day! It was the time of the Troubles and the fight, against the veteran Mike McTigue, was boxed against a background of exploding bombs and gunfire. At the end of 20 rounds McTigue was the winner and new champion. No surprise there then.

The Battler had three more fights in France before heading across the Atlantic for his fight with Kid Norfolk. The Kid was a tough handful for anybody, having fought the top men in America, and Siki knew he had been in a fight. So did Norfolk, after 15 hard rounds, before he received the decision. Siki continued fighting in American rings for a couple of years only to be found dead, lying in the gutter in New York's Hell's Kitchen area, on 15 December 1925. Aged 28, he had been shot twice in the back.

By September, Jack Dempsey was still unemployed. He donned his gear for a stiff workout at Stillman's gym on 8th Avenue while manager Doc Kearns was telling everyone within earshot that 'the champion was in such shape that he would be ready to fight in a week...If Dempsey can get ready in a week then Adam was a seventh son and Carrie Nation ran a cabaret. Jack is wide in the middle and wadded out all over with a distributed thickness which doesn't make him look exactly fat, but certainly gives him no strong resemblance

332 *Lethbridge Herald* Alberta 26 September 1922
333 *Oakland Tribune* 30 September 1922

to the hardened, fine-drawn athlete who slugged that young French movie actor at Jersey City.

'The champion gave Jack Thompson a card to the morgue as soon as they got started. He whacked the brown boy on the left ribs with a moaning right smash that bent him out of shape and then laid in with both big arms pumping against Thompson's belt line. They were terrific hurtful punches but this Thompson is unusually game and durable and he banged Jack on the lips with a right hander pulled clear from the docks. Jack shook his head, pumped a steaming jab into Thompson's face, opened him up and shot over a right smash to the jaw which knocked the negro irresponsible on his feet. Thompson was out for half a minute but didn't fall and Dempsey let him wrestle till his head cleared.

'When his head did clear, Thompson told reporters, "Mister, that man is the hardest man to hit in the world. I can hit him, but he ain't never where you think he is. I miss him closer than any boxer I ever met. He just moves his jaw half an inch, and when you miss – zowie – you get it."

'Talking of the on-off fight with Harry Wills, Kearns said, "we aren't asking half a million dollars at all. All we want is a fair share. They offer us 37.5 per cent of the receipts at the Polo Grounds which would give us $400,000 and Wills $125,000. That would be very nice, but we see that the promoters would get more than half a million dollars for themselves, and that wouldn't be so elegant for us."'[334]

A proposed fight with Billy Miske fell through when Billy performed poorly against Tom Gibbons and New York commissioner Muldoon refused to allow the champion to have another go at Bill Brennan. The Wills fight couldn't take place outdoors until the next summer. A column in the *Bridgeport Telegram* on 22 October was headed 'DEMPSEY IN FOR A LEAN WINTER', 'Here it is coming on winter and the heavyweight champion absolutely is out of work, with coal high and food and lodging not any too reasonable. If this state of affairs continues it might come to pass that a stalwart youth would be seen after the first snows standing at the corner of Forty-Second Street and Broadway calling out to the passersby, "Please help a poor guy who can't get work at his trade." Same stalwart youth will be William Henry (called Jack) Dempsey, champion heavyweight boxer of the world.'

334 *Kansas City Star* 9 September 1922

A week after that item appeared in print, Tex Rickard stated that it was his considered view that Tom Gibbons of St Paul was the only white heavyweight capable of giving the champion a real battle for his title. Tex further stated that he was trying to contact Jack Kearns or Dempsey and hoped for an answer within 24 hours. It was understood that Doc and Dempsey were in Toledo on a theatrical tour that would take them to the Pacific coast, but Rickard thought they would hurry back to New York if there was a chance of a bout at Madison Square Garden. Dempsey wanted action and both Jacks needed some serious money. Playing the Pantages circuit wouldn't give them that.

New York Commission chairman William Muldoon made it known that he wouldn't oppose a Dempsey–Gibbons match, but he thought that the St Paul boxer should meet Brennan, with the winner going into a match with Dempsey for the title. The boys kicked that one around the block and agreed Gibbons deserved a title shot but they couldn't see how Bill Brennan was deserving of another chance.

A Damon Runyon column observed, 'Jess Willard, former heavyweight champion is giving boxing exhibitions out in Los Angeles. Report says he "looks fair". Willard has not given up the idea of getting a fat loser's end out of another bout with Jack Dempsey. He will meet no one else, so he will never meet Dempsey. Harry Wills or Floyd Johnson, heavyweights, can beat Willard. Harry Greb, Gene Tunney or Tom Gibbons, light-heavyweights, would bewilder him. Willard is pugilistically dead.

'Managers may be parasites, as William Muldoon claims, but a crafty fight manager could resurrect Willard. A crafty manager would take Willard about the country, having him meet and knock over "set-ups" or easy opponents. At first few would take these knockouts seriously. After a while you would commence to hear thrilling tales of Willard's great "come back". Finally he would be solidly "built up" to be knocked out by Jack Dempsey. The thing is elemental to those who know the boxing game.'[335]

As the year 1922 drew to a close, it seemed Harry Wills was back in the frame for a go at Dempsey. International News Service sports editor Davis J. Walsh trumpeted in his final column before meeting the New Year, 'Diplomatic revival of the Dempsey–Wills proposition is in order when Jack Kearns arrives in New York in a glow of self-satisfaction and a cutaway coat some weeks hence. This is

---

335 Damon Runyon *Cedar Rapids Evening Gazette* 17 November 1922

the good word that has gone out among the fistic elite. From sources unknown higher up, the tip has been given that all is not well and the interested parties may proceed with their plans without fear of discreet interruptions.

'Al Smith, the new governor, is said to look with a tolerant eye upon the prospect. At any rate he is believed to be in a receptive mood and in no way inclined to interfere as long as the law is obeyed. Gentlemen of the press, therefore, may expect to be duly informed almost any time now that public demand for the match can be restrained no longer. It is believed that Kearns is convinced that neither Floyd Johnson nor Luis Firpo can be built up in a convincing attraction before the summer months and realising that Dempsey is gaining nothing by his protracted idleness, is ready to do business with the first real contender that happens along. The latter and Harry Wills are one and the same. Tex Rickard of course will be a conspicuous bidder, but unless he can get the Yankee Stadium, may not care to erect a new arena capable of accommodating a crowd such as would witness a bout of this magnitude.'[336]

As heavyweight champion Jack Dempsey prepared to meet the New Year, it seemed as though Harry Wills, his black nemesis, just wouldn't go away.

---

336 Davis J. Walsh *Oakland Tribune* 29 December 1922

15

Tough Times Out West

HUGH Fullerton III was an influential American sportswriter of the first half of the 20th century, one of the founders of the Baseball Writers Association of America and best remembered for his role in uncovering the 1919 Black Sox scandal. In a January column in 1923, Fullerton took a fling at the fight game, especially the game being played by Tex Rickard, Jack Kearns and Jack Dempsey. And he couldn't see a happy ending to the game for Mr Rickard with a statement that sent shockwaves racing along 8th Avenue.

'I can tell you that Rickard is about done as a fight promoter in New York – I have inside information that he will not control any of the big matches in which Dempsey will appear. Further, Governor Smith is done with Rickard...Confidentially, Tex Rickard will cease to be the czar of New York boxing.'[337]

According to Fullerton, Kearns had arrived in New York with the news that Dempsey would fight Harry Wills for the heavyweight championship on or about 4 July, and he challenged one and all of the other contenders – Willard, Firpo, Greb, Gibbons or Johnson – to meet him at any time prior to 4 July. Kearns stated that Dempsey wanted three fights in a row, climaxed by the bout with Wills, a bout

---

337 Hugh Fullerton III *Atlanta News Telegraph* 26 January 1923

for which he was now ready to sign articles with Paddy Mullins, manager of the contender.

Tom O'Rourke, a former member of the New York Commission who had taken charge of the Polo Grounds, made an offer of a million dollars to Dempsey to fight three times at the stadium. The offer was for Bill Brennan, Luis Firpo, Tom Gibbons or Jess Willard, with Harry Wills in the third bout.

If Tex Rickard was down for a count, he was getting up and fighting back with the announcement that Luis Firpo, the Wild Bull of the Pampas, would meet Chicago veteran Bill Brennan in a 15-round contest at Madison Square Garden on 12 March. Brennan had just lost a tough fight in the Garden with young contender Floyd Johnson but Rickard decided that the loser would be a better match with Firpo on his return to America. Johnson would keep till later. Rickard promised Firpo a title bout with Dempsey within six months if he could beat Brennan.

Dempsey's name was in an item datelined Los Angeles 13 January, 'A judgment of $250 was awarded Owen Bartlett against Teddy Hayes, trainer for Jack Dempsey, because of a beating administered to him 13 February 1922 when he was discharged as a painter by the defendant. Bartlett sued for $75,000 damages, claiming Jack Dempsey and his brother Joseph Dempsey were defendants in addition to Hayes.'[338] Justice prevailed when a nonsuit was granted the champion as it was shown that he was not present when the altercation took place.

Heavyweight fighter Harry Wills was being used as a political football, according to columnist Damon Runyon, by the Republican State Administration, working through the boxing commission. To gain the votes of the city's coloured population, the commission stated that Dempsey must fight Wills. 'That suited Dempsey,' wrote Runyon. 'It meant much money for him. He signed articles for the bout at once. Then Dempsey and Dempsey's manager, Jack Kearns, were told to forget the match for a while. The Republican Administration did not wish to give reformers a target the size of a black and white prize fight with a campaign on.'[339]

But it was a new year and a new administration had moved into the Empire State and the new governor, Al Smith, was said to be in favour of the Dempsey–Wills fight being held. As long as boxing was

---

338 *Indianapolis Sunday Star* 14 January 1923
339 Damon Runyon *San Antonio Evening News* 1 January 1923

legalised in New York, then Governor Smith had to allow the bout to take place so long as it was held in accordance with the law and the rules of the commission.

However, Rickard was still opposed to inter-racial heavyweight title bouts on principle, after the 1910 fiasco between Jim Jeffries and Jack Johnson led to race riots across America, and he was Dempsey's promoter.

Then Tex received an unexpected way out of the Dempsey–Wills problem. New York Commission boss William Muldoon held a press conference on 4 February to announce that he would not sanction any heavyweight title matches in the state of New York. Muldoon's main concern, he said, was the crass commercialism in boxing, asking how Americans could tolerate a heavyweight champion earning more in ten minutes than the president of the United States could make in four years. 'It is the commercialized condition produced by money-mad promoters and managers,' he said, 'which is responsible for the commission's opposition.'[340] United Press sports editor Henry L. Farrell reported, 'Some talk is going around town that Tammany Hall doesn't think Dempsey is such a good champion, and that the organisation is not going to let him take any money out of New York while they hold the heights of Albany.'[341]

It was known that Dempsey, no doubt prompted by Kearns, had sent a nice fat cheque into the committee before the last city election, and that Tammany sent it right back with some warm remarks about it. Dempsey should have been happy to get his cheque back after reading that his promoter had dropped out of the scramble to make a fight for Jack's title. Towards the end of January, Tex Rickard had given Jack Kearns $1,000 not to talk to any promoters until 1 February. When the option expired, instead of making a big offer for Dempsey's contract, he surprised everyone by withdrawing from the field, announcing to the press, 'I have decided after full consideration not to participate in any bidding for a heavyweight championship contest in which Jack Dempsey will defend his title. I am not convinced in my own mind that the press and the public would support any particular match right now.'[342]

---

340 William Muldoon *New York Times* 5 February 1923
341 Henry L. Farrell *Charleston Daily Mail* 23 January 1923
342 *Oshkosh Daily Northwestern* 1 February 1923

'Tex Rickard did not yet consider that Gibbons or anyone else was enough of a drawing card to make another great fight spectacle,' Dempsey wrote in his 1940 autobiography. 'Both Kearns and I began to feel the need of making some more money. A champion's expenses are unavoidably heavy, and we had lost money instead of making any in business. Consequently, when a group of western businessmen offered us a $300,000 guarantee for a fight with Tommy Gibbons, to be staged at the oil town of Shelby, Montana, we decided it was too good to pass up. There are not many times in the lives of any fighters when they are offered a flat guarantee of $300,000. There were, however, several things wrong with the picture. The promoters were amateurs. They knew no more about the fight business than Doc and I did about coal mining.'[343]

'Early in 1923, Doc saw a chance to leave Rickard out in the cold on the next Dempsey fight,' wrote Samuels. 'This happened when Shelby, a cowtown in Montana, offered the champion $300,000 to meet Tommy Gibbons of Minneapolis. Gibbons was a brilliant boxer but had no punch worth mentioning. Along with almost everybody east of the Great Divide and in many places west of it, Doc had never heard of Shelby. But as soon as Rand McNally's head office assured Doc that there was actually such a place, he happily skipped over to Tex's office and told him about the offer. "They are real serious about putting on a fight out there, Tex. Wanna up their offer?" "I wouldn't pay a nickel for Jack in there with Tommy Gibbons," Tex replied.'[344]

Rickard had already stated that he considered Gibbons the only white boxer capable of giving Dempsey a good fight for the championship, but he couldn't see Gibbons as box office.

In January, Gibbons had filed a formal challenge backed by a cheque for $2,500 with the New York Commission for a championship fight with Jack Dempsey. Harry Wills already had a similar challenge on file but it hadn't gotten him anywhere near Dempsey. Harry's problem was his colour. Promoters and politicians didn't want a black–white battle at any cost. The commission rules stated that a champion must accept a challenge within 60 days. Dempsey and Kearns got round that one by signing a contract dependent on a reliable promoter proposing an acceptable purse, date and venue. That wasn't going to happen.

---

343 Dempsey and Stearns pp. 214–215
344 Samuels p. 263

'Gibbons is too small.' With those words and that excuse, chairman William Muldoon of the New York State Boxing Commission rejected and disposed of the St Paul man's challenge to heavyweight champion Jack Dempsey. 'Gibbons is a good little man compared to Dempsey,' said Muldoon. 'Dempsey is a good big man.' The commission, for banning a Dempsey–Gibbons bout because of the 20lb difference in the size of the two heavyweights, left itself open to ridicule. If Gibbons was too small for Dempsey, then Dempsey was too small for Harry Wills, two inches taller and 20lb heavier.

'Shades of Bob Fitzsimmons,' wrote columnist 'Fair Play'. 'The boxing commission's ruling that because Tom Gibbons is 20lb lighter than Dempsey, make it impossible for it to license such a scrap. How about Dempsey being 50lb lighter than Willard at Toledo?'[345]

Looking over the heavyweight field, sportswriter Billy Evans wrote in a February column, 'A year ago Gibbons was considered a certainty for a Dempsey meeting. Then came the upset by Harry Greb which cost Gibbons at least $100,000...Dempsey fought Brennan, Carpentier and Miske in championship bouts and none of the trio had any more to recommend themselves as contenders than has Gibbons.'[346]

When Greb beat Mickey Walker in a middleweight title bout in 1925, Doc Kearns, then Walker's manager, told Mickey he would never let Dempsey fight Greb.

'In my three bouts with Gibbons,' wrote Greb in a newspaper article a few days after the New York bout, 'I had carefully studied his style. My experience had proved to me that Gibbons was a flat-footed puncher, extremely dangerous if allowed to get set...I defeated Tommy Gibbons by refusing to let him get set. He must be set to have any power back of his blows...I know that most of the ring experts were surprised at my carrying the fight to Gibbons. That is the only way to beat Gibbons. Don't let him get set and beat him to the punch by stepping inside as he telegraphs his intentions with his right.'[347]

Tommy Gibbons, who was born in St Paul on 22 March 1891, dropped out of college to follow in the footsteps of his older, famous brother, Mike, as a professional fighter in 1911. Three years older, Mike would become famous as the St Paul Phantom as he dazzled opponents with a boxing style that prompted Nat Fleischer to say

345 'Fair Play' *Syracuse Herald* 23 January 1923
346 Billy Evans *Appleton Post Crescent* 1 February 1923
347 Harry Greb *Lima News* 17 March 1922

Mike was the nearest approach to the superb artistry of Tommy Ryan that the middleweight division ever boasted. Following the untimely death of Stanley Ketchel, Mike Gibbons was one of the claimants to the vacant title but that was the nearest he got to an official world title. As a boy, Tommy idolised his brother, and he would earn his own niche in ring annals. Remarkably, between them the Gibbons boys racked up 233 fights and suffered only seven official defeats.

'Before the brothers staged an exhibition one night, Mike choreographed the performance for Tommy. "Let's dance around for the first couple of rounds," Mike said. "Then in the third round, I'll let you knock me down." "Sounds good, Mike," Tommy said. "When do you get to knock me down?" "Anytime I feel like it," grinned Mike.'[348]

Tommy Gibbons was soon making a name for himself, not just as Mike's kid brother. The boys had a unique system as explained by Mike. 'My brother Tom and I keep books. In it we have a careful résumé of every fighter in the business either of us is apt to be called upon to fight, as well as those we have already fought and are liable to meet again. Every bit of strength that a fighter is known to have is jotted down, along with his weaknesses, temperamental aspects, habits, and how they are liable to affect his ring work…The tough fellow, the slugger who is willing to tear at you, must be made to back up. The clever fellow who is anxious to stand at long range and exchange his "Long Toms" with you, must be made to come to you.'[349]

Tommy went undefeated in his first 11 contests before tackling local rival Billy Miske. It was a no-decision bout over ten rounds with the press seeing it for Gibbons. A year later Tommy was again adjudged the winner over Miske before giving young middleweight Harry Greb a one-sided beating over ten rounds. The kid was developing a punch that saw him win 20 of his 23 fights by knockout in 1921. Moving up, on his way to the Dempsey fight, he defeated Harry Greb three times in four bouts, Billy Miske four out of five, tough Chuck Wiggins four times, Bartley Madden, Porky Flynn, Willie Meehan, Bob Roper, Al Reich, George Chip, Battling Levinsky, George KO Brown, and Buck Crouse.

Gibbons would fight only twice at Madison Square Garden, the Mecca of pugilism, in a career total of 106 bouts, and was beaten both

348 Jason Kelly *Shelby's Folly* (Lincoln, Nebraska: University of Nebraska Press 2010) pp.25
349 Bert Randolph Sugar *Boxing's Greatest Fights* (Guilford, Conn.: The Lyons Press 2006) pp. 315, 316

times. The 15-round loss to Greb in March of 1922 was his first official defeat and was followed seven months later by a disqualification against Billy Miske. By all accounts this was a travesty of justice. Gibbons had dominated the contest for nine rounds, and when he dropped Miske with a body shot in the tenth round it looked like a knockout. But as referee Kid McPartland began his count, one of the ringside judges, Artie McGovern, called the referee over. After a brief discussion, McPartland disqualified Gibbons for an alleged low punch and declared Miske the winner, the signal for a roar of disbelief from the crowd. The St Paul fighter left the ring with their cheers ringing in his ears.

Tommy went back to doing what he did best, boxing. He engaged in six contests in six different states, racking up five knockouts and taking a newspaper decision over Miske in a rematch. Then Tommy got a break. For his big Milk Fund show in March of 1923, Tex Rickard handed Gibbons a $15,000 bout with young contender Floyd Johnson who had just beaten Bill Brennan. But Johnson's manager pulled him out of the bout and it was announced that Johnson would fight Jess Willard on the show. Gibbons was then matched with Jack McAuliffe in the Garden only for commission boss William Muldoon to rule that McAuliffe could not fight Gibbons. Then McAuliffe got the 'flu and Muldoon in his wisdom said that he could meet Luis Firpo in the Milk Fund tournament.

Fed up with the runaround they were getting, manager Eddie Kane posted a challenge on behalf of Gibbons to Jack Dempsey for a fight for the championship, backed by the obligatory cheque for $2,500. Muldoon reportedly returned the cheque saying Tom was too small to fight Dempsey. Then he stated that the St Paul fighter could have a fight with Dempsey if he could defeat Jack Renault. The latter refused to fight Gibbons, and was then chosen as an alternate on the Milk Fund show should one of the principals fail to appear.

'Having failed to get Dempsey in this way,' announced Eddie Kane, 'we will now go after the championship match in the other and the best way. We will fight our way to the match and the commission will not be able to stop it.'[350]

Farrell wrote, 'Wise critics figure that when Dempsey is defeated, unless it happens when he is gone physically, he will go down before a small, fast-punching boxing opponent who can hit with both hands.

---

350 *Oshkosh Daily Northwestern* 22 January 1923

Tommy Gibbons is all of that, and if anyone in the ring is good enough to beat Dempsey, it is Tommy Gibbons.' [351]

If New York didn't want Tom Gibbons in that spring of 1923, out in the Midwest his name was already being linked with Dempsey in a world championship contest.

'Up on the Hi-Line in Montana, where the Great Northern Railroad chugged from horizon to horizon, Shelby evolved into a town almost by accident. Even its namesake did not think much of the potential there. Peter Shelby, an executive for the Great Northern, did not appreciate the gesture his fellow railroad manager Allan Manvel made in naming the town after him. "I don't know what Manvel was thinking of when he named that mudhole, God-foresaken place after me. It will never amount to a damn." Peter Shelby had good reason to doubt the town's prospects. The empty grassland and surrounding hills gave the area the feel of an asteroid crash site. Railroad officials, in their expansion west through the Marias Pass in 1891, threw a boxcar from the train and called it a station. Shelby, Montana.'[352]

In 1921, oil was discovered just north of Shelby and stretching to the Canadian border, bringing an influx of field workers, contractors, land men. There was a further strike in June 1922 and workers and their families brought prosperity to the town. Mayor James Johnson owned most of the town and his developing real estate business was run by his son 'Body' and Mel McCutcheon. The boom in sales following the oil strike slowed down and Johnson, idly looking through the *Great Falls Tribune* one morning, spotted a story out of Montreal about a promoter who was offering $100,000 to stage Jack Dempsey's next title defence. Body had been made chairman of the American Legion Boxing Club even though he freely admitted to knowing nothing or less about the fight game. But he did know about publicity, and turning to McCutcheon he exclaimed, 'If this fellow can make the headlines, so should we. We'll offer $200,000 for a Dempsey fight!'

Former boxer Lyman Sampson had been helping Johnson run the boxing club, bringing a few hundred fans to the Liberty Theater. When he heard Johnson's bright idea, he offered little comment but he did suggest an opponent for Dempsey – Tommy Gibbons. Johnson had heard of Mike Gibbons but Sampson told him that Tommy was Mike's younger brother and a prominent heavyweight. With Sampson's help,

---

351 Henry L. Farrell *Galveston Daily News* 13 May 1923
352 Kelly p. 14

Johnson drafted two telegrams, one to Jack Kearns, the other to Mike Collins, in the mistaken belief that Collins was manager of Gibbons. Collins was editor of the *Boxing Blade* and managed a few fighters on the side. Eddie Kane was manager of Tom Gibbons and he would get to hear of what seemed a crackpot scheme to grab a headline, which is what it started out to be. They got their headlines! The *Great Falls Tribune* spread the story across its sports page. 'Shelby Offers Kearns $200,000 for Dempsey–Gibbons bout.'

When Kearns received his telegram he was inclined to drop it into the waste bin. Mike Collins had sent him a telegram asking his views on the offer and Doc told him it sounded like Montana bull! He still sent a reply to Sampson asking for $100,000 to guarantee the contract. In Shelby, Mayor James Johnson threw his weight and wealth behind his son and they went and saw the Governor, then the Attorney General, both of whom gave their approval. Within five days of the birth of Dempsey–Gibbons, the sum of $150,000 had been raised and there was an offer from oil and real estate magnate Mose Zimmerman stating his pledge of $100,000.

Body Johnson and Sampson sought Mike Collins out for his expertise, but Mike had doubts in his mind, especially when he arrived in Shelby in the early hours before sunrise. 'If it had been daylight,' he recalled, 'I could have looked the town over in a very few minutes and would have likely stayed on the train.' Collins estimated Shelby as a town of about 750 hearty citizens, all of whom appeared to be waiting for his train… 'According to their version of my mission, the big fight was already on and all that was necessary were some little details to close up the whole affair, and that their little cow-town in the hills would surely stage the greatest international sporting event of 1923.'[353]

'The first thing I said to Kearns,' recalled Dempsey, 'was I don't want to fight in no place named Shelby, Doc. It's crazy.' "They're going to give us two-fifty and fifty per cent," he said. "Well, okay," I said. "But I'm going to hold you responsible for the money."'[354]

The money was always going to be a problem. When Collins met with Eddie Kane he was informed that Gibbons wanted $100,000 plus 25% of the gross receipts and film rights. Kearns, informed of the latest terms, said he could no longer agree to a $200,000 deal because he had better offers to consider. Dempsey's guarantee would now be

---

353 Ibid p. 49
354 Dempsey with Considine & Slocum p.144

$300,000. As the fight grew in the press and the public eye, Mose Zimmerman said when he made his pledge of $100,000 he didn't think Shelby was serious.

Loy J. Molumby was an attorney and commander of the Montana American Legion, a man with the legion's distaste for champion Dempsey. 'The sooner he is whipped the better I will like it,' he announced. 'If he is ever licked I don't know any place in the world I would rather see him licked than at Shelby, Montana.'[355]

Molumby proposed he seek subscriptions from American Legion posts around the state to raise $100,000 in exchange for ringside seats in the amount they contributed. He also hoped the fight would finance a hospital for Montana's war veterans. 'Molumby proposed, said Kearns, that Dempsey be guaranteed $300,000 for the fight,' the *Great Falls Tribune* reported on 1 May 1923. 'A certified cheque for $100,000 would be paid when the contract was signed, $100,000 more would be paid within a month, and the third $100,000 at least 48 hours before Dempsey entered the ring.'[356]

Collins would say that the thing that saved the show was Eddie Kane suggesting that Gibbons work on a percentage after Dempsey had been paid. Stating that the only thing holding up the match was the signing of the contracts, Kane said he understood that Dempsey was guaranteed $300,000 and that he had already accepted terms on behalf of Gibbons. Articles were finally signed on 5 May at the Morrison Hotel in Chicago between Kearns, Kane and Molumby.

Body Johnson thought the newspapers had got it wrong in reporting that Dempsey was to receive $300,000 for the fight, and he tackled Molumby about it. 'The publicity is right,' Molumby said, 'that's the contract we have.' He showed the contract signed by Kearns, Kane and himself, saying, 'I signed the contract because Kearns wouldn't go for less.' Kearns had the first payment of $100,000, plus $10,000 for expenses, and the second instalment was to be paid on 15 June with the third and final payment being made on 2 July, two days before the fight. Body's father, Mayor Johnson, was named treasurer and general manager and he had to scramble to get the second payment together, putting in $50,000 of his own money. His son had flown around the state in a small plane with Molumby, collecting the outstanding money, and was injured when the plane

355 Kelly p. 47
356 Ibid p. 89

crashed on take-off. The plane was wrecked, Body ended up in hospital, but Molumby was able to continue by train.

The second payment was duly made at a bank in Great Falls with reporters and cameramen crowding the room. But Doc Kearns was still refusing to state publicly that the fight would definitely go on as planned. Consequently, as Body Johnson would recall, 'Instead of ticket sales coming in we got cancellations of special trains and ticket reservations because of the feeling on the part of everybody that there would not be any fight.'[357]

On 2 July, 48 hours before the big fight, it was agreed to turn the gate receipts over to Doc Kearns who finally made a statement to the press that the fight was on.

---

357   James W. (Body) Johnson *Sports Illustrated* 4 July 1966

16

Gibbons Goes All The Way

ON the afternoon of 15 May, the train carrying Jack Dempsey arrived at the railroad depot in Great Falls, Montana. As it clanked to a noisy, steaming halt, it was immediately surrounded by a huge crowd of the local citizens, anxious to get their first look at the heavyweight champion of the world. The welcoming party led Jack to a waiting automobile that headed an impromptu parade leading to the Park Hotel. After a brief session with reporters and cameramen, the champion was once again driven around the town past cheering onlookers and back to the hotel. Once in his room, Jack shook off his jacket, rolled up his shirt sleeves and relaxed. In 50 days he would fight Tommy Gibbons of St Paul, Minnesota, in the little town of Shelby, some 70-odd miles in the north of the state.

Three days later Doc Kearns arrived in the town and Dempsey was among the crowd there to welcome the champion's manager. Training camp had been set up in a former beer garden and the local population was soon turning up in ever increasing numbers, something that prompted Doc to introduce an entrance fee of 50 cents. For the first few days Dempsey just loosened up, did some skipping, punched the bags. He was anxious to get some sparring but Kearns held him off until 25 May. In camp were British light-heavyweight Harry Drake, also known as Draake, and welterweight Billy Wells, a regular performer in American rings. Jack liked the two Brits. Drake had fought for the British light-heavyweight title before making his debut in New York on Tex Rickard's big show for the Milk Fund, beating Joe McCann over four rounds. Dempsey figured Harry's style of jabbing would help him in ducking and countering the Gibbons jab. Billy Wells was good for speed training if Jack didn't hit him too hard.

One guy definitely not welcome in camp was Rocco Stramaglia, a heavyweight from Cle Elum in Washington State. He turned up in camp one day, and they put him in the ring with the champion. Dempsey knocked him down, but he got up and charged into Jack like a bull and when Kearns broke them, his boy had a cut around his left eye. Doc was furious, blamed Rocco for butting, and gave him his marching orders. While Dempsey eased off sparring for a few days and enjoyed himself fishing on the Missouri River, Rocco turned up at Gibbons's camp at Shelby and was hired.

He would tell reporters, 'Dempsey hit me harder but Tom landed on me twice as often. When it comes to landing on them, I found Gibbons three times as hard to hit as Dempsey. In fact I was dizzy from missing punches aimed at Tom.'[358]

Gibbons's chief sparring partner was Bud Gorman, Chicago-born resident of Kenosha, Wisconsin, 26 years old and a solid six-footer. Tom also had light-heavyweight Jimmy Delaney in camp and a feisty Mexican welterweight named Tillis Herman who kept threatening to knock his employer off his feet. He never managed it. Nobody did knock Tom Gibbons off his feet, not until the end of a 106-fight career when Gene Tunney knocked him out in round 12 in New York in the summer of 1925. Aged 34, he never fought again. But this was the summer of 1923 and Tom was in the Montana town of Shelby and he was training for the biggest fight of his career, every fighter's dream, a shot at the world's championship. It was a fight New York commissioner Muldoon had denied him because, in the words of Muldoon, 'He was too small.'

'The tale of the tape revealed Dempsey and Gibbons to be the most evenly matched competitors ever in a heavyweight championship fight. A *New York Times* analysis depicted Dempsey as three-quarters of an inch taller and about eight pounds heavier...From neck to ankle to fingertip, the fighters' physical differences were measured in fractions of an inch. The only area where they didn't look identical on paper turned out to be nothing more than a rumor. Gibbons felt

---

358 Kelly p.132

compelled to correct it for the record. Word got around that he was 34 years old, six years Dempsey's senior...He admitted to only 29 years (32 was the truth), saying any reports to the contrary referred to his brother Mike's age. An honest mistake but significant as a contrast between two fighters otherwise indistinguishable in height, weight, and any other physical artillery.'[359]

Among the press boys covering the fight was little Johnny Kilbane, the veteran Cleveland fighter who had defended the featherweight title for 11 years before time caught up with him in the fiery fists of Frenchman Eugene Criqui, and Kilbane was knocked out in six rounds. Johnny hung up his gloves after that fight and a few weeks later was in Montana, this time working the other side of the ropes. Kilbane observed one significant difference between Dempsey and Gibbons.

'One of the most interesting slants of the fight to me is the different mental viewpoint of the two men,' Kilbane wrote. 'Dempsey fights primarily because he is a fighting animal...Tom Gibbons on the other hand does not love fighting. He made fighting his trade, but fighting is only a business with Tommy. With Dempsey, it's life.'[360]

Away from the training camps, the promoters were still scrambling to raise that final $100,000 and Doc Kearns wasn't helping matters with his constant threat to pull Dempsey out of the fight altogether if the terms of the contract were not adhered to, and he was still refusing to give the press boys a definitive statement that the fight would go on. On a somewhat bizarre note, Kearns was offered a 3,000-acre Montana ranch that was on the market for $150,000. He turned it down, as he did the offer from Mayor Johnson of 50,000 head of sheep, saying, 'Now just what the hell would I do with 50,000 head of sheep in a New York apartment?'[361]

'In two days of his early workouts,' observed Farrell for United Press, 'Gibbons has looked better than he ever has. He is hitting harder and boxing like a flash and his morale is perfect. Bud Gorman, chief sparring partner of Gibbons, says the challenger's timing and judgment of distance were the most perfect he had been called upon to face.'[362]

359 Ibid p. 139
360 Johnny Kilbane *Bismark Tribune* 3 July 1923
361 Kelly p. 153
362 Henry L. Farrell *The Daily Republican* Rushville Ind. 12 June 1923

Some of the newspaper critics who had journeyed to Montana thought that Dempsey did not look like the man who had smashed Georges Carpentier in summary fashion two years before. They thought he looked sluggish when boxing with big George Godfrey and with Billy Wells, but couldn't argue with the display of power the champion turned loose on the unfortunate giant, Big Ben Wray.

Writing from Great Falls, Hugh Fullerton noted, 'Wray, who is seven feet two inches and weighs 245lb, was present for 58 seconds when Dempsey shot over a left hook and pulled and Big Ben heard a thousand alarm clocks. He added another great fall to those already here and it took him almost as long to fall as he was in the ring.'[363]

Wray, a former cowboy and oil rigger from Sayre, Oklahoma, had been looking to spar with Dempsey for a few weeks, convinced the champion could not knock him over. He had come 2,000 miles to try his luck, against the sage advice of his manager, Tex McCarthy, a former heavyweight who had gone in with Dempsey in 1918. Fighting as Tommy Kid McCarthy, he was flattened in one round at Tulsa. Big Ben was sure he could do better than his manager. He left his corner with left hand extended, right hand stuck to his chest, and Dempsey took a few seconds to see what he had in front of him. Then he whipped a left hook that grazed Ben's ear and then another hook that missed. Hook number three crashed on target and the giant stiffened back on his heels, his long arms flew over his head and he toppled backwards as stiff as a board.

Dempsey bent to pick Wray up but his legs wouldn't support him and Johnny Kilbane, who was acting as referee in the training bouts, helped him to his corner. When he left the ring, Wray had a large lump on his jaw, and the medical examiner later disclosed that the blow had broken the lower maxillary bone. To crush a jawbone with 16oz gloves indicated the power of Dempsey's punch. Small consolation came from Ben's manager, McCarthy, who said, 'It will do the big stiff good.'

Dempsey had planned to visit Wray in hospital but Big Ben had left before the champion could be informed. His jaw was still in a cast, but he told reporters, 'I'm going to learn how Dempsey knocks them over and then some of these boys in the game will have to watch out.' He thinks the crack on the chin he received entitles him to a ringside seat 4 July and Dempsey plans to see that he gets it.'[364]

---

363 Hugh Fullerton III *Washington Post* 23 June 1923
364 *Evening Courier and Reporter* Waterloo, Iowa 26 June 1923

As the big-name writers prepared to leave New York for the distant west, Manhattan fight fans seemed in a take-it-or-leave-it frame of mind. 'It doesn't look to date as tho there'd be a mad rush to the Pullmans en route to Shelby for the Dempsey–Gibbons fight,' wrote Sparrow McGann. 'The feelings hereabouts is that Dempsey will surely win the scrap and that Montana is a long way off for a visit to see something of which the outcome looks foregone.'[365]

Yet Damon Runyon had met one Doubting Thomas among his press row colleagues, as he cabled from Chicago on his journey westward. 'The writer knows of but one man who seems honestly convinced that Gibbons has a good chance of beating Dempsey,' wrote Runyon. 'The man is Walter St Denis, a judge of boxers and boxing of such capability that his opinion makes one wary of an inclination toward cocksure predictions that Dempsey will win in a few rounds.'[366]

Runyon himself firmly believed that Dempsey would win in a few rounds, allowing that Gibbons was a better fighter than Billy Miske, Bill Brennan or Georges Carpentier, the champion's last three challengers; a better boxer, a better ring general and a better hitter. It was when Gibbons was crowded, hard pushed, he didn't show up so well, and Damon considered Dempsey the greatest 'crowder' the game had ever known.

The Hearst-Universal Service columnist, together with William McGeehan, sporting editor of the *New York Sun-Herald,* arrived in Great Falls a week before the fight, only to have Dempsey tell him, 'I've had a harder time getting in condition than I expected. I laid off too long. I'm all right now however,' added the heavyweight champion. Later that night he asked Runyon what sort of fighter was Gibbons. 'Gently the writer reminded Dempsey that they had sat together at the Gibbons–Greb fight at Madison Square Garden a year ago, so Dempsey must know what sort of fighter Gibbons is as well as anyone else.'[367]

Runyon recalled Dempsey watched that fight very carefully through the 15 rounds and remarked that Gibbons was not fighting Greb the right way to beat him. Tommy didn't beat Greb that night as the Pittsburgh Windmill romped to a comfortable decision.

A few nights later Runyon asked Jack Kearns how long did he think the fight would last. '"Oh, maybe six rounds," replied the

365 Sparrow McGann *Oakland Tribune* 24 June 1923
366 Damon Runyon *Davenport Democrat & Leader* 23 June 1923
367 Damon Runyon *Davenport Democrat & Leader* 24 June 1923

manager of the champion. "If it takes Dempsey six rounds to beat Gibbons, you'd better never match Dempsey against Luis Firpo," we remarked. "Well," said Kearns, revising, "maybe it won't go over two or three rounds." As the writer sees the thing it isn't a contest.'[368]

With the second $100,000 in the bank, Dempsey recalled, 'Doc was still jumpy, and on more than one occasion Runyon told me to shut him up because he was driving everyone nuts.'[369]

Dempsey himself was becoming concerned about the final hundred grand materialising and would often say to Kearns, "Doc, I told you if they don't get the money up I'm not going to fight." "I'll get it," Doc would say. "You can count on me." I was beginning to wonder just how much I *could* count on Doc.'[370]

A couple of days later, Dempsey got Rickard on the phone and told him what was happening. Without hesitating a minute, Rickard said he'd get hold of the promoters, Kearns, Gibbons and everybody else concerned, and if it was acceptable to them he'd move the whole fight to New York, and see that everybody got paid what he was promised.

Shelby, however, was going to have its big fight, come what may. One thing that soothed Doc's troubled mind was the arrival in town of James F. (Jimmy) Dougherty, Kearns's hand-picked referee who would control the world championship contest. Dougherty was known throughout the fight game as the 'Baron of Leiperville'. He lived in a section of Philadelphia called Crum Lyn which was originally called Leiperville, after the Leipers, one of the first families to settle there. Dougherty went there as a poor young man and took control of a small tavern close by the Baldwin Locomotive Works. He played a little pro baseball and ran a few fighters out of a gym which was frequently used by Joe Gans and Jack Dempsey. He promoted small shows and in all his association with boxing there was never a whisper against the Baron of Leiperville.

'Dougherty is red-headed and nearly always smiling. He must be beyond 50 and looks ten years younger. He wears heavily checked suits and diamonds and has an enthusiasm that belongs to a boy.'[371]

With a week to go, Dempsey concentrated on speed in his training, working with Billy Wells, the British welterweight, Connie Curry, a

368 Damon Runyon *Oakland Tribune* 1 July 1923
369 Dempsey with Piattelli p. 153
370 Dempsey with Considine & Slocum p. 145
371 *The Indianapolis Star* 8 June 1923

115-pounder from Sioux City, and Lee Moore, a lightweight from Los Angeles.

Associated Press reported, 'Dempsey met Wells's rushes with a perfect defense, contenting himself with blocking the punches or taking them on the shoulders or side of the head while riding with the blows. As a result, Wells, regarded as an accurate hitter, missed more frequently than usual.'[372]

'Tommy Gibbons glows with health from toe to crown,' wrote Sparrow McGann after visiting the challenger at his Shelby camp. 'He glows more impressively than does Jack. If he could keep Dempsey from hitting him solidly – and he may be able to do this – he will last out the fifteen rounds with perhaps a balance of points.'[373]

The vexing question for everyone concerned in the little town of Shelby as fight day approached was, would there be a fight at all? And the answer to that poser was held by one man, John Leo McKernan, famously and infamously known throughout the fight business as Jack Doc Kearns, at this time manager of heavyweight champion Jack Dempsey. Kearns finally gave his answer to Shelby's vexing question at 2.35am on 3 July 1923 in a smoky hotel room in Great Falls, Montana.

'Hope rose against odds as the hours wore on towards dawn. Word came from conference rooms where Jack Kearns was closeted with different "Angels" of the fight that he was standing pat – that he demanded his $300,000 or there would be no fight. But in the end came the final news that Kearns had capitulated.'[374]

His decision was accompanied by a wild cheer and a band, held in readiness by members of an Elks convention in town, burst into sound, horns blaring and drums rolling as the wildest celebration 'within the memory of the oldest inhabitant' began its procession through the town, into the residential section and back into the business section, banners flying, men and women dancing and singing. The oil strike in Montana had hit another gusher!

Fourth of July, Independence Day, and the sun dressed it up a treat. Shelby looked like a Hollywood western on location as cowboys, dressed from Stetsons to spurs with gun belts in between, mingled with colourfully bedecked Indians of the Blackfoot tribe, celebrities like Mrs Raymond T. Baker (formerly Mrs Alfred Gwynne Vanderbilt) Mae Murray, Tom Mix and One-Eyed Connelly, the professional gate

---

372 *Davenport Democrat & Leader* 27 June 1923
373 Sparrow McGann *Oakland Tribune* 1 July 1923
374 *The Lake County Times* Hammond, Ind. 3 July 1923

crasher. And, sweating profusely in the little ticket office with a pile of tickets marked 20 to 50 dollars, Doc Kearns was finally happy to let them go at ten dollars a head. Historian Nat Fleischer recorded the official gate receipts at $201,485 paid by 7,202 persons. Then the crowd outside the arena burst through the fencing and rushed in for a free look at the world championship fight, boosting the attendance to around 12,000.

Dempsey entered the ring at 3.36pm to some hissing from the crowd. They were waiting for Gibbons, the sentimental favourite, Thunder Chief as he had been ceremoniously named by the Blackfeet Indians who were now gathered close to the ring ready with their war whoops to urge the St Paul challenger on to victory.

'A little Indian papoose stood wide-eyed in an aisle yesterday afternoon as Jack Dempsey chased Tom Gibbons 'round and 'round for fifteen long rounds under a blistering Montana sun,' wrote Damon Runyon from ringside. 'Perhaps the child thought it was some strange new game played by those naked white men, and in a manner of speaking so it was.'[375]

It was the fight game, but someone once said it's not a game, you don't play boxing. You don't play with Jack Dempsey at any rate. The champion had weighed in at 188 pounds with Gibbons 174.5 pounds and he looked bigger and stronger. Referee Jimmy Dougherty, bow-tied and cap jammed down on his head, got them away and Dempsey was first to score with lefts to the body, then a left and right to the head forced Gibbons back. Tommy hooked two lefts to the head but Dempsey hammered the body again then shot a right to the face and Tommy was bleeding from his mouth as he backed away. He sent left and right to the jaw and the champion jarred him with a vicious right uppercut. Jack missed a big right as the bell ended round one.

Coming out for round two Dempsey missed a hard left hook in his anxiety and Gibbons got home a hard right to the body. Dempsey was fighting in close, savage short punches finding their mark, and a solid right thudded into the body before Gibbons sent left and right to the face and there was a cut around Jack's eye, an old one from the sparring ring and it didn't bleed much. Gibbons went in with a left and Dempsey fired a big right to the jaw, only for Gibbons to set Jack back on his heels with a left to the jaw. Jack came back with a left that strayed south of the border and the crowd yelled. They hissed loudly when the round ended as Dempsey swung wildly at Gibbons.

Round three and the champion was in with a right and left to the body and Gibbons clinched. He was shaken by a whistling left hook to the jaw, then a right before the champion zeroed in on Tommy's waistline. Gibbons came back with two lefts and a right but Jack grabbed him and tried to swing him off his feet. The challenger hung on and was rewarded with two rabbit punches on the back of his neck. They both fired for the body and Gibbons got home a right to the jaw at the bell.

Dempsey's punishing body blows were forcing Tommy to clinch in round four and whenever they clinched Jack hammered the back of his head. He was ripping in short body punches at the bell. Round five and Gibbons brought blood from the cut over Jack's left eye. The crowd yelled for him as he caught Dempsey with lefts to the head, but the champ roared back with a right and left and another cracking right that shook Gibbons. Then Tom knocked Dempsey into the ropes with a solid left to the jaw to bring shouts from the crowd and they went wild as he landed another just before the bell.

In the sixth referee Dougherty had to break them and Gibbons danced away out of range. Dempsey caught up with him and when Tommy's head went through the ropes, Jack pulled him in with the crowd booing. Next time they clinched Gibbons hit the champion with a rabbit punch, but Jack just snorted and hammered a right and left to the body, hurtful punches that made Gibbons happy he had done his homework in the gym and on the road. Tom landed a hook to the chin at the bell.

Into round seven and Dempsey drove a right to the body and a left to the jaw, then as Gibbons came forward he hooked him with a vicious right to the chin. The St Paul man hung on and backed away after the breakaway. Dempsey swung another right to the jaw and Gibbons sent in a left hook at close quarters. As Dempsey forced the action, Gibbons ducked under a left and moved away from a right swing. Closing in, Dempsey hammered short left and right hooks into the body, then up to the head, and Gibbons backed into the ropes to escape punishment. He appeared to be weakening under Dempsey's relentless body attacks.

In the eighth Gibbons missed two lefts and Dempsey sent a left hook to the chin. Suddenly Gibbons whipped over two lefts to the head to get the champion's attention. Dempsey fired back with a savage right to the body and a left to the head, then Gibbons smashed his own left to the chin and the cowboys and Indians let him know they were there. Tom repeated the blow but signed for a solid left jab in the face. Gibbons backed to the ropes and hooked Dempsey high on the head with a left, then swung a right to the chin. Dempsey ended the round with a barrage of short rights and lefts to Tom's crew-cut head.

Going out for work in round nine, Dempsey had Doc's urgent pleas for a knockout in his ears, but Kearns wasn't having a tough time trying to hit Tom Gibbons with a square shot on the jaw. Jack was. But he kept trying and drove Gibbons to the ropes with a battery of lefts and rights. Gibbons landed two hard lefts and a right to the jaw and the crowd were on their feet screaming his name. His mouth was bleeding at the bell.

Dempsey opened round ten with a furious barrage of lefts and rights, driving Gibbons to the ropes. A big left hook went wild but the right thudded into Tom's body. He countered with a right to the body but took two lefts in return, before shoving Dempsey back into the ropes, the bell stopping his swing for the head. Gibbons nailed Dempsey with a left to the head as round 11 opened but two sizzling lefts had him going backwards. Dempsey crowded in with two left uppercuts, missed with the right but got another uppercut home to send Gibbons running to his corner then along the ropes to escape the champion's fury. Jack felt he was winning the fight but was thwarted in his efforts to bring the man down on his face. Gibbons was clever and he was tough, he had never been knocked down in his long career and he wasn't going down this afternoon even if this guy was Jack Dempsey.

Round 12 and they swapped leather in close before Gibbons danced away from a left hook that was aiming to remove his head from his body. Dempsey hooked another left to the head and when they clinched, he rabbit punched Tom as the crowd shrieked. A right and left to the body, a hook to the head, another left and Gibbons was hurt. He walked into a right uppercut but it skidded off his temple, then a yell from the crowd as Dempsey's body shot went low. A tough session for the challenger.

Coming out for the 13th round, Gibbons became the fighter who had stayed longest against Dempsey since Jack became champion. Miske, Brennan, and Carpentier, none of them made it into round 13. Would this one be unlucky for the man from Minnesota? Dempsey forced him back with two lefts to the head, more hooks to the head then a big right nailed Tom on the jaw. He shook but he didn't go down and he fired back with a right, left to the body then right and left to the champion's nose. They were in a clinch at the bell.

The 14th round and they said it would never go this far, they said Gibbons would be gone by this time, yet here he was still defying the feared champion, clinching when the blows got home and he felt like going home. He punched back as the champion hammered him around the ring looking for the knockout that usually ended the show. But when the bell sent them back to their corners, Tommy Gibbons knew he was going all the way with Jack Dempsey, just three more minutes and they would remember what he did here under a blazing sun on the plains of Montana.

At the bell for round 15, the crowd were throwing seat cushions into the air as their favourite walked out of his corner, fists cocked, rock-jawed, walked into the guns that forced him back around the ring, back but not down. He took the blows when he couldn't make Dempsey miss and he ran like a thief as the seconds ticked away. Dempsey hammered two lefts and a right to the head and as the bell rang out that head was never held higher. Referee Dougherty grabbed Dempsey's sweaty glove and held it aloft in token of victory but the crowd already had their winner.

For United Press, Farrell wrote, 'With a puffed face, a split lip, sore ribs that glared an angry red but covered a heart full of satisfaction, Tommy Gibbons of St Paul came out of his fight with Jack Dempsey with whatever glory was won beneath the broiling sun that beat upon the big pine bowl here yesterday afternoon.'[376]

'It was a great fight,' cabled Runyon from ringside. 'Everybody who saw it will tell you that. It was a great fight chiefly because of the masterly heady manner in which Gibbons fought. The years have brought great boxing knowledge to this sturdy man from Minnesota. He knows how.'[377]

In the opinion of INS sports editor David J. Walsh, 'Dempsey is either a greatly over-played individual or else has slipped back from a form he displayed against Willard, Fulton and Carpentier. His punching yesterday was severe without being actually unpleasant. He was not the man-killer of Toledo and Jersey City.'[378]

376 Henry L. Farrell *Appleton Post Crescent* 6 July 1923
377 Damon Runyon *Wichita Daily Times* 5 July 1923
378 Davis J. Walsh *New Castle News* 5 July 1923

Of Gibbons, Grantland Rice noted, 'After taking a terrible inside hammering in the seventh round he suddenly braced and slugged Dempsey with a whistling right upon the mouth. The force of the blow drove Dempsey's upper lip between his teeth. It was a lusty crack, a free untrammeled blow, and for ten seconds Dempsey worked to get the bruised flesh free.'[379]

'Tom Gibbons out-thought Dempsey Wednesday,' Runyon reflected two days after the fight. 'Had Gibbons fought as well as he thought he might today be champion of the world. He never made a mistake from a boxing standpoint. He could never have won fighting as he did; he never will win an important battle fighting as he did... But defensively Gibbons' work was perfect.'[380]

However, the general feeling among the sportswriters leaving Shelby and heading back to their city desks was perhaps best summed up by William O. McGeehan who would write in the *New York Herald* of 5 July 1923, 'The inference now must be that Dempsey is going back.'

379 Grantland Rice *Winnipeg Free Press* 5 July 1923
380 Damon Runyon *Davenport Democrat & Leader* 6 July 1923

17

Doc Knocks
Out Shelby

IF the Carpentier fight was Tex Rickard's masterpiece, the
Gibbons fight was surely the crowning moment in the gaudy life
of boxing's greatest hustler, Jack 'Doc' Kearns. He had held the
little town of Shelby in Montana to ransom with his demand for a
$300,000 guarantee before he would allow his heavyweight champion
Jack Dempsey to enter the ring with Tom Gibbons on a sun-baked
Independence Day afternoon in 1923. Two days before the fight,
Kearns had $210,000 in the bank, but the third payment of $100,000
was proving difficult for the local promoters to round up, despite Doc's
threats to call off the fight if his demands were not met.

With the fight 48 hours away and the clock ticking, the gambler
in Kearns had surfaced and he announced that he would take over the
box office on the understanding that all of the gate receipts would be
held by him until the final hundred grand was collected. He cleaned out
the till in the ticket booth, taking the cash and the remaining tickets.
The first preliminary bout went in at noon with only 1,500 people in
the place. But there were thousands milling around outside the arena.
Then some guy with a foghorn voice set up a chant, with the crowd
joining in: 'Ten dollars! Ten dollars! We'll come in for ten dollars!'

Doc was not about to pass up all those waving ten dollar bills. The
main difficulty was that all the tickets were stamped from $20 to $50
and the Treasury Department men were on hand to make sure the
proper tax would be paid.

At this point, Kearns suggested to the chief Internal Revenue collector, 'It's going to be just as good for the government as it is for us to forget the price of the tickets and sell them at a flat ten dollars each. I'll pay you ten per cent of whatever we take in.' He thought it over a few minutes, then agreed...'A fat pile of bills and silver, it came to $80,000. It was all ours, still being $20,000 short of our total guarantee, although I had to give the government $8,000. That left me a table-top crammed with $72,000 in cash.'[381]

Doc was strapping up the two bags stuffed with money when one of the Revenue men took him aside and said he thought the chief was going to renege and ask for tax on the face value of the tickets. Thinking quickly, Kearns said he was just going across the street to deposit the money in the bank, then he would be back to buy the government men a drink. The chief tax collector watched him cross the dusty street and enter the bank, but he didn't see Doc walking straight through the bank and out the back door, into the alley and up to the railroad office where he offered the depot manager $500 to hook up a calaboose and locomotive and take him down to Great Falls. He slipped the guy an extra 50 for himself. Thus did Doc Kearns leave the little cow town of Shelby, Montana, the town that for one crazy day in 1923 was the centre of the sporting world.

Long after the dust had settled, Ken Merrit wrote in a magazine article, 'Kearns would look back and laugh about the time he closed the banks in Montana. It should be noted, however, that these were voluntary closings, and in the end no depositors got hurt.'[382]

On the 43rd anniversary of the fight, James (Body) Johnson wrote an article in *Sports Illustrated*, stating, 'The whole thing started as a gag, then developed into a good publicity stunt, then into a financial nightmare...No one connected with the promotion of this fight profited one nickel, but at least I can say it was an honestly held fight promotion with no shady negotiations on the part of the original and final backers of the show.'[383]

In his book *Shelby's Folly*, author Jason Kelly recorded, 'In a letter to the local American Legion Boxing Club, James A. Johnson did the math and arrived at a net loss of $164,500...all of this loss was stood by James A. and the James A. Johnson and Company. Body Johnson said, "No banks participated in this loss. No banking organisations

381 Kearns pp. 173, 174, 176
382 Ken Merrit *Sports Illustrated* 9 April 1990
383 James W. (Body) Johnson *Sports Illustrated* 4 July 1966

had anything to do with the loss and no Legion organisation lost any money on the fight.'"[384]

As Associated Press saw it, 'The hot sports of this locality, having wished themselves into a colossal bloomer, are ready to pay the price. It will be a stiff one. Only a miracle can bring the investors fifty cents on the dollar.'[385] The wooden arena had cost $80,000 to erect, but a lumberman reckoned that the second rate pine boards, of odd lengths, would hardly be worth $5,000 as salvage.

One man going into the fight with no expectations of making any money was Tom Gibbons. 'I knew before entering the ring that I would not receive a penny for my services, other than the $5,000 paid to me for training in Shelby,' he told George Barton, veteran sportswriter for the *Minneapolis Tribune*. 'I was so confident of my ability to beat Dempsey that I was willing to fight him for nothing. I knew I could make a fortune with the championship.'[386]

Tommy didn't beat Dempsey so he didn't make a fortune with the championship, but as the *Bakersfield Californian* pointed out, 'Gibbons's trip to Montana was not entirely barren of profits. He received $5,000 from Shelby for training expenses, from $100 to $400 per day during nearly three weeks of training in admissions to his camp. A tour of the state immediately preceding the fight netted him $5,000.'[387]

Some years later, when asked why he fought, Gibbons replied that he had a big family and he had to support them. He said he fought Dempsey on a percentage basis and Jack got just about every penny that made its way through the gate. 'I did however get a vaudeville contract. I had to compete with trained seals to get enough money to feed the wife and kids.'[388]

The contract, with the Pantages circuit, brought Gibbons a tidy $50,000. Before Tommy set off on his tour, he returned home with his wife and three children to a riotous welcome and the news that the civic leaders and businessmen of St Paul were adding a Gibbons Day to its municipal calendar.

Two months after the fight, a newspaperman went back to Shelby to report, 'Since 4 July the town's two banks have closed their doors,

---

384 Kelly pp. 188, 189
385 *Evening Courier & Reporter* Waterloo, Iowa 26 June 1923
386 George Barton *Ring* November 1959
387 *Bakersfield Californian* 5 July 1923
388 Dempsey with Piattelli pp. 154–155

ten mercantile houses have failed, most of the saloons and gambling houses are closed, and the orchestras in the dozen dance halls are silent…half a dozen roadhouses are deserted, heavy boards are nailed over the windows and "closed" signs hang over the doors.'[389]

The reporter found scores of men and women who had invaded Shelby hoping to make it rich with concessions, were left with thousands of dollars worth of fight souvenirs for the crowds who didn't turn up, and now didn't have enough money to get out of town. Residents of the town however, were in good spirits. North of Shelby the oil fields hadn't been affected and during July and August a large number of new wells had been brought into production. The big pine bowl where Dempsey fought Gibbons under a blistering sun, was being torn down, the lumber sold for a bargain $5,500.

In New York, Tex Rickard, busy with his Luis Firpo–Jess Willard fight scheduled for 12 July at Boyle's Thirty Acres in Jersey City, took time out to praise Gibbons for the showing he made against the champion. 'I have said all along that Gibbons is the best man of his weight in the country and his fight proved it,' Tex told reporters. 'He was under a heavy handicap in weight but battled gamely and cleverly. I don't think that Dempsey has gone back. He simply had a hard man to beat.'[390]

Willard and Firpo had already signed an agreement whereby the winner would be matched with Dempsey for the heavyweight title later in the year. The champion and his manager were expected to arrive for the big fight, and Rickard was ready to negotiate with Kearns to match Dempsey with the Jersey City winner.

Heavyweight champion Jack Dempsey was still the favourite whipping boy of the American Legion. The Legion was founded in 1919 by veterans returning from Europe after the First World War and was later chartered as an official American patriotic society under Title 36 of the United States Code. Although the champion had been acquitted in the 'slacker' trial, many veterans could not forgive him for never serving in uniform. As already chronicled in these pages, various Legion posts had cabled Carpentier wishing him luck against Dempsey, and when Jack won his fight, one Legion post suggested a fund of quarter of a million dollars be raised for any serving or ex-serviceman who could whip the champion. They were at it again after the Gibbons fight.

---

389 *Hamilton Evening Journal* Ohio 6 September 1923
390 *Oakland Tribune* 5 July 1923

From Prescott, Arizona, it was reported on 5 July, 'Resolved: That the executive committee of the American Legion, department of Arizona, having been informed at the conclusion of its general session of the result of the Gibbons–Dempsey fight, regrets that Gibbons failed to knock Dempsey's block off.'[391]

Associated Press, Chicago, 5 July – 'Reports that moving picture films of the Shelby fight were en route to Chicago by airplane today led to the announcement by United States District Attorney Olson that any exhibitor who attempts to show the pictures will be arrested on warrants charging violation of the federal law prohibiting interstate shipment of fight films.'[392]

A few weeks later, district attorney Edwin A. Olson announced that both Jack Dempsey and Jack Kearns would be prosecuted if the fight pictures were shown in Chicago. The films, reportedly shipped by air to Chicago, had disappeared and Mr Olson stated that Kearns and Dempsey owned 70 per cent of the films.

Dan Streible's book *Fight Pictures* recorded, 'Motion pictures of Dempsey's 1923 defense against Tommy Gibbons were shot and exhibited, but not boldly marketed. Aggressive law enforcement initially stemmed their distribution. Federal agents in Los Angeles impounded the Dempsey–Gibbons pictures just as they were being developed at the lab of Horsley Studios. Harry Grossman, who filmed the Fourth of July fight in Shelby, Montana, was found nearby at Dempsey's Hollywood home, but no one was arrested for transporting the goods.'[393]

The ban on the interstate shipment of fight films came out of the one-sided defeat of Jim Jeffries by Jack Johnson in their fight at Reno, on 4 July 1910, which caused racial conflict resulting in many deaths and injuries. The screenings of the fight film added to the problems, and following heavy lobbying by such interested groups as the United Society of Christian Endeavor, the films were soon barred from many individual cities and 15 states went further by banning all prize fight films.

When another Johnson fight, against 'Fireman' Jim Flynn a year after the Jeffries bout, threatened further civic unrest, the legislation was passed. It then became a federal offence to transport fight films

391 *Oakland Tribune* 6 July 1923
392 *Manitowoc Herald News* 5 July 1923
393 Dan Streible *Fight Pictures* (Berkley & Los Angeles: University of California Press 2008) p. 275

over state lines. It would be June 1939 before the Senate passed a bill permitting interstate shipment of prize fight films.

Years later, James (Body) Johnson recalled that he still had a copy of the original moving picture contract made with a guy named Harry Grossman. Grossman took the film and $1,000 he was advanced for printing, and Johnson never heard from him again. 'The only time I ever saw the damn thing,' recalled Johnson, 'was one night in Chicago, I strolled into a Loop theater, paid my buck and sat through two showings.'[394]

'Meet Luis Angel Firpo, the next heavyweight champion of the world,' exclaimed the Argentine fighter when given the result of the Dempsey–Gibbons fight. 'I always thought I could beat Dempsey, but now I'm sure that I can knock him out. I never gave Gibbons much consideration.'[395]

Columnist Sparrow McGann had a different slant on Firpo's opinion of Tom Gibbons, writing, 'The report today that Luis Firpo might sidetrack an immediate bout with Jack Dempsey and go up against Tommy Gibbons has been denied by all concerned...Gibbons would show up Firpo and probably cut him to pieces and that is the last thing the promoters would want, having built up the South American slowly and carefully.'[396]

The big Argentine fighter cemented his championship crack at Dempsey when he clubbed former title-holder Jess Willard to defeat in eight rounds at Boyle's Thirty Acres in Jersey City. The manner of his victory was summed up by Westbrook Pegler who wrote, 'All the schooling, the text book learning, the tireless coaching of Jimmy De Forest, was wasted on Firpo. Luis Angel won by sheer weight of his right hand swing.'[397]

Leaving his ringside seat, Jack Kearns paused by the press section to tell newsmen that his man Dempsey was ready for Firpo, anytime. 'Labor Day?' someone shouted. 'Anytime,' replied Kearns.[398]

'Jack Dempsey v Luis Firpo. If anything like that happens within the next year,' wrote Frank G. Menke, 'the likelihood is that they'll carry that dear Luis out on a stretcher before six rounds of warfare

394 James W. (Body) Johnson *Sports Illustrated* 4 July 1966
395 *Bismark Tribune* 6 July 1923
396 Sparrow McGann *Lacrosse Tribune* 15 July 1923
397 Westbrook Pegler *Daily News Standard* 13 July 1923
398 Jack Kearns *Sioux City Journal* 14 July 1923

are over…A great guy against set-ups and has-beens – that's Luis. But against Dempsey – boy, page the undertaker!'[399]

A similar inference was implied by another commentator who wrote, 'Tex Rickard has refused Luis Firpo's plea to postpone his bout with Jack Dempsey. All that is left for Luis is to write a few letters home and make his will.'[400]

Paddy Mullins, erstwhile manager of Harry Wills, was becoming a desperate man. In a long-distance telephone call to his fighter, Paddy ordered Wills to travel to New York where his presence was required. The fighter had been training at Dan Morey's camp in East Cheshire, Mass., for the past two weeks, and before leaving Harry told locals that he hoped to return as he would like nothing better than to train in the Berkshires should a title bout be arranged for him. Mullins had something else arranged for his tiger.

'MULLINS CLAIMS RING TITLE FOR NEGRO BATTLER – Paddy Mullins, manager of Harry Wills, negro challenger for the world's heavyweight title, has issued a formal statement in which he claimed the world's heavyweight title for Wills, and proclaimed the negro's readiness to defend the title against any heavyweight rival, Dempsey and Firpo preferred.'[401]

Mullins had decided to claim the title with a public proclamation following his failure to have the New York State Athletic Commission declare Dempsey's title vacant and establish Wills as the recognised champion. The commission, however, pointed out that Dempsey had accepted Wills's challenge as they had instructed him to do and that was as far as they could go in the matter. All that was missing was a promoter willing to go with the fight.

Rickard had always said that he would never again promote a mixed bout for the big title after the Johnson–Jeffries fight, yet a news item dated 30 August, two weeks before the already announced Dempsey–Firpo fight for the championship at the Polo Grounds in New York City, stated, 'Jack Dempsey and Harry Wills will meet in Stamford, Conn., before the present outdoor boxing season closes if plans now under consideration by Tex Rickard should materialize. Tex wants to bring Wills and Dempsey together in a 15-rounds battle

399 Frank G. Menke *Steubenville Herald Star* 20 July 1923
400 *The Times* Hammond, Ind. 1 September 1923
401 *Evening Independent* Massillon, Ohio 30 August 1923

for the heavyweight championship of the world in a Stamford arena that will seat upwards of 100,000 persons.'[402]

Stamford was a little more than an hour from New York with excellent train services, and the mayor and some influential businessmen were eager to have the much-discussed fight there. Rickard, according to reliable sources, had already taken an option on a suitable site and local contractors were ready and willing to erect the proposed arena. Jack Kearns had recently stated that a fight with Wills was worth no less than half a million dollars to Dempsey, adding, 'I may ask for a million for Dempsey's end if the gate receipts are big enough. Dempsey is entitled to all he can get. He brings the dough into the box office and makes these big gates possible.'[403]

'Because of this announcement,' commented W.O. McGeehan, 'the Dempsey–Wills bout is merely in the conversational stage and probably will remain that way for some time. Also, unreasonable as it may seem, Harry Wills, the stevedore, will want payment of some sort for meeting Dempsey…Wills is sure to insist upon enough to make his retirement comfortable.'[404]

Maybe it was left to INS sports editor Davis J. Walsh to put the Dempsey–Wills fight to rest. 'Some fine day,' Walsh wrote, 'when Harry Wills is ancient and ring rusty and there isn't a remote chance that the honor of the white race will be impugned, there may be a bout between Harry Wills and Jack Dempsey. It isn't that Dempsey fears Wills, he merely respects him.'[405]

The salutary lessons learned by the financial backers of the Dempsey–Gibbons fight in Shelby, Montana, seemed to have been lost on some people. A committee of five persons, headed by J.L. Baugh, president of the Union Steel and Wire Company, proposed holding a world championship fight between Jack Dempsey and Tom Gibbons on the military reservation at Fort Benjamin Harrison in Indiana. Mr Baugh, who had engaged an attorney, stated that Fort Harrison was not within the jurisdiction of the state of Indiana. Governor McCray, upon learning of the plans, declared, 'It is my impression, however, that I am Governor of all Indiana and not just part of it. Jack Dempsey will not fight in Indiana as long as I am the chief executive.'[406]

---

402 *Biddeford Journal* Maine 30 August 1923
403 *New Castle News* 12 July 1923
404 W.O. McGeehan *New York Sunday Herald* 16 July 1923
405 Davis J. Walsh *Logansport Pharos & Tribune* 1 August 1923
406 *Fifth Corps News* Louisville 21 July 1923

The governor had already barred a Dempsey fight in his state. In 1922, when he learned that Jack Dempsey and Bill Brennan were matched to fight at Michigan City, he called on local authorities to stop the match. The fight was cancelled. So was the Dempsey–Gibbons bout headed for Fort Benjamin Harrison.

A few weeks later, a similar scenario was enacted in Los Angeles where a group of sportsmen, headed by Mr A.E. Santweir, came up with the idea of holding a Dempsey–Gibbons fight at Fort MacArthur at Los Angeles harbor, for the benefit of Disabled Veterans of the World War. The group went to San Francisco to try to obtain permission from General Charles C. Morton, commanding the Ninth Army Corps Area, to hold a 15-round bout to a decision between champion Jack Dempsey and Tom Gibbons. If Santweir was successful in San Francisco he intended travelling to Washington to seek permission from Secretary of War Weeks, and later to visit New York to confer with Jack Kearns.

Mr Santweir claimed that $500,000 had been subscribed for the fight purse and it was now in the bank. From Spokane, where Tommy Gibbons was appearing in vaudeville, manager Eddie Kane announced, 'We'll fight Jack Dempsey again, anywhere, and what's more, they don't need to have $500,000 to get us together, either. However, the time to talk terms is when they get permission to have the fight on the military reservation as they propose. The only condition we would make would be that Dougherty should not referee.'[407]

Since the rematch between Dempsey and Gibbons never happened, at least the $500,000 was still in the bank, gaining interest.

Champion Dempsey meantime was meeting old pal Billy DeBeck, cartoonist creator of the 'Barney Google' strip. Taking a jab at Dempsey, Billy boasted, 'Shelby proves I can draw better than you.' Dempsey and DeBeck spent a lively two minutes sparring, the cartoonist's form surprising the champion. When asked what he thought of Billy as a boxer, Jack, fixing his gaze on DeBeck's fancy hose, observed, 'His socks are like Benny Leonard's the last time I saw him.' Billy, en route for Honolulu, promised to send Jack a native ukulele and Jack said he would call it 'Firpo'.[408]

Señor Firpo was still reaching for every dollar not nailed down. In Boston he boxed exhibitions with countryman Natalio Pera and Pat

---

407 *The Times* Hammond 2 August 1923
408 *New Castle News* 26 July 1923

McCarthy, with Damon Runyon noting in his syndicated column, 'Only once lately has Firpo's business acumen failed him. He got $5,000 flat for appearing three days in Boston at an amusement park and is said to have drawn over 55,000. He could have had 50 per cent had he been willing to gamble.'[409]

Six days after leaving Boston, the Argentine's big hope for the championship was in Battle Creek, Michigan, to knock out Joe Burke inside a couple of rounds; a week later Homer Smith lasted ten rounds in Omaha, Nebraska, then it was Philadelphia and veteran Charley Weinert who flopped in two rounds, winding up with a ten-round no-decision bout against Joe Downey in Indianapolis. That little exercise in pursuit of the almighty dollar brought Firpo back to New York with the Dempsey fight less than a month away. A relieved Tex Rickard announced, 'You can say for me that Dempsey and Firpo will box at the Polo Grounds 14 September as originally announced by me. There will be no postponement. In this connection I want to say that Firpo's lack of knowledge of our language probably has caused someone to misquote him.'[410]

409 Damon Runyon *Indianapolis Star* 26 July 1923
410 *Kansas City Star* 31 July 1923

18

Dempsey's Here, Where The Hell Is Firpo?

A S August 1923 rolled up on the calendar, heavyweight champion Jack Dempsey was in Chicago, en route for New York City. While in the Windy City, Jack visited Mayor Dever at City Hall after discovering they would be travelling east on the same train. The mayor bemoaned the fact that boxing was not permitted in the state of Illinois, but said the only solution would be the appointment of a boxing commission and the lifting of the sport from the control of promoters who had temporarily killed it.

'Chief of Police Collins looked Dempsey over and offered him a position on the police force. "You are a wonderful specimen of physical manhood," said the chief. "The only man who will ever beat you in a fight is Father Time."'[411]

The champion talked with reporters before boarding his train for New York where he would hook up with manager Jack Kearns and head for White Sulphur Spring, Saratoga, to establish his training camp for the fight with Luis Angel Firpo on 14 September at the Polo Grounds.

'Dempsey said he was anxious to meet the Argentine fighter, although he would rather fight Harry Wills first. He expressed a desire

---

411 *Danville Bee* 4 August 1923

to meet Tommy Gibbons again, "after I've got a few good fights under my belt. Fighting is my business and I'll fight anybody." He scoffed at the suggestion that Firpo was afraid of the champion.'[412]

'Don't worry, he's a dangerous fellow and not afraid of anyone,' Dempsey said. 'If he was afraid of me he never would have signed for the fight. I'm not underestimating him. Anyone who can punch like he can is dangerous, and I won't take any chances with him.'[413] Dempsey said he expected his next fight to be against Harry Wills, provided he came through the Firpo bout with his title intact. He admitted he had been a bit rusty in the Gibbons fight in Shelby which he attributed to his two-year layoff after the Carpentier bout at Jersey City in 1921.

The White Sulphur Spring Hotel was located on the south end of Saratoga Lake in the town of Stillwater, New York, some 183 miles north of New York City. The hotel was named after a spring on the property and dated from 1874. Thomas C. Luther purchased the hotel in 1888 and he and his family would operate the property until his death in 1937. In its heyday the hotel hosted many famous celebrities of the early 20th century, including famed actress and singer Lillian Russell, 'Diamond Jim' Brady the larger-than-life millionaire, financier and railroad baron Jay Gould – and Jack Dempsey.

'Jack Dempsey established his training quarters here tonight,' Associated Press reported from White Sulphur Spring, Saratoga Lake. 'Dempsey with Jack Kearns spent the afternoon at the race track and came out to look over the quarters in the evening. "This is great," said Dempsey, bounding out of his car at the hotel. "When do we eat?"'[414]

The champion walked down to the training ring which was erected midway between the shores of Saratoga Lake and the state highway, took a quick look at Fern Lodge which would be his home for a month, then returned to the hotel for supper. The hotel was renowned for its fish and game suppers. Among the first to greet Jack was the little Filipino Pancho Villa, who had just knocked out Jimmy Wilde to become flyweight champion of the world. They made an odd pair – boxing's lightest champion and the heaviest. Dempsey would ask Villa to box with him when he started training but Pancho thought better of it. Jack took things easy the day after reaching camp, spending the day swimming, taking short strolls, and enjoying a motor trip to Saratoga Spring, 11 miles away.

---

412 *Waterloo Evening Courier* 2 August 1923
413 *Lima News* 2 August 1923
414 *Syracuse Herald* 4 August 1923

'Tomorrow, erection of a new training ring will begin, the one used by Frank Moran years ago and by eight victorious fighters so far this year, apparently being a bit too shaky for the champion's tread. Dempsey's living quarters Fern Lodge and the camp of his sparring partners adjoining will be fenced in to keep out the curious.'[415]

'The Jack Dempsey who journeyed to Saratoga yesterday was the same Jack Dempsey the writer saw out in Montana a few weeks ago,' wrote Damon Runyon, 'yet he was not the same. The Jack Dempsey of Montana was a somber, strained Jack Dempsey, a changed man from the Jack Dempsey of a couple of years ago.'[416]

The writer was concerned that the champion had something on his mind when he trained at Great Falls for the Gibbons fight. Looking for an explanation, Runyon decided that Dempsey was not satisfied with his condition, not achieving the condition he expected to be in for a defence of his title. Therefore he could well start thinking that he was no longer the man he used to be, that he was going back, something that would have accounted for Dempsey's depressed state of mind.

'Dempsey's mood passed with the Gibbons fight,' observed Runyon. 'Dempsey found that he was all right, that his fears were groundless...The writer now suspects that Dempsey's worries over the Gibbons fight were greater than anybody but Dempsey ever knew. Dempsey was probably not worried about Gibbons, he was worried about Dempsey.'[417]

Runyon had travelled up from New York on the train with Dempsey and was happy to see that his friend was once again the Dempsey he had known through the years, had lived with in America, in Europe. The sportswriters who had been at the Gibbons fight and, like Runyon, had noted the change in the champion, would see the old Dempsey when they arrived in Saratoga. He was interested in everything about him, in the people who came into the drawing room to talk with him at the races. He stood on the lawn in front of the clubhouse, greeting the jockeys as they jogged past him, hanging on the rails watching the finishes. It appeared as though Luis Angel Firpo was the last thing on his mind.

With Dempsey comfortably settled in Saratoga, Luis Angel Firpo continued to barnstorm through the Midwest with four fights still to

415 *Oakland Tribune* 5 August 1923
416 Damon Runyon *Indianapolis Star* 6 August 1923
417 Damon Runyon *Davenport Democrat & Leader* 6 August 1923

193

fill on his dance card. Joe Burke at Battle Creek, Michigan – Homer Smith at Omaha, Nebraska – Charley Weinert in Philadelphia and Joe Downey at Indianapolis, four fights in three weeks, while back in his office in Madison Square Garden, promoter Tex Rickard had everything crossed as the foolhardy Firpo was seemingly ignorant of the fact that his hunt for the Yankee dollar was jeopardising the biggest fight of his life, and his biggest purse ever.

Rickard even ordered Firpo to return and start training, which would have prevented the South American from filling engagements on his tour and a loss of earnings in thousands of dollars. Through his acting manager Hughey Gartland, the Argentine fighter gave his answer. 'He would go through with all the bouts on his program regardless of what Tex Rickard or anyone else said. "Just tell Tex that," Gartland added. Firpo got in bad with Rickard earlier when he told newspapermen he was not at all anxious to fight Dempsey this year.'[418]

So the Wild Bull carried on regardless. He gored Burke and Weinert inside a couple of rounds apiece, but journeyman Smith made him look bad in going ten rounds and the Downey farce/fight was embarrassing for a man about to fight for the world championship. And if Firpo was not impressing the folks on his whistle-stop tour, he was even less impressive on the movie screens across the nation showing his training bouts and gymnasium antics. The pictures showed Firpo on the road, in the gymnasium boxing and punching the bag. Old light-heavyweight champ Philadelphia Jack O'Brien and a big amateur heavyweight donned the gloves with the Angel in the sparring bouts.

A reporter for the *Oakland Tribune* watched the films at the local Franklin Theater, writing, 'If Luis Angel Firpo does not box better in the ring than he does in the gymnasium, Jack Dempsey should have a picnic when he meets the South American next month...nobody that uses a left hand like Firpo does has any license in the same ring with Dempsey...his boxing is crude and his defense wide open.'[419]

Nevertheless, the giant from the Argentine had punched his way to a crack at the biggest prize in sports with his Wild Bull strength and a sledgehammer of a right hand that had decimated 12 of his 14 victims since arriving in America.

---

418 *Chester Times* 2 August 1923
419 *Oakland Tribune* 2 August 1923

Yet despite his runaway success and the backing of the greatest promoter in the world in Tex Rickard, Firpo and his countrymen were still suspicious, were still not convinced that he would get a fair deal when going against the world champion. Some Spanish-language newspapers in New York were even openly hinting that Luis Angel was being discriminated against because of his colour. In this respect they pointed to Firpo's recent victory over former champion Jess Willard at Jersey City when a rally by Willard in the fifth round brought the big crowd to their feet with cries of 'Come on, Jess, come on.' This was considered an act of hostility against the Argentine fighter, an indication that he might not get a square deal when fighting Dempsey.

This prompted United Press sports editor Henry L. Farrell to write of Firpo, '...his doubts about the sportsmanship of fans in this country are absolutely without foundation. Some wise old follower of fistiana could have told him that crowds practically always lean toward the underdog...that the shouts for Willard to "Come on" were inspired more by a loser making a rally than by a spirit of animosity toward a "brown man".'[420]

To further allay the fears of Firpo and his friends, Farrell cited the terrific ovation given to Georges Carpentier when he faced Dempsey in Jersey City and the demonstration that was staged in Shelby when Tom Gibbons was introduced from the ringside before making his gallant stand against the champion, the man Farrell described as perhaps the most unpopular heavyweight champion that has ever held the title. The columnist added that when Dempsey and Firpo do meet it would be very likely that Firpo would get the better hand from the crowd.

Comprising almost the entire southern half of South America, Argentina is the eighth-largest country in the world, and in August 1923 it was becoming one of the world's greatest nations in sport. A band of horsemen; Louis Lacey, J.D. Nelson, J. Miles and David Miles won title honours at polo in England before winning the open championship in the United States. In the world of tennis, Argentina sent a team to Europe to play in the elimination matches of the Davis Cup. They played well but were defeated by the Swiss team. Marathon swimmer Enrique Tirabocchi set a record by swimming the English Channel from the French side in 16 hours 33 minutes. They called him the 'Iron Man of the Argentine'.

---

420 Henry L. Farrell *Iowa Press Citizen* 1 August 1923

Luis Angel Firpo was being called the Wild Bull of the Pampas and now he was set to challenge for the world heavyweight championship. As heavyweight contenders go, Firpo's challenge was being orchestrated in a rather unique way, masterminded and manipulated from thousands of miles away in Buenos Aires, where Felix Bunge was pulling the strings, sending his instructions daily by cable to Horatio Lavalle in Atlantic City. Señor Bunge stated that under the direction of Señor Lavalle, Firpo's new trainer and himself, the boxer had made a careful study of Jack Dempsey's technique as revealed in motion pictures.

'We have trained him in methods we believe to be superior to North American methods,' claimed Bunge. 'He will beat Dempsey because he is stronger, quicker and more scientific and because we know Dempsey while Dempsey does not know us.'[421]

That statement drew comment from INS sports editor Davis J. Walsh. 'Neither Bunge, the director, nor Lavalle, the mouthpiece, has seen Dempsey in action. Firpo himself has never watched his prospective opponent under fire. They, as a combination, are sublime in their ignorance of the champion's strong points and weaknesses, if any. They apparently air the style of men who sit around and solve the crossword puzzle.'[422]

Señor Lavalle arrived in New York on 21 August, accompanied by several other boxing enthusiasts from the Argentine, and were met by Firpo. The fighter and his new trainer held a short conference with promoter Rickard before going off to Atlantic City where the challenger had established his training camp. Lavalle, described in the press as a millionaire sportsman and patron of Luis Angel Firpo, an amateur boxer of prominence in South America and scion of a wealthy and aristocratic Argentine family, declared that he had no definite plan for Firpo's training.

'That must wait until I have had the opportunity to discuss these matters with Firpo,' he said. 'My theory of training however, adds nothing new to present knowledge. It calls for hard work, good food, regular hours and proper adjustment of conditioning activity.'[423]

Lavalle said that he had nothing but the highest regard for Jimmy De Forest, the veteran American trainer discarded by Firpo after he had

---

421 *Emporia Gazette* Kansas 18 August 1923
422 Davis J. Walsh *Syracuse Herald* 27 August 1923
423 *Indianapolis Star* 22 August 1923

conditioned the South American for his fights with Bill Brennan, Jack McAuliffe and Jess Willard.

'De Forest is an excellent trainer,' said Lavalle, 'but he has certain drawbacks to Firpo. The primary one is that he does not speak Spanish...I have known Firpo for more than 15 years. I know his weaknesses as well as his virtues in the boxing game, and I think I can correct the more glaring of his defects.'[424]

Lavalle went on to say, 'I have never seen Dempsey fight, but I have studied motion pictures of him in action and have every confidence in the ability of my friend. Firpo should win easily. How quickly he will land the decisive punch I naturally am not in a position to say but I feel sure that the fight will not last long.'[425]

Señor Lavalle would have taken comfort from the statement of veteran columnist Robert Edgren when he wrote, 'If Dempsey started against Firpo as he started against Bill Brennan he'd take a big risk of being knocked out...Now Firpo is the hungry wolf. Dempsey has been well fed on everything the championship brings for four years. There's a big difference between going after something you want and defending something you already have.'[426]

Meanwhile, in his 'Sportlight' column, Grantland Rice was asking 'Who is the greatest drawing card in sport today? Babe Ruth or Jack Dempsey?' William J. 'Kid' Gleason, much-loved manager of the Chicago White Sox, was the first to answer Rice. 'Ruth, as a drawing card, outclasses them all. He's out beyond Dempsey. Dempsey fights on average about once a year...Ruth draws them out every day for six solid months. Does anyone believe that any champion boxer could draw out great crowds every day for six months? No chance.'[427]

'The heavyweight champion is a great sight to watch, in action there is no one else who has a greater lure,' countered Rice, before adding, 'Ruth and Dempsey are the main cards, who at every appearance entice forth the pulse-throbbing masses. Many of those arriving at the scene may come to see one struck out and the other knocked out – but they keep on coming.'[428]

And as long as they kept coming to watch Dempsey, he'd be there for them. One night at Saratoga, Damon Runyon asked the champion

424 *Bridgeport Telegram* 22 August 1923
425 *Ogden Standard Examiner* 22 August 1923
426 Robert Edgren *Kansas City Star* 5 August 1923
427 Grantland Rice *Bridgeport Telegram* 6 August 1923
428 Grantland Rice *Ogden Standard Examiner* 5 August 1923

if he'd ever think of retiring with the title. 'No, I never do,' replied Dempsey. 'I'll retire only when some fellow hits me on the chin and takes the championship away from me. Maybe I won't retire even then, unless I'm too old to fight anymore…I'll fight as often as Kearns can get me the matches from now on, until someone knocks me over.'[429]

Would that someone be Luis Angel Firpo? Not according to Dempsey trainer Teddy Hayes, who told the *Oakland Tribune* on 10 August, 'They say Firpo is fast, but no 215-pounder who is still learning the game can hope to be as fast as Dempsey…Firpo's newly learned stuff is easily brought into play against setups, but he is going to forget all his lessons when the champ sets the pace and smacks him a couple of times.'

Runyon was of the same opinion as Hayes, although he had told the champion more than once that Firpo was a dangerous fighter. The big man from the Argentine certainly packed a wallop in his right hand and when it landed the end was usually in sight for the other fellow. His left hand, however, Runyon observed, 'seems of no use whatever to him in a fight. He holds it out in front of him but knows nothing of jabbing or hooking with it. Sometimes when he is attacking he drops his left at his side and leads with his right. Firpo seems unable to keep his face out of the way of a left.'[430]

Jack Skelly, one-time amateur champion who famously fought world featherweight champion George Dixon in his first pro fight in 1892 (he was knocked out), was in the corner with both Jack McAuliffe II and Jess Willard when they fought Firpo and he had them using a strong left hand to keep the Argentinian off balance. But Willard was too old and McAuliffe was not strong enough to take Firpo's right-hand thunderbolts. Both were knocked out.

In one of his Saratoga sessions with Runyon, Dempsey said, 'I don't see how anyone can say Firpo is a poor fighter when few people have seen him off his feet. He has met some pretty good hitters and they haven't been able to put him down…Firpo is the biggest and strongest man I've met since I fought Willard. I'll be giving height and reach and poundage to him.'[431]

That first week in camp Dempsey took it easy. He played golf with Kearns and Remy Dorr, the New Orleans sportsman, swam in the lake, and took in the races. Late in the afternoon the champion

429 Damon Runyon *Davenport Democrat & Leader* 7 August 1923
430 Damon Runyon *Davenport Democrat & Leader* 9 August 1923
431 Damon Runyon *Davenport Democrat & Leader* 12 August 1923

worked in the open air pavilion, punching the heavy bag and shadow boxing. For light relief Jack chased his pal Joe Benjamin, the California lightweight, around the ring for a couple of rounds. It was the first boxing Dempsey had done since the Gibbons fight.

'Benjamin has a theory that the only way to make a good showing against the champion is to start the first day he boxes, open up at a fast clip and get in everything possible before Dempsey gets fully warmed up. At that period Joe argues it is a good scheme to retire.'[432]

A welcome face at the camp was that of Ike Dorgan. John L. Dorgan was the brother of Joe Dorgan and famed sports cartoonist 'Tad' Dorgan, and he was an old friend of Kearns and Dempsey. He was a bookbinder before throwing his cap into the fight ring as a manager, press agent for Rickard and a founding partner of Nat Fleischer's *Ring* magazine in 1922. When he arrived at Saratoga, Ike was manager of Chicago lightweight contender Charley White, and he was keen to show Charley the place he had discovered as a training camp when he was managing Frank Moran, the Pittsburgh heavyweight. Ike trained Moran there at Luther's building, the same one Dempsey was using, in 1916 when the 'Fighting Dentist' was preparing to challenge then champion Jess Willard for the big title. Moran had gone from pulling teeth to knocking them out with his right hand, tagged 'Mary Ann' by the sportswriters. But Willard would emerge with his teeth and his title intact at Madison Square Garden (the second Garden 1890–1925).

Another visitor to the camp was promoter Tex Rickard, keeping a weather eye on his champion meal ticket. There was a good crowd of folk from the races on hand and they saw the champion box two rounds with Jack Burke and two rounds with big George Godfrey. A Pittsburgh light-heavyweight, Burke was National Amateur Athletic Union champion in 1920 and since turning professional had boxed Gene Tunney twice and Bill Brennan. In the ring with Dempsey, Burke would talk to the champ, calling him names which made Jack smile.

A regular sparring mate of Dempsey, Godfrey was 6ft 3in and bounced the scales at 225lb. Born Feab Smith Williams in Mobile, Alabama, he took the fighting name of George (Old Chocolate) Godfrey when he became a money fighter in 1919. He had boxed with such men as Sam Langford three times, Bill Tate and Jack Renault.

---

432 *Indianapolis Star* 13 August 1923

The *Eau Claire Leader* reported on 23 August, 'With an urgent demand for more human punching bags, Kearns using wires today to get more spar-mates for Dempsey. Jules Rioux, French-Canadian, is beginning to yearn for the north woods and Burke needs plenty of rest between beatings. Godfrey is the only willing one in camp but says he doesn't want to take it all.'

Luckily for the hired help, with three weeks still to go, the champion was not putting everything into his ring work. Manager Doc Kearns told International News Service, 'The champion's greatest fault lies in the fact that when he once tears into work he doesn't know when to slow down...When I figure it is time for him to tear loose he will do the tearing and will continue to tear along right up to the moment he jumps into the ring with Firpo.'[433]

Dempsey's hired help would have been surprised to hear Doc's statement that the champ was not yet going all out in the training ring. Godfrey and Burke were actually still suffering from the Shelby sparring sessions and Rioux went missing for a few days. British welterweight Billy Wells left camp with a badly bruised left hand after going a few fast rounds with Jack.

Watching the sparring one day, Runyon heard someone ask Kearns if he had made any arrangements with Firpo for a return match with Dempsey in case Firpo beats the champion next month. Kearns laughed. 'No sir,' he exclaimed. 'If Firpo wins we won't want a return match. He'll be too tough.'[434]

Trainer Jimmy De Forest, who had shaped Firpo into a reasonable facsimile of a heavyweight contender through his American fights up to the defeat of Willard, had, even after that fight, stated that he was still of the opinion that it would be suicidal to send the South American against Dempsey. However, talking with columnist Davis J. Walsh, Jimmy had partially revised his previous statement. 'Dempsey is up against a tougher fighter than he realises,' said the trainer, 'if he fails to take the coming match seriously. Firpo is not to be trifled with. He is a dangerous fighter. However I will repeat what I have said before, that Firpo is not yet ready for the championship.'[435]

De Forest was philosophical about his relationships with both Dempsey and Firpo, dropped by the new champion after Jack annihilated Willard at Toledo, and now being fired by Firpo as he

433 *Oakland Tribune* 22 August 1923
434 Damon Runyon *Davenport Democrat & Leader* 24 August 1923
435 David J. Walsh *Waterloo Evening Courier* 22 August 1923

prepared for his biggest fight. He stated that there was no trouble of any kind between Firpo and himself, but admitted that the arrival of Horatio Lavalle to take over Firpo's training chores had come as a surprise to him. When the South American had left on his barnstorming tour of the Midwest, he had told Jimmy in his broken English that they would stick together to the end. De Forest told Walsh that Firpo didn't send word to him that he was making a change of trainer. He just went ahead and made it.

19

Training Camps

'FOR the first time since he signed to fight Jack Dempsey, heavyweight champion, at the Polo Grounds on 14 September, Luis Angel Firpo today gave his undivided attention to preparation for the title bout,' stated a news bulletin from New York on Monday 20 August.[436] Shortly after his return from Indianapolis where he ended an exhibition tour of several weeks, Firpo left for Atlantic City to inspect his training quarters. Then he motored back to New York to await the arrival of Señor Lavalle from Buenos Aires, due next morning. Upon learning that his people were having the same trouble as Dempsey in hiring what some of the sporting press referred to as 'punch catchers', Luis signed up Cliff Kramer, the San Francisco heavyweight. A pro for four years, 195lb Kramer had won 14 bouts with six by KO. He had boxed Floyd Johnson four times, recording a win, a loss and two draws.

While Firpo was in town, Tex Rickard stuck a pen in his big fist and obtained his signature on not one, but two contracts. Both were to fight Harry Wills in Argentina in April 1924, one contract to hold if he beat Dempsey for the title and the other if he lost to the champion. This news brought a quick response from Paddy Mullins, manager of Wills, who declared that he wouldn't even think of signing up with Firpo unless he did beat Dempsey.

'There wouldn't be the slightest point in fighting Firpo in the Argentine unless he held the world's heavyweight championship,' Paddy told the press. 'Wills wants a fight with the champion whoever

---

436 *Findlay Morning Republican* 21 August 1923

that man is, and not with an ex-contender.' Rickard said, 'I have Firpo signed for the fight. Mullins can take it or leave it.'[437]

Mullins didn't want any part of Luis Firpo, he wanted Jack Dempsey for his man and he was prepared to pay. 'If Kearns wants $250,000 for Dempsey's signature on a contract I will give it to him,' he told reporters. 'Let Kearns name his own terms. Just before Dempsey and his manager left for the Gibbons fight, I had a talk with Kearns and he assured me he would come back and fix things up for a go with Wills.'[438]

Paddy had a financial backer in Simeon Flaherty who was willing to post the amount of $50,000 to bind the match. Flaherty was willing to stage the bout at Ebbets Field in Brooklyn. He had an option on the home of the Brooklyn Dodgers and had already drawn up plans to increase the seating capacity. Mullins did meet up with Kearns after the Shelby fight and once again Doc assured Paddy that Dempsey was willing to fight Wills and everything would be arranged shortly. Mullins and Flaherty took a cab to the offices of the New York State Athletic Commission to state their case.

The commissioners were sympathetic but until they could see a contract with the name of Jack Kearns on the dotted line, nothing could be done, which left poor Paddy somewhat confused. They had told him to get a promoter, he had brought a promoter before them, now they wanted Doc's signature on a contract. Talking to the press again, Mullins stated that papers had been signed a year ago and as recently as a few weeks ago commissioner Muldoon had told him that they had signed for the bout once and that was enough. All of which left Paddy Mullins a very frustrated Irishman and Harry Wills venting his feelings on the heavy bag in the gym. It was almost a year since his last fight, when he defended his colored heavyweight title against Clem Johnson. It would be the only heavyweight title Harry ever held.

On Tuesday 21 August, veteran manager Tom O'Rourke resigned as promoter and matchmaker for the Polo Grounds Athletic Club in New York City. Aged 67, the Boston-born O'Rourke had done it all in sports but mainly boxing. His star fighters were world champions George Dixon, bantam and featherweight, and Barbados Joe Walcott, welterweight. Tom also handled heavyweight contenders Tom Sharkey and Al Palzer. He operated in some of New York's most

437 *Kokomo Tribune* 22 August 1923
438 *Oakland Tribune* 22 August 1923

well-known fight clubs, including the National Sporting Club and the Coney Island Athletic Club. He promoted the Pancho Villa–Jimmy Wilde world flyweight title bout at the Polo Grounds in 1923, his last big show. When he died in 1936, Harry Grayson wrote of 'the last of the really old guard of colourful figures in early American boxing history. O'Rourke was the country's standout promoter long before 1906 when Tex Rickard so dramatically entered the field with his Nelson–Gans marathon in the goldfields of Nevada.'[439]

Tom O'Rourke died of a heart attack in Max Schmeling's dressing room an hour before the German went to the ring and sensationally knocked out the unbeaten Joe Louis at Yankee Stadium. He had advised Schmeling to cross his right as Louis dropped his left after jabbing.

As O'Rourke stood down at the Polo Grounds in August of 1923, it was announced that Tex Rickard had taken active management of the club and appointed Frank Flourney, matchmaker at Madison Square Garden, to the same job at the Polo Grounds.

Rickard was too busy to attend a meeting of the Boxing Commission with the articles of agreement covering the Dempsey–Firpo fight, 'and in consequence William Muldoon, chairman of the license commission, stated that until he did the bout simply "didn't exist" in the eyes of the commission...The applications of Dempsey and Kearns for a boxer's and manager's license, respectively, were returned owing to the fact that they had not been properly filled out.'[440]

With 23 days to go to the fight that was not yet officially recognised by the commission, Luis Angel Firpo reckoned he better do something about getting ready for battle. Up at daybreak he took a brisk walk of eight miles along the boardwalk before breakfast, accompanied by Horatio Lavalle. Then the challenger helped move his personal equipment to the cottage on Windsor Avenue, in the Chelsea district, which would house the entire party during the training period. Lavalle had good news for his fighter, a voracious eater, in that Albertino, a famous chef of Uruguay, was to take charge of the training camp cuisine. He had been loaned to the Firpo camp by the Uruguayan consul general in New York.

Damon Runyon was on hand that first day of training at Atlantic Field, which was used for greyhound racing in the evening. Going

---

439 Harry Grayson *Indiana Evening Gazette* 1 July 1936
440 *Capital Times* Madison 22 August 1923

through some warming-up exercises were the hired help. Newark heavyweight Joe McCann, who once put Firpo down for a count before being knocked out; Jeff Clark, the once famous 'Joplin Ghost' who had boxed such men as Harry Wills, Sam Langford, Joe Jeanette, Kid Norfolk and Battling Levinsky; and Argentine light-heavyweight Natalio Pera.

'There was no pep in the atmosphere,' observed Runyon. 'The boxing with McCann was sluggish, but the bout with the Joplin ghost was quite lively. The old ghost once had a great left hand and he was trying to stab the remnant of it into Firpo's face. He reached Firpo's features occasionally. Firpo is as open as ever to a left hander.'[441]

Leaving the camp, Runyon thought that Dempsey would prove too fast for Firpo but he would have to put his speed on very early as he did when fighting Willard for the title at Toledo. The columnist was suitably impressed with Firpo's size, and punching power and thought he was the strongest man he had ever seen in the ring.

The South American was also one of the shrewdest men to ever pull on boxing gloves. Since his arrival in America, he had steadfastly refused the offers of fight managers to look after his business. 'I am the manager of Luis Firpo,' he would say and he had the money to prove it. And in August of 1923 he shocked Runyon when he informed the columnist that he was in the process of taking over an agency for the distribution of a well-known American car in South America.

'Why, you can make more money in one fight here than you make in a year selling cars down there, can't you?' queried Runyon. 'Firpo said no. If what he and Vega say is true all the salesmen in the land should take the next boat.'[442]

Apparently a car called medium-priced in the States would sell for $5,000 in Buenos Aires and beyond. And the car Firpo had in mind was the Stutz Bearcat, no less. Richard A. Wright recalled, 'One of the most legendary stars in the American automobile firmament is Stutz. "Stutz Bearcat" conjures an era, the Roaring Twenties, flappers and gangsters and college men in raccoon-skin coats.'[443]

In 1923 the Stutz Bearcat, powered by a 109 hp engine, had a retail price of $2,765. And Luis Angel Firpo had just bought 100 Stutz cars with a United States retail value of $250,000. He had cabled his bankers to make arrangements for suitable sales rooms and service

441 Damon Runyon *Indianapolis Star* 24 August 1923
442 Damon Runyon *Davenport Democrat & Leader* 15 August 1923
443 Richard A. Wright *www.stutzmotor.com/history*

stations in Buenos Aires and Montevideo, capitals respectively of Argentina and Uruguay, both of which were included in his trade territory.

'Firpo is not a fighting man at heart,' says G. Widmer, Firpo's secretary and interpreter. 'His real ambitions are along business lines. He is a businessman by nature, one of the keenest minds I have ever known. Being the idol of the Argentine, any venture that he undertakes down there is certain to prove a success.'[444]

If Firpo could go home as heavyweight champion of the world the Argentine folk would most likely elect him president. 'I am confident,' he said, 'but I never make predictions. All I can promise is that I'll fight. I'll do my best whatever the outcome.' Señor Lavalle, angry to hear that some people were saying the fight was a setup for Dempsey, exclaimed, 'Firpo has a record that speaks for itself...He is a match for Dempsey at Dempsey's best.'[445]

Talking to the press in Chicago, former champion Jess Willard sized up the forthcoming heavyweight title fight as a toss-up. 'Dempsey and Firpo are both hard hitters,' he said. 'I ought to know. Firpo is a good tough fellow, probably the hardest white man in the ring today. Pitted against his bull strength will be Dempsey's shift and speed. Firpo is a heavier hitter than Dempsey but not nearly so fast.'[446]

Sports columnist Sparrow McGann figured there was something mysterious about the challenger for the title. He didn't think that Firpo was putting all his goods in the shop window. 'Down at Ridley Park where Jimmy Dougherty holds forth, Firpo went through a couple of exhibition rounds and put on stuff no one knew he possessed. He jabbed with his left in a manner that made the old timers think he had been working for months with Jim Corbett or Kid McCoy.'[447]

'Firpo went into the ring against Charley Weinert and looked like a truck horse,' said McGann. 'Perhaps because he was in Philadelphia and not New York, Firpo unmasked his real ability at bag punching. Believe us he put up a classy performance at Ridley Park where he cavorted with the skill of a lightweight at the expense of Spike McFadden.'[448]

---

444   *Charleston Daily Mail* 25 August 1923
445   *Davenport Democrat & Leader* 29 August 1923
446   Jess Willard *Wichita Daily Times* 26 August 1923
447   Sparrow McGann *Davenport Democrat & Leader* 26 August 1923
448   Sparrow McGann *The Decatur Review* 26 August 1923

Firpo was beginning to look better in his workouts at Atlantic City. In the morning he went on the road for a short spell, roughing around with Joe McCann and Pera before a quarter-mile race which ended at the door of the cottage. Luis easily beat his sparring partners before tucking into breakfast, prepared by Albertino. Rested for an hour, he pounded the heavy bag which hung in one of the rooms. In the afternoon it was time for the hired help to earn their money.

'Jeff Clark stepped into the ring at Luis Angel Firpo's training camp today and gave the South American the stiffest and best workout he has had. The shiny head of the ghost bobbed in and around the Argentine and caused him to miss heavy rights sent straight from the shoulder, but Jeff could not keep away all the time...'[449]

The engagement lasted only two rounds but was rough enough to keep a crowd of about 2,000 spectators shouting. Firpo boxed a further two rounds each against McCann and with Frank Koebele, the Brooklyn light-heavyweight who had developed a right hand with considerable power behind it and he landed often on the Argentine's jaw, without seeming to bother him too much, any more than did McCann's heavy swings to the midsection. Relaxing after the workout, Firpo walked over to where the greyhounds were quartered. One of the fastest hounds had been named after the challenger, and after watching it being schooled he stated that he might buy it for a mascot.

One night before dropping off to sleep in his cottage by the shores of Saratoga Lake, heavyweight champion Jack Dempsey recalled a time in 1916 when he was riding the rods looking for work. He landed in Kansas City and took a job as sparring partner for Carl Morris who was training for a fight with Frank Moran. Carl Morris was everything everyone said. He was fast and he was good. He was also obnoxious. Jack's daily pay was 75 cents, which went towards room and board – whatever board he could afford with the money.

One day, when Jack was eating a doughnut in a lunchroom, Morris walked in and sat down next to him. He called the waitress over and ordered a steak with all the trimmings and then turned his attention to his sparring partner, commenting that he sure must have been hungry judging by the way he wolfed the doughnut. Dempsey looked at him and told him that he still was – just as the waitress arrived with Carl's full, steaming hot plate which was set down in front of him. Hoping he would offer to buy his sparring partner something, Jack stared at

---

449 *The Arizona Republican* 26 August 1923

his meal. He ignored Jack, devouring the food as if he hadn't eaten in months. Then he turned to Dempsey and said, 'Listen, kid, why don't you get someone to buy you something to fill your belly and quit staring at my grub. I'm sure you can manage to hustle someone.' Jack was angry and humiliated, 'I rose and said so long. I hoped he would choke.'[450]

Young Dempsey wasn't too upset when the Moran fight was called off. Morris was a mean taskmaster in the sparring ring and at 6ft 4in and 235lb to Jack's 180lb, he delighted in punching the smaller man all over the ring. Retribution would come a couple of years later when Dempsey was matched with Morris in New Orleans. He knocked him to the mat in 14 seconds of the first round. He didn't get up.

When he became champion, Dempsey respected the men who shared a ring with him, especially in the training ring. In a 1935 issue of *Ring* magazine, T.W. McNiel wrote, 'Though it took an exceptionally durable fellow to hold a job around Dempsey's camp, he paid 'em well – being just that sort of a guy. One of Jack's favorites was Martin Burke, the New Orleans Irishman. Jack used to pay Burke a "grand" a week and lodging for the missus and the little Burkes.'[451]

Another favourite of Dempsey was Big Bill Tate, all 6ft 6in and 240lb of him. Born in Montgomery, Alabama, Tate fought out of Chicago and held the colored heavyweight title in 1917, winning and losing to Sam Langford. He tangled with Langford, Harry Wills, Joe Jeanette and Ed 'Gunboat' Smith but his colour barred him from a title bout. But Dempsey loved him as a sparring partner.

Although Dempsey did not fight many black opponents, most of his sparring partners were black. When he trained for his (18-second) fight with Fred Fulton in 1918, he used Battling Jim Johnson, who had boxed a ten-round draw with then champion Jack Johnson in Paris in 1913. Then there was big George Godfrey, who had a huge appetite for chicken and chops. There was a story that Dempsey hit George so hard in the breadbasket, he had to go on a diet. Godfrey was with Dempsey at Saratoga and he had been with the champion for the Gibbons fight at Shelby. Godfrey left camp very suddenly and it was rumoured he had knocked Dempsey out.

The champ was training at a Prohibition-closed roadhouse a mile out of Great Falls. Sportswriter Robert Edgren was covering the fight and, visiting the place one afternoon, found it empty. The rooms were full of sweaty training clothes, shoes, punching bags and other equipment, but there wasn't a soul in the building. Sitting on the back porch however, Edgren found a huge black man who turned out to be Godfrey. When asked he said that Dempsey had gone on the road, taking everyone with him, even the cook. Edgren queried why George hadn't gone along, whereupon Godfrey pulled up his shirt revealing adhesive tape, stuck on strip after strip on his left side until it was a quarter of an inch deep.

Recalling his father's meeting with Godfrey in a 1939 issue of *Ring* magazine, Bob Edgren Jnr related the sparring partner's tale of woe. 'Mistah Dempsey done hit me here. Why, that man hits something terrible. Them ribs sorta caved in. I thought they was all busted. But the doctor, he looked at 'em and he says, "They're not busted. All the ligaments are torn loose, that's all." I was gonna get a thousand dollars fighting in the semi-final.'[452] A few weeks later, the affronted Mister Godfrey was back in the punishment pit, sparring with Dempsey at Saratoga as the champion prepared to meet the challenge of Luis Angel Firpo.

Associated Press reported, 'The power of Jack Dempsey's punches was revealed today when the heavyweight champion came dangerously near knocking out Jack Burke and George Godfrey in one of the roughest workouts in which the titleholder has engaged since establishing camp two weeks ago…Falling into a clinch probably saved them from hitting the floor.'[453]

Godfrey had a stormy session for two rounds in which he failed to connect solidly. 'The giant negro was in retreat continually and within a few seconds blood was spouting from his mouth from a vicious right swing. A left to the chin sent Godfrey reeling into the ropes. He quickly grabbed Dempsey's arms and shot an appealing glance to Kearns who was refereeing, as to indicate that Dempsey was hitting much too hard.'[454]

Jack Burke had scored freely with right hand punches on Dempsey the day before but was soon put in his place. As round two opened, 'Dempsey drove Burke in a corner, whipped over a left hook to the chin, a right to the head and another left to the jaw. Burke sagged to the ropes but quickly recovered. With eyes flashing angrily and a snarl

452 Bob Edgren Jnr. *Ring* August 1939
453 *The Arizona Republican* 26 August 1923
454 *Indianapolis Star* 26 August 1923

on his lips, Burke let punches fly with both hands until the smiling Dempsey trapped him into a clinch.'[455]

Reporters noted a marked improvement in Dempsey's work, despite a cold that was bothering him. Instead of missing punches, the champion exhibited good judgment of distance and impressive speed through the six rounds of boxing. Jack was so eager for a strenuous workout that manager Jack Kearns had to call a halt when Dempsey belted a punching bag from its moorings.

Next day, a crowd of over two thousand gathered around the training ring to see Dempsey go through the equivalent of ten rounds. 'When the champion, his broad shoulders covered by a flashy bathrobe, entered the canvas-walled arena, the crowd was so dense with fashionably gowned women and their escorts that he had to shoulder his way to the ring. The cold from which the champion is suffering was reflected in his work.'[456]

Dempsey complained of stiff muscles and was not so aggressive as usual, which was a relief to Godfrey and Burke. The black giant managed to keep Jack busy with a long left jab, keeping him off balance so he was unable to get off his favourite hooks. He still managed to rock Godfrey back on his heels with a few meaty rights to the head. Burke received the same treatment as he jabbed to the head but Jack caught him in the corner enough times to keep him honest.

Walter 'Farmer' Lodge boxed out of St Paul. He had been a wrestler before becoming a fighter and was a favourite of Dempsey's. 'When Farmer came upon hard times, Jack sent him a sympathetic wire: "Don't worry. Everything is going to be all right. Come stay with me. Your pal, Jack." After less than a week in Dempsey's camp, Farmer groaned, "What a pal! He knocks me out every day."'[457]

The sparring partners had a chance to nurse their bruises when Doc Kearns gave his champion a three-day lay-off that last week of August. Jack started his welcome break by trying to pick winners at the race track with a party of friends. He placed a modest bet on every race but refused to reveal his winnings or losses. While seated in the clubhouse, Dempsey was introduced to Lord Birkenhead, the former chancellor of England, who was on a speaking tour of America. Dempsey posed for a photograph with him and Lord Birkenhead,

455 *Davenport Democrat & Leader* 26 August 1923
456 *Indianapolis Star* 27 August 1923
457 Jim Allan *Boxing Illustrated & Wrestling News* April 1963

unlike the champion, admitted to having a good day by winning some $5,000 on the horses.

'Rather than risk the danger of further aggravating his cold, Jack Dempsey postponed his contemplated fishing trip today and remained in his cottage to keep out of a cold drizzling rain that was still falling when he crawled under the blankets for the night. Jerry Luvadis, his faithful little trainer, smeared his chest with liniment.'[458]

Ever an outdoors man, Jack didn't take kindly to being confined to his cottage, spending the time playing cards, reading and grinding out jazz tunes on an old phonograph. Having tried every remedy in camp his cold was refusing to go away and he just hoped to work it out of his system when he got back in the gym, which sounded like bad news for the long-suffering sparring partners.

458 *Bridgeport Telegram* 29 August 1923

20

Firpo Trains On The Cheap – Dempsey KOs A Reporter

IRPO was starting his second week of training in Atlantic City and the hired help was beginning to take the strain. 'Banging away with lefts – straight lefts, hooked lefts, and uppercut lefts – Firpo punched four sparring partners dizzy in eight rounds of a fairly heavy workout this afternoon. The sharp commands of Lavalle could be heard above the thudding of the punches, directing the challenger to work only with the left.'[459]

Frank Koebele, the young Brooklyn light-heavyweight whose style was similar to the champion, gave Luis a stiff workout, his straight lefts to the jaw and left hooks to the body finding a home on the 220lb torso in front of him, but Luis took most of them going away, reducing the full force of the blows. In the two rounds they sparred, Firpo shot his left straight to Koebele's face and found his jaw with left hooks. Jeff Clark, the old Joplin Ghost, bobbed and weaved but he was caught in the leather storm, as were Joe McCann and Pera, the Argentine pretty boy. Señor Lavalle smiled his satisfaction at the end of the afternoon. Koebele, Clark, McCann and Pera were also happy; bruised but happy.

---

459 *Bridgeport Telegram* 28 August 1923

'Firpo rolls out of bed promptly at 6.30 every morning and is on the road or the boardwalk by seven o'clock. He enjoys his early morning workout, running, walking and playing leapfrog with Lavalle, Pera and Carlos Vega, the interpreter and general liaison man. The heavy sand bag hanging in the garage gets a pummeling after breakfast, which is prepared by Albertino and prescribed by Felix Bunge in his daily cables to Lavalle. Luis is in bed by 9.30pm every night.'

The heavy rain in Saratoga found its way to Atlantic City with Associated Press reporting, 'A cold driving rain falling throughout the early part of today compelled Luis Angel Firpo to pass on his daily workout. The South American champion started out for his regular jaunt along the beach and the boardwalk and had walked briskly for about a mile when the rain began falling in sheets.'[460]

The rain fell heavily until the afternoon, then eased off. Señor Lavalle organised his sparring party and they motored to the dog track where the ring was pitched in the open air. But the canvas was waterlogged and with a chill wind blowing off the ocean, the trainer called it a day.

'Like the small-town youths that hover about a circus tent awaiting a chance to peek inside, a crowd of Atlantic City boys are to be seen daily about the small frame hut that is called Luis Firpo's dressing room. These youngsters look upon Luis Angel as their hero and they'll be sadly disappointed if he doesn't defeat Jack Dempsey.'[461]

Always eager to do chores for the fighter, they got their chance one afternoon when Firpo decided he wanted to bathe after his workout. His dressing room didn't boast a shower bath, so Lavalle shouted for buckets of water. One of the kids offered to fetch the water, an offer Lavalle readily accepted. Immediately there was a mad scramble for fire buckets hanging around the grandstand at the dog track. Soon half a dozen boys were carrying water to the dressing room, and while Luis Angel took one bucket after another, held it over his head and let the water run over his sleek-muscled body, the boys peeking through a window chortled gleefully, 'Say, now, betcha Dempsey can't do that.'

'A mysterious dark woman accosted Luis Firpo as he returned from his training camp last night. "Let me read your palm," said she.

---

460 *Uniontown Morning Herald* 29 August 1923
461 *Syracuse Herald* 27 August 1923

"I will tell your future." "No," replied Firpo as he passed along. "My future is not in my palm. It's in my fist and the strength behind it.'"[462]

Gamblers in the city were not so confident that the strength of Firpo's fist would prevail over Jack Dempsey. 'Betting at two-and-a-half to one has opened here that Dempsey beats Firpo when they meet 14 September for the world's heavyweight championship,' wrote Henry L. Farrell from New York. 'One bet of $5,000 to $2,000 has been placed in Wall Street. Another wager of $3,000 to $5,000 has been offered by backers of the Argentine giant.'[463]

'Considering the fact that practically all of the experts look rather lightly upon the chances of the South American, the odds in the opening offers are considered rather short,' commented Farrell. 'Expert opinion however has gone wrong so many times on big fights that it may be that the public thinks Dempsey is not a sure winner.'[464]

Promoter Tex Rickard had always maintained from the time he started directing the destiny of Firpo that the South American was a great fighter and that he had a good chance to win the championship. Tex always held up Jim Jeffries as the best heavyweight he ever saw and he likened the Argentine giant to the Californian, who was berated by so-called experts as being as slow and clumsy as a truck horse who would be cut to pieces by a clever man. He wasn't.

But if not yet a great fighter, 'FIRPO IS GREAT EATER' proclaimed a headline in the *Danville Bee* of Virginia on 31 August. According to the Associated Press story, 'The Argentine gladiator is one of the greatest eaters the boxing ring has ever known, declared Dr Juan Reilly. Insofar as eating is concerned Firpo is following an idea directly opposite to those of all the great American trainers and specialists. He eats eggs and meat and fruit three times a day in great quantities.'

Dr Reilly was an Irish-Spanish specialist who was making a study of Firpo for the University of Pennsylvania and various health institutions and foundations. In a single day, the food that Firpo took contained, according to Dr Reilly, about 7,000 calories more than those in the food of the huskiest longshoreman.

Firpo's gargantuan appetite was certainly agreeing with him. 'Firpo shows no more anxiety about the coming fight than the player piano which beats out music all day long without the inducement of

462 *Davenport Democrat & Leader* 23 August 1923
463 Henry L. Farrell *Oakland Tribune* 28 August 1923
464 Henry L. Farrell *Eau Claire Leader* 28 August 1923

a nickel,' observed Farrell for United Press. 'It plays all the popular jazz tunes and upon its rack are several of the latest hits from the Argentine, one of the most recent is, "Firpo, Firpo. You're going to get it Dempsey."'[465]

One of his handlers told Farrell that before the Willard fight Firpo was the only one in the house who slept. He was not worried a bit and the others were all worked up. Luis, his friend said, had a fine memory on all ring topics and could tell the round and the punch that won every big fight for years back.

At Saratoga, Jack Dempsey was training so that Luis Angel Firpo would remember the round and the punch that ended his bid for the world's heavyweight championship. 'When I start going this afternoon I'll keep right on training until possibly two days before the fight,' he announced on 30 August. 'For the next ten days I intend to go at top speed.'[466]

Jack McAuliffe II had arrived in camp and the champion was anxious to quiz him about Firpo, who had knocked out the Detroit heavyweight in three rounds. A couple of days later, Mac was wishing he hadn't got off the train when it steamed into Saratoga. McAuliffe, all 6ft 2in and 206lb of him, was all but knocked out in less than three minutes of his first training session with Dempsey. After the disastrous first round McAuliffe was unable to continue for the second. He crawled out of the ring with his right eye half closed and bleeding from a ripped left ear. In the three minutes he shared the ring with the champion he did not land a solid punch on his boss, while Dempsey, seeing McAuliffe's condition, held his punches to avoid a certain knockout. The man from Detroit walked to his corner on shaky legs but gamely offered to go another round. Dempsey urged him to quit.

In the rubbing room, McAuliffe, having hot towels applied to his eye, declared if the giant Argentinian was able to go two rounds with Dempsey he would be the most surprised man in the world. When asked if Dempsey hit as hard as Firpo, McAuliffe exclaimed, 'Why there is no comparison. Dempsey is 100 per cent a better hitter with either hand. He is the snappier puncher and can step around with such speed that Firpo won't know what it is all about. All Firpo has is a right-hand wallop. Dempsey, in my opinion, will tear him to pieces with left hooks.'[467]

---

465 Henry L. Farrell *Sandusky Star Journal* 30 August 1923

466 *Hutchinson News* Kansas 30 August 1923

467 *Logansport Free Press* 31 August 1923

While McAuliffe nursed his wounds, Jack Burke was in the ring exchanging furious punches with Dempsey in a terrific two rounds that held the watching crowd spellbound. Burke's right hand found the champion easily enough but Dempsey was always crowding his man, driving him into corners and into the ropes. A short right hand exploded on Jack's jaw and the Pittsburgh puncher did well to last out the round. Dempsey finished with a round lugging at the weights, two rounds of shadow boxing before pulling on the leather and hammering the heavy boxing dummy for two rounds, ending with a session on the light bag. Manager Kearns seemed satisfied with his tiger.

Jack's pals were less than satisfied when he turned out for their baseball game on the shores of the lake. 'Jack Dempsey was knocked out today but not on the floor of a ring. He was knocked out of a pitcher's box when his offerings were batted to every corner of the lot...After one disastrous inning on the mound, Dempsey was shifted to first base where he performed like a major leaguer.'[468]

Jack collected a half-dozen hits, driving runs in ahead of him every time he smashed the ball.

After days of idleness enforced by heavy rain that soaked his training ring and chilled the air so that his trainers were frightened of him catching cold, Luis Firpo was back at work today. 'Firpo was eager to get going and he fairly eats work these days. Encouraged by progress made with his left hand, he is anxious to carry on when trainers say stop. They want him to take things slow until spar-mates arrive of lighter poundage. Luis also wanted Young Bob Fitzsimmons to join him, they are good friends.'[469]

Watching Luis Firpo go through his training routine in Atlantic City, Henry Farrell noted for United Press, 'Firpo is showing a nice left in his sparring and he has acquired a hook to supplement the conventional jab. In training for Willard he showed the same thing but when he started to fight the former champion he apparently forgot he had anything hanging on his left shoulder.'[470]

In Firpo's first year in America, press stories had him the son of a wealthy railroad builder and a Cantilonean noblewoman. Farrell was on hand when Luis told a reporter, 'Yes, my father is a railroad builder, but he builds with a pick and shovel.'

468 *Uniontown Morning Herald* 29 August 1923
469 *Hutchinson News* 30 August 1923
470 Henry L. Farrell *Lebanon Daily News* 31 August 1923

Now, a week before the Dempsey fight, Associated Press ran a story out of Atlantic City announcing Luis Angel Firpo was a direct descendent of the Italian nobility of the 12th century. 'Luis Angel received an official-looking sheepskin, decorated with gold seals, a coat of arms and Latin writing. There is some Latin below the shield telling about the audaciousness of the Firpo family and then the history of the family, it is said that the Firpos, as far back as known were of the highest caste, owned castles and were intrepid warriors.'[471]

If this was the result of a Rickard press agent's over-active imagination, it put a smile on the more often sombre visage of the South American heavyweight and he was delighted as he showed the sheepskin around among his companions. That afternoon he went out to the training ring and knocked seven bells out of his unfortunate sparring partners. Joe McCann was able to stand up to the barrage of leather thrown at him for two rounds, but Frank Koebele and Natalio Pera didn't make it through the second round of their sessions. Leo Gates, a New York heavyweight with ten wins in his 19 fights, was due in camp the next day, along with Young Bob Fitzsimmons.

During his fighting career in the United States, Firpo had been labelled the Wild Bull of the Pampas, some termed him a gorilla, others found in him the modern version of the mastodon. Watching Firpo train, two turfmen found in him the idea of a dray horse. 'Let me explain that,' one of them said. 'No one to look at Happy Thoughts would think that she is a great horse. She almost goes to sleep at the post. She acts as lazy and as sluggish as a nag on a milk wagon, but when the barrier springs she is all run. That's the way Firpo looks before he goes into action.'[472]

Another spectator with an opinion was Billy Nolan, veteran manager of immortal Battling Nelson who fought Joe Gans at Goldfield, Nevada, in 1906, billed as new promoter Tex Rickard's 'Greatest Fight of the Century', Gans winning when Nelson was ruled out for a low blow in the 42nd round. Nolan had seen them all and he was not too impressed with Luis Angel Firpo. 'The question in my mind is whether he can stand the gaff,' said Billy. 'He is sure to take a terrible beating for I never saw a challenger with less defense than that man has. His own left is a joke. He might as well tie it behind him, for then the temptation of trying to use it would be removed.'[473]

---

471 *Logansport Morning Press* 6 September 1923
472 *Port Arthur News* Texas 6 September 1923
473 *The Mansfield News* Ohio 11 September 1923

Firpo knockout victim and Newark heavyweight Charley Weinert weighed in with his two-cents' worth; 'FIRPO CINCH FOR JACK' appeared over Charley's by-line. 'I don't think he will go a round with Jack Dempsey. I found Firpo so easy to hit in the first round of our fight in Philadelphia that I thought the scrap was going to be a cinch for me to win. I did not think it was necessary to cover myself the way I got to him in that first round.'[474]

Unfortunately for Charley, Firpo got to him in the second round and closed the show.

A reporter, matching hands with the challenger, found Firpo's fingers extended beyond his own by an inch and a half and they measured ten and a half inches from thumbtip to little finger. The scribe called the hand probably the biggest and most compact known to man. The size of Firpo's wardrobe was also worthy of note, with Associated Press reporting, 'He has an even half dozen suits of coloured tights; black ones for Sunday, blue for Monday, red for Tuesday, green for Wednesday, maroon for Thursday and Friday, and lavender for Saturday. He is having a set of trunks made to order for the title fight, in these trunks will be woven the Argentine national colours, baby blue and angel white.'[475]

Along with his ghost-writer, Luis Firpo penned an article for the North American Newspaper Alliance on his chances with the champion. Recalling his fight with former champion Jess Willard, the Argentine said that he'd had doubts as to his ability to defeat Willard – was the giant Kansan too big for him to hurt? And then Luis said he got the feeling one day that he knew he could whip Jess. 'As soon as that feeling came to me that he could not hurt me and I could knock him out…I do not know how I knew but I knew…If I have that feeling about Jack Dempsey then I know I will win from him. I do not have that feeling yet. If it comes to me I will say so, and if I say so I will win.'[476]

Champion Jack Dempsey was not holding his breath for that feeling to come to Señor Firpo; he was expending his own breath in every workout and his sparring partners were searching the want-ads for another line of work. Jules Rioux, the 200lb French-Canadian lumberjack, was one of them but his fiery little manager, Dr Gadbois of Montreal, had other ideas. Dr Gadbois paced nervously alongside

474 Charley Weinert *Indianapolis Star* 27 August 1923
475 *Indianapolis Star* 26 August 1923
476 *Kansas City Star* 30 August 1923

the ring as his protégé tried to avoid Dempsey's lethal fists. He didn't succeed. Rioux was knocked spark out inside the first round by a left hook that didn't travel more than six inches. The big Canadian crashed to the floor and rolled over on his back as though he had been shot.

After Rioux had been dragged to his corner and revived with cold water, Dr Gadbois was asked if Jules would be going back to the woods. 'No, no,' he exclaimed, 'He must remain. It will do Rioux good to get knocked. Experience you know. Yesterday was the first time for him. Now he knows what it is to be knocked out. It is very good practice.'[477]

Jules should have taken the advice being freely dispensed by manager Jack Kearns as to how Firpo could possibly beat Dempsey. Kearns was telling the press boys that the only person who could win the fight for Luis was Babe Ruth. 'Ruth has a big baseball bat,' explained Kearns. 'If he loans it to Luis and lets the latter use it, why maybe Luis can knock out Jack, but it cannot be done any other way. When Dempsey loses it will be on a decision, not through a knockout.'[478]

Kearns painted a lurid word picture of what would happen should Firpo make Dempsey angry on the night of 14 September. If he did, Jack described the somewhat weird scenario that would unfold, with the spectators seeing six tigers, two lions and a couple of panthers all rolled up in one, loose and swishing around a prize ring. A tough job for even a wild bull!

Not too tough, according to one reputable witness. Old Jack McAuliffe, the former undefeated lightweight champion, writing for United Press from Atlantic City, stated, 'I have seen the angel and I think he is a devil. Luis Angel Firpo...has the brains and the brawn to reach the top. I dislike to forecast the passing of a championship but after seeing both boxers one is constrained to the cruel task.'[479]

Another veteran of the square ring with a different point of view was Jimmy De Forest, a view to be respected. De Forest trained Dempsey to take the title from Willard and he conditioned Firpo for his contests with Bill Brennan, Jack McAuliffe II, and Willard. 'De Forest, standing at the side of the ring with several other boxing experts, watched every move the champion made yesterday. After it was over, Jack Kearns, manager of the champion, said to De Forest,

477   *Olean Evening Herald* 1 September 1923
478   *The Mansfield News* 6 September 1923
479   Jack McAuliffe *Lebanon Semi-Weekly News* 10 September 1923

"Well, Jimmy, he's ready isn't he?" De Forest smiled and replied, "Yes, pretty fair. He's pretty fair."[480]

Well, it was Sunday, 9 September, and although the champion boxed six rounds, he only worked earnestly in four of them. One of the rounds was somewhat unique, as Paul Gallico told it in his 1937 book *Farewell to Sport*.

'I had been assigned to my first training camp coverage, Dempsey's at Saratoga Springs, where he was preparing for his fight with Luis Firpo. For days I watched him sag a spar boy with what seemed to be no more than a light cuff on the neck, or pat his face with what looked like no more than a caressing stroke of his arm, and the fellow would come apart at the seams and collapse in a useless heap, grinning vacuously or twitching strangely. My burning curiosity got the better of prudence and a certain reluctance to expose myself to physical pain.

'I asked Dempsey to permit me to box a round with him. I had never boxed before, but I was in good physical shape, having just completed a four-year stretch as a galley slave in the Columbia eight-oared shell. When it was over and I escaped through the ropes, shaking, bleeding a little from the mouth, with rosin dust on my pants and a vicious throbbing in my head, I knew all that there was to know about being hit in the prize ring. It seemed that I had gone to an expert for tuition.

'I knew the sensation of being stalked and pursued by a relentless, truculent professional whose trade and business it was to injure men. I saw the quick flash of the brown forearm that precedes the stunning shock as a bony, leather-bound fist lands on cheek or mouth. I learned, too, that as the soldier never hears the bullet that kills him, so does the fighter rarely, if ever, see the punch that tumbles blackness over him like a mantle, with a tearing rip as though the roof of his skull were exploding, and robs him of his senses.

'There was just that – a ripping in my head and then a sudden blackness and the next thing I knew, I was sitting on the canvas covering of the ring floor with my legs collapsed under me, grinning idiotically. I held on to the floor with both hands because the ring and the audience outside were making a complete clockwise revolution, came to a stop, and then went back again counter clockwise. When I struggled to my feet, Jack Kearns was counting

---

480 *Daily News Enterprise* Thomasville Ga. 10 September 1923

over me, but I neither saw nor heard him and was only conscious that I was in a ridiculous position and that the thing to do was to get up and try to fight back.

'The floor swayed and rocked beneath me like a fishing dory in an off-shore swell, and it was a welcome relief when Dempsey rushed into a clinch, held me up, and whispered into my ear, "Wrestle around a bit, son, until your head clears." And then it was that I learned what those little love taps to the back of the neck and the short digs to the ribs can mean to the groggy pugilist more than half knocked out.'[481]

In his 1977 autobiography, Dempsey recalled, 'While I was training, a young kid fresh out of Columbia University approached me with the idea of getting into the ring with me. He was a cub reporter of the *New York Daily News*. His name was Paul Gallico...Now, in September 1923, he decided that the only way to write good colour was to become my sparring partner, to see for himself what it was really like to be in the ring with me...Gallico told me his editor had sent him to spar with me. I couldn't help ribbing him. "What's the matter, son? Doesn't your editor like you?" Doc acted as announcer and kept glaring at me, hoping that Gallico would change his mind at the last minute. I came bobbing and weaving toward him and he put out his left. The next thing he knew, he was sprawled out on the canvas. Gallico somehow managed to get up and Doc whispered, "Get rid of this bum." I pulled Gallico into a clinch and said, "Hang on, kid, 'til your head clears." I gave him a few rabbit punches. Doc, seeing Gallico's eyes spinning, stopped the fight. His lip was bleeding and his eyes were glazed. But he had been a sport. And the fact that I had kept my promise meant a lot to him.'[482]

In his book *The Million Dollar Gate*, Doc Kearns would recall that Sunday afternoon in August when a towering young guy he'd never seen before came to the workout and introduced himself as Paul Gallico of the *New York Daily News*. Doc thought he had a peculiar request. He wanted to spar a few rounds with Dempsey so that he could write a story about how it felt to be hit by the champion. As Doc pondered his request, wondering what kind of nut he was talking to, he was beginning to get that old uneasy feeling from the vaudeville build-up days that he might be some kind of a ringer trying to build a quick reputation by making Dempsey look bad. Doc made a quick

481 Paul Gallico *Farewell to Sport* (London: Simon & Schuster Ltd. 1988) pp. 291–292
482 Dempsey with Piattelli pp. 157–159

appraisal of Gallico, standing roughly 6ft 3in and going about a stripped-down 190lb and in top condition.

Then Doc figured the other newspaper guys in camp certainly would know if he was on the level, so he buttonholed Runyon, and asked what he knew about this Gallico. Damon pulled Doc nearer and whispered that he figured the guy was a ringer. So did little Hype Igoe. That was enough proof for Doc. Mouthing threats, he headed back to the training ring and young Gallico, while Runyon and Igoe tried to keep a straight face as they took their ringside seats.

Kearns quietly warned Dempsey that he thought Gallico might be a ringer from the Firpo camp and to get rid of him as soon as he could. Wanting Dempsey really warmed up before Gallico got into the ring with him, Doc started him against a middleweight to make him work up a quick sweat. Dempsey next worked out against a heavyweight named Farmer Lodge. That didn't last long. Dempsey feinted the Farmer, Lodge dropped his guard and Dempsey hit him a hook straight out of the slaughterhouse. That was all for the Farmer. Then Doc, acting as referee, called Gallico into the ring.

'I told Dempsey as the bell rang, "Nail this guy as quick and as hard as you can." Dempsey bobbed forward, ignored a couple of jabs and then threw a right hand that would have busted down a brick wall. It hit Gallico on the chin and he went down. I began the count and was up to five when I heard Runyon yell, "Hey, Doc, tell Dempsey to take it easy. It's a gag. Gallico really is from the *Daily News*." He was game, the big guy. At eight he staggered up on rubbery legs, but I moved in between them, grinned at Dempsey and whispered for him to take it easy. Dempsey wrestled Gallico into a clinch, trying to hold him up. But the habit is a strange thing. Dempsey forgot himself and automatically belted Gallico a couple on the back of the neck. Down he went again. I counted him out at 1.37.'[483]

In his 1964 book *The Golden People*, Gallico would recall of his first meeting with Dempsey on the porch of his cottage at Saratoga, 'I remember how he looked, not quite as tall as I, clad in an old gray sweater, still crinkle-nosed then, three days growth of beard, with his curiously high-pitched voice and body always restless and moving. Much has been written about Dempsey in his heyday, about his viciousness, his cruelty, and the killer in him, but the truth is that he was basically a good-hearted man. It was a kindly act for him to

---

483 Kearns pp. 182–185

consent, on the eve of an important defense of his title, to take on an unknown reporter in order that he might not fail in his assignment; one incidentally, who stood an inch and a half taller and outweighed him by ten pounds.

'You might not consider it a kindness to deal out a split lip, a bloody nose, and a knockout left hook to the chin of a tyro, but it is results that count and the ten seconds I spent unconscious on the canvas were the turning point of my career. For so amused was Captain Patterson by the affair that shortly afterward he made me sports editor and gave me a daily column to write.'[484]

That knockout left hook certainly made an impression on young Gallico, and triggered a lifelong friendship between the fighter and the writer.

---

484 Gallico *The Golden People* p. 84

21

Who Do You Like, Dempsey Or Firpo?

THE Jack Dempsey–Luis Angel Firpo fight for the world heavyweight championship had become the Battle of the Beards. On Tuesday, three days before the Friday night fight, champion and challenger dispensed with their shaving gear to allow the whiskers to sprout on those sturdy chins. Firpo merely stated that he wanted to look as tough as he felt. Dempsey made the 12-mile trip into town for a haircut and his final shave. 'He wants to have at least three days' growth of black stubble on his face, because he says there is less danger of cuts from a rasping blow. The chin would be too tender by shaving, the champion contends.'[485]

The champion's visit to Saratoga Springs excited no interest apart from that taken by the barber in cutting Jack's hair. "I've laid a hundred bucks, Jack, on you," the barber confided. "Well, I hope you win," the champion replied, and settled down to the business of waiting for the barber to quit talking and finish the haircut.'[486]

Before making the trip into town, Dempsey rested in his cottage, played a few games of pinochle with Mike Trant, the Chicago police sergeant who regularly acted as his bodyguard, and enjoyed going through his daily mail bag. Among the hundreds of letters received from all over the country with messages of good luck, were two

---

485 *Hutchinson News* 11 September 1923
486 *The Bridgeport Telegram* 13 September 1923

letters from unknown admirers who enclosed a pair of leather wrist and thumb protectors and a wishbone. Jack couldn't figure why the protectors had been sent to him. He did welcome a group of six guys from Butte, Montana, who arrived in a dust-covered motor after a cross-country trip that had taken them 11 days. After a brief chat they wished Dempsey luck for the fight and proceeded on their way to New York City. A hand-painted sign on the back of the car declared 'Butte to New York – Dempsey–Firpo bout'.

'There was a haunted appearance about the deserted camp today as the champion prepared for his departure. The sparring partners were gone; the two cottages in which they lived were empty; the outdoor ring in which Dempsey unleashed his punches in five weeks of training for battle, was being dismantled.'[487]

Dempsey was not sorry to be leaving the White Sulphur Spring complex at Saratoga. 'He regards the place as the most uncomfortable and most undesirable ever selected for him, especially with the chill of autumn settling down on this region. He contracted a cold as a result of the dampness and the chilly winds sweeping off the lake and has not been satisfied with the cramped little cottage in which he lived.'[488]

Thursday was a day of hand-shaking for the champion as he went among the friends he had made to bid them goodbye. Jack had elected to travel to New York on the 13th because he believed it would bring him good luck. Along with Trant, Joe Benjamin, trainer Jerry Luvadis and his brother Johnny, Jack motored to Albany, some 40 miles away, where the party boarded a private compartment for the rail journey to the city. Doc Kearns would meet them at Grand Central to escort them to the Hotel Belmont for the overnight stay.

Luis Firpo and his party had travelled in from Atlantic City the day before and the challenger woke up that Thursday morning within 20 minutes' drive of the ring in the Polo Grounds where he would attempt to relieve Jack Dempsey of the title of world heavyweight champion. After dressing, Luis left the apartment for a brisk walk along Riverside Drive, returning greatly refreshed to sit down to a breakfast fit for a champion.

'Like a lion in a cage, Luis Angel Firpo awaits in the seclusion of a sixth floor apartment uptown for the call to battle with Jack Dempsey in an arena just out of sight across the flats and heights of Harlem,'

---

487 *Olean Evening Herald* 13 September 1923
488 *Hattiesburg American* 13 September 1923

reported Associated Press. 'If a caged lion were to be denied his daily rations of meat for a week, he would be like Firpo is today.'[489]

'The big man of the Argentine...is fighting mad. This madness, a sort of ferociousness, is exactly what the South American's trainers have labored to develop in the three weeks of preparation at Atlantic City. It is Firpo the gladiator. The gladiator's friends think him invincible. His mighty right will not be denied, they predict.'[490]

Friday 14 September 1923, a day of destiny for Luis Angel Firpo, a day he had waited for since first pulling on boxing gloves as a young man in his native Buenos Aires. The day began at 10.30am when he arose, after retiring at 11pm the night before. Luis headed for the breakfast table where he was already a champion. He consumed a large steak, six eggs, some toast and seven glasses of milk. Later, shortly before 1pm, he entered a Broadway restaurant with his party where he devoured a small steak, six eggs, some assorted fruit and several glasses of milk. His presence in the restaurant was soon noticed and by the time he was ready to leave, police reserves had to be called to clear a way through the crowd for his exit. It was time for the official weigh-in at the offices of the New York State Athletic Commission. Firpo arrived late after Dempsey had already weighed-in and left the building.

The commission's medical officers in attendance were Drs Lindenbaum, Hyman, McCaffery and Walker, the regular commission physician. 'I have never seen any better physical specimen,' announced Dr Walker after examining the champion. 'He is full of energy and as well trained as anyone could be.' Dempsey weighed in at 192.5lb.[491]

After Jack had been cleared by the doctors, he was called to one side by William Muldoon, chairman of the commission who told the champion he would have to observe certain conditions. One of these was to shave before the fight, not necessary as Dempsey had already got rid of this three-day growth. Muldoon also stated that Jack would not be permitted to wear an American flag and dark trunks in preference to white ones. He was also asked to leave the ring immediately after the contest. An escort of six policemen had been assigned to the champion who were to protect him before and after he entered the Polo Grounds. These rules would also apply to the Argentine challenger, who wore his three-day stubble when he

489 *Cumberland Evening News* Maryland 13 September 1923
490 *Wichita Daily Times* 13 September 1923
491 *New Castle News* 14 September 1923

stepped on the scales. Firpo was also pronounced fit following his examination.

When Dr Walker was asked what he thought about Firpo, he made no mention of the dislocated left elbow suffered by the South American, merely replying, 'I'll leave that to your own judgement,' adding, 'he is not the athlete that Dempsey is.'[492]

Dempsey had been first to arrive at the weigh-in and he was the first to arrive at the arena that night. His police escort brought him from the Riverside apartment where he had spent the afternoon to the main gate where a slight problem arose. The milling crowd spotted his car as it approached the gate and in no time at all a howling mob surrounded the vehicle, jumping on the running board and cheering their champion. One of the gates to the grounds was broken as they forced an entrance for Jack. Firpo did not arrive until sometime after Dempsey. He was taken to a private gate by his bodyguard and was able to enter without being noticed by the crowd.

Rickard would later announce that 88,228 people had paid gate receipts of $1,127,800 to see the fight, with an estimated 35,000 turned away from the gates. It was Tex's second million-dollar gate. 'Rickard...was pleased by the mass of people who attended the fight. But he was overjoyed by the quality of those present. The leaders of American industry and society were gathered in the first twenty rows around the ring. Archie and Kermit Roosevelt sat close to those faithful fans. A.J. Drexel Biddle, Sr., and Jr. Elihu Root was in shouting distance of W.K. Vanderbilt, George Gould, Forbes Morgan, L.H. Rothschild, William A. Brady, and Henry Payne Whitney.

'The rich and influential, and the sons and daughters of the rich and influential, were seated next to the most illustrious show business entertainers and athletes in America. Florenz Ziegfeld, John Ringling, James J. Corbett, Mickey Walker, John J. McGraw, and Jess Willard were ushered to their seats without notice. Some excitement was caused when Babe Ruth took his seat during the second preliminary, but that thrill vanished when the rumor began circulating that the Prince of Wales, who had been visiting Canada, was present at ringside. The Prince was not there, but, as far as East Coast society was concerned, everybody who was anybody was present.'[493]

---

492 *New Castle News* 13 September 1923
493 Roberts p. 183

The *New York Times* of 15 September 1923 noted, 'The roll call of ringside ticket holders, in addition to reading like an abridged edition of the Social Register, contained the names of well-known persons in every walk of life.'

One well-known person not listed in the Social Register was Charles 'Lucky' Luciano, although he was listed in the files of the New York Police Department as a leading organised crime figure. In his book *The Last Good Time,* Jonathan Van Meter wrote, 'Lucky Luciano and Nucky Johnson met for the first time at a boxing match in New York City. On 14 September 1923, heavyweight champion Jack Dempsey fought Argentine boxer Luis Angel Firpo in front of 88,000 people at the Polo Grounds in Manhattan, and Lucky Luciano moved heaven and earth – and paid $2,500 – for 200 ringside seats. It was all part of a deliberate campaign to rehabilitate his tarnished reputation after a drug bust that brought a storm of bad press and turned him into a pariah, even among underworld figures. Selling drugs – especially heroin – was considered the dirtiest business of all to the Mob. Luciano figured if he could invite cops, politicians and society muckety-mucks to a fight that was impossible to get tickets for, he would have everyone eating out of the palm of his hand again – and it worked.

'Luciano, Costello, Lansky and Siegel leaked the word out that Luciano was going to invite one hundred people and their dates as his guests to the fight. Within twenty-four hours, people from all over the country were calling for tickets. His guests that night included Al Capone with twelve friends; Florenz Ziegfeld and Earl Carroll, rival Broadway producers who met that very night; Bernard Gimbel of Gimbel's department store; Jimmy Hines and Al Marinelli from Tammany Hall; Boss Jim Prendergast from Kansas City; and Charles 'King' Solomon from Boston. One pair of those tickets went to none other than Nucky Johnson.'[494]

The original Polo Grounds stadium was constructed in 1876 and was located at 111th Street between 5th and 6th Avenues as a field for playing polo. By 1883 the New York Giants and the New York Metropolitans took over the field and played there until 1889 when it was abandoned for the new site at 155th Street. By then the name of the 155th Street ballpark was changed. It was destroyed by fire in

---

494 Jonathan Van Meter *The Last Good Time* (London: Bloomsbury Publishing plc 2003) pp. 49–50

1911, forcing the owners to rebuild with concrete and steel instead of wood.

Like a giant horseshoe, the Polo Grounds sat in the shadow of Coogan's Bluff which was above the western side of the stadium, an excellent vantage point to watch the events without paying. Of the three arenas to carry the name, only the original structure was used for playing polo. One of several trivial stories to come out of the Polo Grounds was that of the hot dog. The name was coined by Tad Dorgan, sports cartoonist on the *New York Journal,* who couldn't remember the spelling of dachshund, used to describe the red hot dachshund sausage that was sold at the ballpark.

When Jack Dempsey faced up to Luis Firpo that September evening in 1923, he was hoping not only to beat the South American but to beat the jinx that had beset all world boxing champions who had fought at the Polo Grounds that year. Featherweight champion Johnny Kilbane was the first to meet defeat at the Giants' ballpark, being knocked off his perch by Frenchman Eugene Criqui, who was then beaten by Johnny Dundee. Game little Jimmy Wilde was hammered loose from his flyweight title by Filipino Pancho Villa, then came middleweight champ Johnny Wilson who lost his title to Harry Greb.

Would Dempsey fall victim to the jinx in this, his fifth championship defence? Tex Rickard's million-dollar crowd at the Polo Grounds was about to find out...

22

The Battle Of
The Century

ACOUPLE of minutes after 10pm, Charles Schlegler, the official timekeeper appointed by the New York State Athletic Commission, rang the bell for round one. This is what happened next as recorded by the writers gathered around that ringside.

Dawson of the *New York Times* reported, 'Quick as a flash Dempsey rushed across the ring, struck up Firpo's guard or the place where his guard might have been and wasn't, but the challenger didn't go down. Instead, the champion, half-slipping, half-knocked over by Firpo's right hand counter, was down on one knee, down for the first time since that ancient fight with Jim Flynn, the Pueblo fireman, long before he won the title. He was up again before they could more than start counting, and as he got up on his feet 90,000 people got up on their feet, too, and not one of them sat down before the round was over. Ninety thousand people realised in one breath that they were about to see one of the classic fights of all ring history.'[495]

Henry L. Farrell was at ringside for United Press, 'In the very first round of the fight, a staggering right hand that seemed to come up from the floor, caught Dempsey on the jaw after he had missed a left

---

495 Gene Brown ed. *New York Times Scrapbook* (New York: Arno Press 1980)
    pp. 24–26

hook and the champion went to one knee. Dempsey came up dizzy and he fought the rest of the round as though he was out of his head.'[496]

'The fighters flew at one another like savages,' reported Associated Press. 'Dempsey hurled himself across the ring, slipping to one knee with the fury of his rush which carried the South American against the ropes. Then a right to the body and a left to the jaw and the challenger crashed to the canvas.'[497]

International News Service sports editor Davis J. Walsh recorded, 'Dempsey stepped out for the first round, led for the body with a left that was short and took a right over the heart that he will remember to his dying day. It was probably the hardest punch he had ever received in his life and forthwith he abandoned all pretense of boxing skill.'[498]

Universal Services had put former heavyweight champion James J. Corbett in a ringside seat with a pencil in his big right fist, and he wrote, 'Dempsey might have won the fight in the first round if he hadn't been hit with the fearful right hander Firpo threw at him. That punch came closer to winning the fight for Firpo than anything that happened afterward. Dempsey missed a left lead and Firpo, like lightning, ripped over a right that almost knocked Dempsey to his knees.'[499]

Ford C. Frick was working for the *New York Evening Journal* that night. He would go on to become a sportscaster and serve for 14 years as commissioner of baseball, from 1951 to 1965, but that night in September 1923 it was boxing that held his attention. Frick recorded, 'Eighty-five thousand persons rose to their feet as one man when the bell called the two fighters together for the opening, and eighty-five thousand persons were still standing at the finish. It was a slugging match, pure and simple. Science was tossed to the wind; footwork was discarded and the laws of jab and feint were forgotten.'[500]

Sportswriter Frank G. Menke wrote, 'From the moment the first gong banged…there was action so rapid, so cyclonic that the eye could not follow, nor the brain record the exact details. With the clang of the first gong, Dempsey fairly catapulted from his corner to meet a huge, hairy giant from the Pampas of South America; rushed, crouched, swirled upward and swung a terrific left hand punch to his foeman's

496 Henry L. Farrell *Traverse City Record Eagle* 15 September 1923
497 *Alton Evening Telegraph* Illinois 15 September 1923
498 Davis J. Walsh *Oakland Tribune* 15 September 1923
499 James J. Corbett *Wichita Daily Times* 15 September 1923
500 Ford C. Frick *New York Evening Journal* 15 September 1923

jaw. It was short – by two inches. As Dempsey steadied to try again, Firpo's powerful right hand whistled through the night and struck Dempsey full and solid upon the point of the chin. Every ounce of the South American's gigantic body was concentrated in the blow, one of the hardest ever landed in ring annals. The knees of a world's champion buckled under him; a world's champion pitched forward. He was toppling, face forward to dethronement.

'One punch – the first of the fight – seemed to have sent him to his doom. If Firpo had been six inches farther away at that very fraction of a second, Dempsey probably would have crumpled into the resin dust, either to rise no more, or, in rising, to be met by a fusillade of blows which probably would have crushed the consciousness from him. But as Dempsey pitched forward, Firpo was so close that the champion fell against the body of the giant. Instinct made him grab. And hold. Desperately, wildly, Firpo tried to shake off Dempsey. Before he could achieve his purpose the brief rest saved Dempsey. Strength and a little power came back to Dempsey's legs, the floodgates of reserve energy opened, revived him, refreshed him – refreshed and revived, however, only the body of him, because Dempsey afterward said he remembered nothing about that first round after he had been hit by that first pile-driver.'[501]

Lightweight champion of the world for eight years (1886 to 1894), Jack McAuliffe retired undefeated after a 42-bout career. The former 'Napoleon of the Prize Ring' would prove as adept as a writer as he had been a fighter, and United Press were happy to feature his columns. Jack was at the Dempsey–Firpo fight and after watching the fighters in training, had picked Firpo to become the new champion. The old champ reported, 'I don't believe that Dempsey knew what he was doing after the first punch of the fight, a right to the jaw which knocked him to one knee. He fought through the whole round on instinct and it was proved that he didn't know what he was doing when he hit Firpo twice after the gong rang.'[502]

Farrell recalled, 'Between 85,000 and 100,000 spectators saw the heavyweight crown topple three times from the scowling brow of Jack Dempsey, and they saw it grabbed back and set in place three times because a champion with a champion's brain didn't lose the

501 Frank G. Menke *The Fireside Book of Boxing* W.C. Heinz ed. (New York; Simon & Schuster 1961) pp. 291–293
502 Jack McAuliffe *Oakland Tribune* 15 September 1923

instinct when his senses departed…Dempsey was never nearer to being knocked out in his life.'[503]

Davis Walsh commented, 'The Latin was not supposed to be versed in the technique of ring business. He was and is a primitive fighter. Dempsey furnished the surprise. He went out at the sound of the bell like any preliminary boy and mixed it with the foreign entry, an almost suicidal policy.'[504]

In his book *The Tumult and the Shouting*, Grantland Rice quoted Dempsey, 'Rickard asked me to carry Firpo for four or five rounds, to give the customers a run for their money. I told Tex to go to hell, that Firpo was too strong and hit too hard to play with. I told Rickard I'd put Firpo away in the first round – if I could. Well, in that first round I got in a little too close and Firpo's first shot – a full right – caught me on the chin. I almost went down but kept punching. I was dazed… At that time I wasn't fighting for any championship or any million dollars. I was fighting to keep from being killed.'[505]

Doc Kearns would recall in his autobiography, 'Firpo, a giant of a man with a tousled black mane, glowered from his corner…the bell clanged harshly and I scrambled out of the ring. Dempsey burst into action just as we had planned. Racing across the ring, he belted up Firpo's guard with his left and started to throw a right. But then Jack half slipped and at that moment Firpo caught him with a wild right swing. Dempsey fell to one knee…Dempsey bounced up before referee Jack [sic] Gallagher could even start a count, and now he was the old raging tiger I had worked so hard to develop…'[506]

In his 1964 book *The Golden People*, Paul Gallico recalled his day as sportswriter on the *New York Daily News*. 'The first fight in which I ever saw Dempsey engage was that tremendous heart-stopping brawl at the Polo Grounds in New York City on the night of 14 September 1923, against Luis Angel Firpo, which was rightly called the Battle of the Century, for nothing like it has been seen since for thrills, chills, and pure animal savagery…In this uninhibited contest there was revealed a barbarity that echoed the earliest battles of primitive man or the awful, slashing death struggle of wild beasts hidden in the depths of some jungle. Indeed the giant Firpo had been nicknamed

503 Henry L. Farrell *Evening Chronicle* Marshall, Minn. 15 September 1923
504 Davis J. Walsh *Syracuse Herald* 15 September 1923
505 Rice *The Tumult and the Shouting* (New York: A.S. Barnes & Co. Inc. 1954) p. 93
506 Kearns p. 186

and likened to a wild bull and if this was so, Dempsey was the tiger attacking for the kill.'[507]

Long-time *Ring* magazine writer Daniel M. Daniel would remember Dempsey talking to Bob Edgren, cartoonist and ring expert of the old *Evening World*. 'Bob, I would like to tell you something from the inside,' Dempsey revealed. 'Firpo actually stopped me with his first punch. My head was knocked out but my legs were alive. I fought the rest of the fight in a daze.' As a matter of fact, wrote Daniel, the punch to which Dempsey referred was Firpo's third, not his first. Luis's first was a right to the face. His second was a left to the temple. Then he cut loose a right swing which Jack blocked with his arm. Then Firpo whipped a right to the body and Dempsey's knees sagged. That was the punch. Jack's knees touched the canvas but he grabbed Firpo about the body and pulled himself erect... Dempsey said, 'I went into the fight determined to win with one punch if I could. The cheer that rang through the Polo Grounds when Joe Humphreys introduced me made me feel great. I said, "These people call on you as an American to knock this guy silly." I remember that right at the start I cut loose with a left hook. Had it landed the fight might have ended then and there. Though I will say that big guy could take it, and plenty. I missed that left hook and then the grandstand hit me. Some of the reporters were charitable and said I slipped. I didn't slip, I was knocked silly.'[508]

Recalling the opening moments of the fight some ten years later, Robert Edgren wrote, 'Dempsey sprang at Firpo like a big cat. Dempsey's left arm hooked viciously at Firpo's unprotected stomach... Firpo's right hand had dropped to his thigh. Suddenly it shot up and his glove smashed under Dempsey's chin. Dempsey dropped to his knees as if he'd been shot, but as his knees hit the floor with a thump he leaped up instantly.'[509]

In two of his three autobiographies, Dempsey himself admitted he did not have total recall of the fight that would be the toughest of his 82-bout career. In his 1940 book, written with Myron M. Stearns, Jack stated, 'Exactly what happened during the battle is, in my own personal recollection, exceedingly uncertain. A heavy blow on the head has sometimes the peculiar effect of not only destroying your memory of whatever happened directly afterward, but also of destroying the memory of what happened *immediately before*. As I

507 Gallico *The Golden People* pp. 84–85
508 Stanley Weston ed. *Best of the Ring* (Chicago: Bonus Books Inc. 1992) p. 83
509 Robert Edgren *Moorhead Daily News* Minn. 4 March 1933

remember the fight, I waded in at the gong and shot a hard left at Firpo's jaw. I was confident that he could be hit, and that I could avoid, or withstand, his counter blows. Whether or not my left to the chin landed, I do not know. It may have missed entirely. Firpo was quicker, both in avoiding blows and delivering them, than I believed possible.

'My left on the other hand, may have landed. Firpo could also withstand a heavier blow than I had believed almost any fighter could take and survive. Anyway, I can remember weaving and throwing that left hook at his chin. Accounts of the fight say Firpo countered with his right and that I went to the canvas. That seems to be correct. After I got up and fought on, more or less instinctively, as I had in my first fight with Gunboat Smith, it may have been, however, that my head cleared at this time, and that as a matter of fact I fought fairly intelligently throughout most of that first round, even though I haven't since been able to remember doing so.'[510]

In 1959, Dempsey fashioned another autobiography with sportswriters Bob Considine and Bill Slocum. Recalling the Firpo fight, Dempsey stated, 'It's a good thing I fought Gibbons, because it put me in shape. If I had fought Firpo in the same shape I was in when I met Tommy, I'd have been knocked out for sure. I didn't know much about Firpo except that he had beat up some guys I never heard of in South America and then he came up here and knocked out Willard in six [sic]. In my mind he was just a big clumsy ox. "You watch this guy," Rickard told me after we had signed. "He's a good fighter, good right hand puncher." But I still didn't think he could fight a hell of a lot. I sure under-estimated Luis. They're still talking about the Firpo fight, and I guess they always will.

'When the introductions and boos were over that night in September 1923 at the jam-packed Polo Grounds, I went across the ring after the big fellow as fast as I could move. I jabbed him, hit him with a kind of sounding-out left. Then I missed a right. I reared back and just as I did he caught me with a right hand on my cheekbone. If I hadn't been going away it would have knocked me cold. As it was it knocked me out on my feet. If you've seen the movies of the fight, you know what happened the rest of the round. Seeing the pictures the day after the fight was the only way I ever learned about what happened.'[511]

---

510 Dempsey with Stearns pp. 223–224
511 Dempsey with Considine & Slocum pp. 147–148

What happened is still called the most sensational fight ever staged for the heavyweight title, or any title for that matter. After he went to his knees in that initial encounter with Firpo's big right fist, the champion was up without a count to crash a right to the body and a left to the jaw and Firpo went to the canvas, perhaps 30 seconds into the round. Referee Gallagher 'proceeded to drone the count', recorded Frank G. Menke. 'He had reached nine when Firpo started to rise. Then he stopped counting – when he should have gone on – for Firpo was not in a boxing position and should have been counted out then and there. It was at least 13 full seconds before Firpo was back in a fighting pose.'[512]

Nat Fleischer would write, 'The punch that actually started Firpo on the road to defeat was a crashing left hook to the jaw in the first round which landed as the men were breaking from a clinch. Firpo, slow to get away, presented the opening that enabled Dempsey to hook that left which dropped Luis like a log. It appeared, even from the press box, like a short jolt, but it was Dempsey's favorite short-arm hook – it travelled less than a foot. Firpo arose, an enraged bull. He swung wildly, but Dempsey avoided his swings. In he rushed, and as he did so, the Argentinian fell into a beautiful right to the jaw and again he went down. He got up at the count of two, only to fall into a left and right to the body and a crashing left to the jaw that sent him sprawling for the third time.

'The crowd hissed as Dempsey stood over his fallen rival, ready to shoot in the telling punch. Weak, badly hurt, Luis got to his feet again, his courage undimmed. He was subjected to another fierce body attack and he collapsed, remaining down on his fourth count, for nine. Still showing a he-man's courage, Firpo dragged himself up and went furiously at his opponent only to be sent down for a fifth time with a right to the jaw, but he was up before the count started. In a jiffy he went down again from a left to the jaw, delivered by Dempsey who stood right over the fallen man. Again Firpo displayed fighting instinct, arising only to sink again from another left.'[513]

'I actually stepped over Firpo, after he went down for a count of seven, as I made my way to a corner,' recalled Dempsey. 'The reason I did that, instead of doing the natural thing and walking around him,

---

512 Frank G. Menke *Fireside Book of Boxing* pp. 291–293
513 Nat Fleischer 1929 pp. 114–115

or going to another corner, is probably that I didn't dare let go the rope, for fear I would fall over on top of him.'[514]

'Firpo...came up swinging. He hit Dempsey with a long overhand right that crashed into Dempsey's head, behind the left ear. Dempsey fell to all fours and took a three count.'[515]

By this time the crowd was going crazy and no one was using the seat they had paid for. At ringside, sportswriter Bill McGeehan said to his neighbour, 'This isn't a boxing match. This is a fight!'

McGeehan was right, but it wasn't just a fight. It was sensational, exciting, brutal, two superb athletes hurling thunderous punches at each other, punches that were absorbed and shaken off until the bodies began to resist, cry enough, at which time it became a battle of the spirit, who wanted it most!

After two frantic, frenzied minutes of a first round that had developed into a savage exhibition of free-hand hitting never before seen inside a prize ring, Jack Dempsey, the heavyweight champion of the world, had been down twice, and his adversary, Luis Angel Firpo, the pride of all South America, had been hammered down seven times. But this big brute of a man had climbed off the canvas seven times, snorting defiance, shaking his black shaggy mane as he went forward to face the guns that had never ceased firing since the first clang of the gong had brought them from their corners.

'The man could take it,' reported the *New York Times*. 'He could take the best, the frantically repeated best, of the greatest heavyweight of the age, and still bounce back to his feet to go on fighting. Could he be beaten at all? And then, as Dempsey came toward him again, Firpo's long driving right caught him on the point of the jaw, and head first, feet pointed in the air, the heavyweight champion shot out through the ropes and to all appearances out of his championship.'[516]

Damon Runyon saw it this way. 'Out of the wildest, maddest flurry of human fists that men have ever seen in a prize ring, out of a brawling, crazy struggle that had 85,000 men and women on their feet screaming, the wild bull, Luis Angel Firpo, clubbed Dempsey to his knees, clubbed him clear out of the ring.'[517]

Recalling that crazy moment, Frank Menke wrote, 'My seat was in the first row, alongside Jim Corbett. My view was wholly

514 Dempsey with Stearns p. 225
515 Kahn p. 344
516 *New York Times Scrapbook* p. 26
517 Damon Runyon *The Salt Lake Tribune* 15 September 1923

unobstructed. THIS IS WHAT I SAW. Dempsey was backed to the ropes with Firpo crowding with the left side of his body. Firpo's right arm was free. Six times in succession he hit Dempsey on the chin or head without a return, because Dempsey was in such a position that his arms were practically handcuffed. Dempsey decided to slide out of the trap. Bending his head low toward his own right arm, he attempted to move along the ropes until he was clear of Firpo. At the exact moment that Dempsey's head was below the upper strand and at the exact fraction of a second that his right foot was off the floor, Firpo hit the champion on the chin with a right. The middle of Dempsey's body was up against the middle strand of the ropes.

'The result was this. Dempsey's legs shot off the ground and his head shot backward. And in a head-first backward dive, Jack Dempsey went into the press row, while 85,000 persons looked on in hushed amazement. Much has been written about how reporters saved Dempsey in his fall and how they helped him back into the ring. The real truth is that the reporters handicapped, more than helped Dempsey in his ring re-entry. When 192.5 pounds of humanity came hurtling through the air directly at their heads, those reporters did only the natural thing. They pushed up their hands to protect themselves. Dempsey landed among the group. Squirming, twisting, lunging with arms, kicking with legs, he strove to get himself steered in the right direction so that he could climb back through the ropes. In one of his wild lunges, his fist hit Kid McPartland, one of the judges, in the eye – and blackened it for ten days.

'Never did a man look more bewildered, more "all gone" than Dempsey, back in the ring just as the referee counted nine, flat-footed, legs spread wide for balance, against the ropes. His hands were helpless at his sides. His eyes showed no brain light. His whole body slumped. This was Firpo's second golden opportunity for world conquest. And for the second and final time it slipped from him. But Firpo, not sure whether Dempsey was faking, decided to take no chances. He went in cautiously. He finally decided to strike. He swung – and missed – because Dempsey instinctively ducked as energy came back to him.'[518]

Grantland Rice recalled the incident in his book, writing, 'At ringside my typewriter was next to Jack Lawrence's. During the final prelim bout, we were discussing the main. "They're two big guys," said Lawrence. "If somebody goes through the ropes I hope it's Dempsey.

---

518 Frank G. Menke *Fireside Book of Boxing* pp. 291–293

At least he's lighter than that truck Firpo." Just before the bout started, I moved down four seats, next to Bob Edgren of the old New York *Evening World*. Well, for the record, Lawrence got his wish. It was Dempsey who came hurtling through the ropes in that madhouse first round. He landed, back first, on top of Lawrence, who had put his hands up to protect himself. But nobody, including Lawrence, had to help Dempsey back through those ropes. He was all for helping himself – but fast!'[519]

In the 1950s, Arthur Mann, a well-known magazine writer, disclosed he had made a definitive study of the incident and put the facts in true perspective, 'The man Dempsey really had to thank was Perry Grogan, long a top Western Union Morse operator. Grogan told me, "I was supervising the blow-by-blow. As I saw Dempsey coming, I instinctively put up my left hand to protect my sending set, which I was working with my right. Dempsey's sweaty back skidded off my left hand and he landed on Lawrence's typewriter, wrecking it. I stopped sending, grabbed Dempsey under his back and shoulders and pushed him up. Jack Lawrence helped. I had to sit down quickly to my telegraph instrument because somebody at the other end kept flashing a signal: Is there anything wrong?"'[520]

Reporting Dempsey's tumble through the ropes, Davis Walsh '...thought he would never come back. He finished the fall with his feet on the middle strand of the ropes and his head on someone's typewriter in the press row...No champion was ever closer to being knocked out than Dempsey was when he hung over the ropes, four feet higher than his dizzy head.'[521]

In a magazine article some years later, Hype Igoe recalled, 'It wasn't much of a punch, it was a push, and Dempsey was flipped right over the middle rope. He landed, laughing, in the arms of the writers directly under him. He was four feet from my fingertips. As the news scribes shoved him upward, Dempsey shouted "allez oop". He wasn't in the least dazed.'[522]

There was a lot of discussion about Dempsey's plunge from the ring with many claiming that the champion was out of the ring for more than ten seconds. Long-time ring expert Bob Edgren, a couple of

519 Rice p. 93
520 Lester Bromberg *Boxing's Unforgettable Fights* (New York: The Ronald Press Co. 1962) pp. 145–146
521 Davis J. Walsh *Indiana Evening Gazette* 15 September 1923
522 Hype Igoe *Ring* September 1938

hours after the fight, managed to get a strip of the movie film, taken at 16 pictures to the minute, and checked the timing of Dempsey's ring exit and re-entry at exactly six seconds. Edgren also quoted the rules as stating that a fighter cannot receive assistance from his seconds during a round. He wasn't responsible for the action of the crowd, or in this case, reporters. Edgren further reasoned that being knocked out of the ring was an accident, the rules merely stating that the referee 'may' count over a man knocked out of the ring, and in this instance there was no reason for the referee to count – although he did. And, officially, Dempsey was back in the ring at the count of nine and therefore perfectly entitled to resume the fight, if able. And he was able!

As Jack stood up alongside the ropes, Firpo rushed at him, throwing that big right hand, but he was wild and Dempsey grabbed him in a clinch. Breaking away, they punched at each other until the bell ended the most dramatic three minutes in boxing history. Neither fighter heard the bell above the roar of the crowd and referee Gallagher had to grab Dempsey and send him across the ring to his corner where confusion reigned. Kearns, Benjamin and Jerry the Greek couldn't find the smelling salts. They were in Doc's shirt pocket and shoved under Jack's nose before the bell summoned him for round two.

'Dempsey was refreshed by the minute's rest and decided to end matters by forcing the fighting from the bell,' recalled Fleischer. 'Seeing an opening, Dempsey rushed toward his man who stood flat-footed, on his face a look of bewilderment as he prepared to meet the champion. A left to the jaw and Firpo went down for a count of two. That was the beginning of the end. Firpo was beginning to show the terrific effects of the body battering. He arose, but a series of lefts and rights to the body and a solid smash to the jaw sent him down again for a count of five. He got to his feet again only to be met with a left hook to the jaw followed by a right to the jaw as he was falling and the most sensational bout of modern ring history was over.'[523]

It had lasted a mere three minutes and 57 seconds, yet no one in that million-dollar crowd asked for their money back. They would never forget this one, not as long as they lived. It truly was the Four-Minute Fight of the Century!

---

[523] Fleischer p. 115

23

All Over Bar
The Shouting

'FRENZIED fans crashed down on the press section, stormed it, captured it, leaped to the ring itself. For a moment it seemed as if the police would lose control of the situation, but finally victor and vanquished were escorted to their dressing rooms.'[524]

'Once in my dressing room,' recalled Dempsey, 'I was in pain, my backside aching from bruised bones. I guess it was a good thing that my fall had been broken by hands and typewriters. All I wanted was to be left alone and to sleep.'[525]

'Firpo recovered with sufficient speed,' wrote Roger Kahn, 'to consume a huge spaghetti supper at Perrona's Restaurant on West 46th Street. He walked in, removed his fedora, and proceeded toward a back room, bowing to the other diners, who cheered him as though he had won.'[526]

Workmen were still dismantling the ring at the now-empty Polo Grounds when the press boys started hammering their typewriters, pounding out their mostly-inaccurate reports of what they had or hadn't seen in that furious four-minute fight. INS sports editor Davis J. Walsh spoke for his press row colleagues when he wrote, 'It may seem a bit garbled, but all accounts of those hectic moments that

---

524 *The News Palladium* Benton Harbor Mich. 15 September 1923
525 Dempsey with Piattelli p. 161
526 Kahn p. 348

marked the bout were just that and the writer is duly proud of the fact that he can garble with the best of them.'[527]

'He held the title, a ton of weight in the golden money that Firpo loves so well, in the very palm of his hand – and he didn't know what to do!' wrote Runyon. 'Dempsey did know what to do. That was the real difference that saved a world's championship title, the very wide difference between brain and brawn.'[528]

Commenting on Dempsey's sudden exit from the ring, old champ Jack McAuliffe saw that as a break for the champion. 'If he had not been knocked clear out of the ring into the press box he would have been knocked out…Had he remained in the ring, Firpo surely would have finished him. Dempsey had a chance to revive while he was being pushed back into the ring.'[529]

There was criticism in the press of Dempsey's disregard for certain niceties of ring combat as the rules of the New York State Athletic Commission took as big a beating as did Señor Firpo. Yet Dempsey was not a dirty or foul fighter, he was a rough fighter, and where he learned to fight the number one rule was survival of the fittest. In the *Chicago American* a few days after the fight, Ed W. Smith wrote, 'The critics have been whacking both sides of it, many claiming that Dempsey was entirely within his rights in everything that he did and others insisting that he fought a foul, unsportsmanlike battle.'

Wilbur Wood reported, 'The Wild Bull has legitimate grounds for his complaint that he was not accorded his full rights by the referee. But in such a fight as that one, everyone concerned is likely to forget such minor things as rules. The charitable way of looking at it is to say that Dempsey and the referee forgot them.'[530]

Henry Farrell allowed that Firpo was partially right in claiming that he was fouled by Dempsey when the champion punched on the breakaway and again when Firpo was struck before he was in a fighting position after a knockdown. But Farrell argued that Dempsey's offence when hitting his man on the breakaway did not make Jack liable for disqualification. In the referee's pre-fight instructions, both fighters were told that they were to defend themselves at all times, and when Firpo failed to do so it was his own fault. Farrell further stated that Firpo should have known that the rules infractions were committed in

527 Davis J. Walsh *New Castle News* 15 September 1923
528 Damon Runyon *Davenport Democrat & Leader* 15 September 1923
529 Jack McAuliffe *Lebanon Daily News* 15 September 1923
530 Wilbur Wood *New York Herald* 15 September 1923

a frenzy of excitement and when both fighters were punched so dizzy that they had no idea that rules existed and when they were influenced only by the savage dictates of self-preservation.

With Firpo admitting after the fight that he did not hear the timekeeper counting at any time during the bout, Farrell wrote, 'He should take the word of unprejudiced writers in the press box who KNOW that he was knocked out before Dempsey had done anything about which he complained. Early in the first round Firpo was on the floor for the count of ten.'[531]

As Farrell pointed out, Firpo was not declared out because the new system of counting established in New York failed to work perfectly under the stress and intense excitement of the moment. The New York rules provided for two timekeepers at the ringside, one to handle the bell and the other to arise on a knockdown and call the count from his watch. The referee follows the count of the timekeeper. 'When Firpo went to the floor this particular time, the timekeeper reached ten, beyond all question of doubt,' reported Farrell. The timekeeper hesitated then, apparently expecting the referee to call 'out'. The referee looked at the timekeeper and apparently thought it was his duty to declare the bout ended. In those fleeting seconds of hesitation, Firpo got to his feet to find Dempsey waiting for him and the fight went on, although Firpo had really been knocked out. As recorded in the previous chapter, this happening was reported by Frank Menke when, with Firpo rising from an early knockdown, the referee counted to nine and then stopped when he should have carried on.

At its regular weekly meeting held on 18 September, the New York State Athletic Commission discussed the Dempsey–Firpo fight but issued no formal statement of its proceedings, despite reports that it might act upon the criticism directed at referee Johnny Gallagher because of his failure to make Dempsey follow his instructions during the fight. It was understood, however, that the boxing solons felt that, though there may have been some grounds for finding fault with Gallagher's conduct, his judgement in the ring, nevertheless, was final and could not be questioned after the bout.

Dempsey was declared by thousands of spectators not only to have struck Firpo viciously after the call of time and to have disregarded the referee's instructions on retreating to a neutral corner during a knockdown count, but to have technically lost the fight on a foul when

---

531 Henry L. Farrell *Bakersfield Californian* 1 October 1923

he was assisted back to the ring by reporters after having been knocked through the ropes by Firpo in the first round. Chairman Muldoon said after the fight that had Firpo's seconds claimed a foul when Dempsey was pushed back into the ring, the State Boxing Commission would have recognised the claim and declared Firpo the winner. No such claim was made at the time.

'The decision of the referee is sufficient for Luis Angel Firpo and despite the protests of his friends and many spectators of his fight with Jack Dempsey, that he was unfairly treated and fouled, he asks nothing more than another match with the world's champion, when he has rested and his arm has healed.'[532]

'The referee, stunned by the fury of the fight, let Dempsey get away with it,' recalled Teddy Hayes. 'Johnny Gallagher, who refereed the Firpo fight, was never to be given another important bout. The Boxing Commission knew he had lost control. Years later, he would come around Billy LaHiff's Chop House and ask for a little money. One day he lay down in a gutter and died.'[533]

The day after the fight, Dempsey was still suffering pain from his crash landing on the press benches.

'I landed on and wrecked a typewriter that was proudly exhibited in a store window for months afterwards,' he recalled. 'Besides that, my head struck the table with a force that completed whatever addling was needed to befuddle me entirely. In addition even to that, my back and hip struck the edge of the ring platform as I fell, inflicting an injury that was far more serious than I, or anyone else, realised at the time.'[534]

Long after the fight, Dempsey would recall, 'Through the years it has amused me to hear this or that person take credit for breaking my fall and throwing me back as if I were a prized baseball...Even Frank Menke of the International News Service, who wrote all his stories with a pencil, claimed the "honor" of having broken my fall with his typewriter.'[535]

The night before the fight, Dempsey checked into the Hotel Belmont. Tex Rickard arrived and asked for a few words in private. 'Keep this bout going, Jack,' Rickard said. 'Don't let it end too quick.' 'Go to hell,' Dempsey said. 'And something else, the cheque for $500,000 goes to me.' 'Of course, Jack. You can have it now, if you

---

532 *Evening Tribute Times* 20 September 1923
533 Hayes p. 64
534 Dempsey with Stearns p. 225
535 Dempsey with Piattelli p. 161

want.' 'I mean to me, not Kearns, and, yeah, I'll take it now.' Rickard gave Dempsey a $500,000 cheque...Dempsey thanked him and put the cheque in one of his suitcases.[536]

On 15 September 1923, when Rickard told Doc Kearns he had given the cheque to Dempsey, Kearns turned furiously on his champion, demanding to know what he had done with the money. Dempsey calmly told his manager he had put $200,000 into an annuity.

Jack Dempsey, heavyweight champion of the world, was starting to think on his feet. The business with the Firpo cheque widened the chasm between him and Kearns and there would be no more big purses to cut up. In fact, Jack would not fight for three years and when he did Kearns was no longer pulling the strings. The break came when Kearns insulted Estelle Taylor in a nightclub, the beautiful movie star his champion had fallen in love with. Women were all right for Doc's fighters for one-night stands. Marriage was a non-starter. Trouble was, Dempsey was in love with Taylor and was going to marry her, just as soon as she divorced her husband. With that complication out of the way, William Harrison Dempsey married Estelle Taylor in San Diego on 7 February 1925. Joe Benjamin was Jack's best man. Doc Kearns was not on the guest list.

That September, it looked as though the championship dream of Harry Wills was about to come true. He signed a contract, along with Dempsey, for promoter Floyd Fitzsimmons who would stage the long-awaited contest at Michigan City, Indiana, in September 1926. Fitzsimmons handed a cheque for $50,000 to Paddy Mullins, manager of Wills, and promised Dempsey a cheque for $25,000 the next day, a down payment on $300,000 due at the contract signing, with Jack to receive a balance of $700,000 before entering the ring, giving him one million dollars and Doc Kearns nowhere in sight! But Dempsey–Wills was a fight for tomorrow and tomorrow never came. The $25,000 cheque Dempsey presented at the bank bounced like a rubber ball and Jack told Fitzsimmons what to do with his contract. At least Harry Wills got to keep his fifty grand and when he died in 1958, he left an estate valued at $100,000, including a 19-family apartment building in Harlem.

Doc had another champion by then, Mickey Walker, the Toy Bulldog who was welterweight, then middleweight champion of the

---

536 Kahn pp. 340, 349

world. Dempsey rested, and rusted, and when he fought Gene Tunney on a rainy night in Philadelphia in September 1926, the former marine outboxed and outpunched him over ten rounds to end Jack's seven-year reign as champion. They would fight a return a year later, in Chicago, in what became known as the 'Battle of the Long Count'.

Rickard made Jack earn his return shot at Tunney by matching him with Jack Sharkey at Yankee Stadium and it was another million-dollar gate paid by a crowd of 75,000. Champion or ex-champ, Dempsey was box office magic. But in the ring he wasn't doing so good as the man from Boston had one of his best fights, for six rounds anyway. Sharkey got careless in the seventh round and Dempsey got his knockout. With the New York State Athletic Commission still insisting that Harry Wills be in one corner of a heavyweight championship fight, Tex Rickard took his fight to Chicago and a crowd of 104,943 paid a whopping record gate of $2,658,660 to see Dempsey go for his old title.

In better shape than he had been in Philadelphia, Dempsey brought a savage left hook out of his past to floor Tunney in the seventh round. But, as was his habit, Jack stood over his fallen opponent in the nearest corner instead of retreating to the farthest neutral corner. Referee Dave Barry refused to pick up the count from the timekeeper until he did so, and when Jack eventually obeyed, Barry picked up the count from 'one'. Tunney got up at 'nine' with unofficial timekeepers having him on the deck for 14 seconds, and backpedalled around the ring as Dempsey tried to finish him. Gene survived the round and even decked Dempsey in the next round on his way to retaining his title on a ten-round decision. Dempsey never fought again. In his 82-bout career, the Manassa Mauler racked up 50 knockouts in 61 winning fights and only six defeats. In retirement, he boxed exhibitions, promoted and managed fighters and refereed many boxing and wrestling bouts. In the Second World War he served as a commander in the Coast Guard, seeing action in the Pacific, and owned a popular New York restaurant. He was still The Champ to millions of Americans.

The morning after his fight with Dempsey, Luis Angel Firpo was up early to complete a deal to import a special sports car into Argentina. It was a Stutz Bearcat, red with the head of a bull painted in white on one side. Firpo would be the exclusive importer and dealer. The car sold well. Everything Luis Firpo associated himself with following his shot at world championship glory did well. He had the Midas touch in that hammer of a right hand.

John V. Grombach, a former athlete from New Orleans, specialized in boxing. He won 60 of 66 fights and the inter-collegiate heavyweight championship in 1922 and 1923 as a cadet at West Point. He was training for the 1924 Olympics when he sparred with Firpo, 'probably the worst looking tyro ever to invade McLevy's training gym in the old Madison Square Garden. I boxed with Firpo in training and often talked with him, and I feel that I may know more about his ideas and boxing psychology than many newspapermen. Luis Firpo had a failing which did not make him popular with the hangers-on of boxing. According to many he was the stingiest man that ever laced on a glove.

'I will bet anybody any amount of money anywhere that no one ever got even a thin penny out of Mr Firpo. Every dollar ever paid to Firpo stuck to him. In addition, most of his waking hours in the United States were spent figuring out ways and means to obtain the necessities of life without recourse to his bank roll. The main reason he used me as a sparring partner was because, as an amateur training for the Olympics, I could not accept any pay. He got his clothes, shoes and hats by autographing pictures or boxing gloves for shop windows.

'We should respect Firpo notwithstanding his penny-pinching for he came to this country for one purpose, to make a fortune, and this he accomplished. There never has been a more straight-forward, never-say-die fellow than Luis Angel. He knew what he wanted, and he went after it, without cutting corners or making any circuitous approaches...Firpo, the Wild Bull of the Pampas, is much too colourful a figure ever to be forgotten. He returned to his home in Argentina without the championship, but with his pockets full of gold and an untarnished reputation. After abandoning boxing, he entered commercial competition finally as a real estate operator and made another fortune. According to Argentine newspapers, he was worth approximately $2m and owned about 40,000 acres of land in the pampas. He probably was the richest ex-professional pugilist in the world.'[537]

In 1924, Firpo had made another bid for fistic fame. He knocked out Farmer Lodge and Al Reich and beat the Italian heavyweight Erminio Spalla in 14 rounds. In September, almost a year to the day since his battle with Dempsey, Tex Rickard paid him a few hundred thousand dollars to fight Harry Wills at Boyle's Thirty Acres in Jersey

---

537 John V. Grombach *The Saga of the Fist* (Cranberry N.J.: A.S. Barnes & Co. Inc. 1977) pp. 57–59

City. In a drab 12-round maul, Firpo was outclassed by Dempsey's nemesis who was awarded every round bar one by the bored newsmen. The only excitement came in round two when a long right hand from Wills sent Firpo to the canvas for a count of six. Wills failed to take advantage and seemed content to outbox the Argentine the rest of the way.

At ringside for United Press, Henry Farrell wrote, 'With a big pair of brown hands that spread out in front of him like a fan and that pumped into action like an air hammer, Harry Wills, former stevedore of New Orleans, took all the wildness out of Luis Angel Firpo in Jersey City last night and gave him a severe beating in twelve rounds.'[538]

Paying gate receipts amounting to $509,135, the crowd of 70,000 waiting in vain for the fireworks that fizzled out long before the final bell. One man who decided he couldn't wait that long was champion Jack Dempsey who walked out after seven rounds. Former champion James J. Corbett told his ringside neighbour it was the worst fight he had seen in 40 years watching from the safe side of the ropes. In Buenos Aires, crowds estimated at 100,000 stood in drizzling rain in front of newspaper offices before drifting away at the news that their hero had been beaten by a wide margin. Two months later, Firpo met former knockout victim Charley Weinert and was adjudged a loser of the newspaper decision over 12 rounds in Newark.

Luis would box once in 1926, beating Spalla in Buenos Aires. Ten years later, he tried that big right hand out again but after flattening a couple of sparring partners he came unstuck against the tough Chilean Arturo Godoy, who finally ended Firpo's career in the third round. Forty-two and fat, the Wild Bull would fight no more.

Luis Angel Firpo died of a heart attack at his home in the Palermo Chico section of Buenos Aires on Sunday 7 August 1960, aged 65. He was survived by his widow Señora Blanca Lourdes Firpo. There were no children of the marriage. 'I am very sorry to hear of his death,' said Jack Dempsey. 'Firpo's punch, ruggedness and raw courage gave boxing one of its greatest boosts. He not only knocked me out of the ring in our fight, but he had me out on my feet. They called him the Wild Bull of the Pampas, and that was an understatement. He came at me like a herd of wild bulls that day.'[539]

---

538 Henry L. Farrell *Sandusky Star Journal* 12 September 1924
539 *Pacific Stars and Stripes* 9 August 1960

Firpo's body lay in state at the Luna Park boxing arena in Buenos Aires as thousands of fight fans and admirers filed by the coffin to pay their respects. His body was later laid to rest in La Recoleta Cemetery in Buenos Aires. A life-size statue of him in his boxing robe stands before his tomb.

In the 1970s, Dempsey suffered a number of minor strokes. 'When last I saw him,' recalled Kahn, 'he was using a cane...After that his stout heart began to fail and doctors implanted a pacemaker. He died on a mild spring afternoon, 31 May, 1983, at the age of 87. Better than most, he had reached out and seized life with two strong hands.'[540]

What Jack Dempsey and Luis Angel Firpo did with their two strong hands on a September evening in 1923 will never be forgotten. To remind us, there is the iconic painting of the fight, showing Dempsey falling through the ropes, that was the work of George Bellows, an American artist who had been commissioned by the New York *Evening Journal* to make sketches of the fight between Dempsey and Firpo. Bellows sat ringside sketching, and later decided to turn one of the sketches into a painting. Sadly, in 1925, shortly after completing the work, Bellows died of complications from a ruptured appendix. But his painting became an American classic that hangs in the Whitney Museum of American Art. During the Second World War, the United States Armed Forces distributed prints of the painting to soldiers in camps and hospitals. However, artistic integrity was a primary concern and the artist was widely criticised for showing the right-handed fighter (Firpo) punching from his left.

In retrospect, Dempsey would have preferred Firpo using his left more than his devastating right. But if he had, then this would have been just another fight, instead of a sensational Battle of the Century.

---

540 Kahn p. 434

Bibliography

Books

Bromberg, Lester. *Boxing's Unforgettable Fights*. New York: The Ronald Press Co. 1962

Brown, Gene ed. *The Complete Book of Boxing*. New York: Arno 1980

Carpentier, Georges. *Carpentier by Himself*. London: Hutchinson 1955

Dempsey, Jack with Bob Considine & Bill Slocum. *Massacre in the Sun*. London: William Heinemann Ltd. 1960

Dempsey, Jack with Myron M. Stearns. *Round by Round*. New York: Whittlesey House 1940

Dempsey, Jack with Barbara Piattelli Dempsey. *Dempsey*. London: W.H. Allen 1977

Fleischer, Nat. *50 Years at Ringside*. New York: Fleet Publishing Corp. 1958

Fleischer, Nat. *The Heavyweight Championship*. New York: G.P. Putnam's Sons 1949

Fleischer, Nat. *Jack Dempsey The Idol of Fistiana*. New York: The Ring Publishing Co. 1929

Gallico, Paul. *The Golden People*. New York: Doubleday & Co. 1964

Gallico, Paul. *Farewell to Sport*. London: Simon & Schuster Ltd. 1988

Grombach, John V. *The Saga of the Fist*. Cranberry N.J. A.S. Barnes & Co. Inc. 1977

Hayes, Teddy. *With the Gloves Off*. Houston: Lancha Books 1977

Heinz, W.C. ed. *The Fireside Book of Boxing*. New York: Simon & Schuster 1961

Kahn, Roger. *Flame of Pure Fire, Jack Dempsey and the Roaring Twenties*. New York: Harcourt Brace & Co. 1999

Kearns, Jack with Oscar Fraley. *The Million Dollar Gate*. New York: The Macmillan Co. 1966

Kelly, Jason. *Shelby's Folly*. Lincoln, Nebraska: University of Nebraska Press 2010

Kimball, George ed. and John Schulian. *At The Fights*. New York: The Library of America 2011

Lardner, John. *White Hopes and Other Tigers*. Philadelphia: J.B. Lippincott 1947

Mee, Bob. *The Heavyweights*. Stroud, Gloucestershire: Tempus Publishing Ltd. 2006

Moyle, Clay. *Billy Miske The St. Paul Thunderbolt*. Iowa City: Win by KO Publications 2011

Rice, Grantland. *The Tumult and the Shouting*. New York: A.S. Barnes & Co. Inc. 1954

Roberts, Randy. *Dempsey The Manassa Mauler*. Baton Rouge: Louisiana State University Press 1979

Samuels, Charles. *The Magnificent Rube*. New York: McGraw Hill Book Co. 1957

Schulberg, Budd. *Ringside*. Chicago: Ivan R. Dee 2006

Streible, Dan. *Fight Pictures*. Berkley & Los Angeles: University of California Press 2008

Sugar, Bert Randolph. *Boxing's Greatest Fighters*. Guilford, Conn. The Lyon's Press 2006

Van Meter, Jonathan. *The Last Good Time*. London: Bloomsbury Publishing 2003

Waltzer, Jim. *The Battle of the Century*. Santa Barbara: Praeger 2011

Weston, Stanley ed. *Best of the Ring*. Chicago: Bonus Books Inc. 1992

Magazines

Boxing
Boxing Digest
Boxing News
Boxiana Review
Boxing Illustrated
Boxing International
Boxing & Wrestling
Ring
Sports Illustrated
Time

Websites

Newspaperarchives.com
Boxrec.com
Cyberboxingzone.com
Espn.com
The sweetscience.com
www.stutzmotor.com/history

Newspapers

Alton Evening Telegraph
Altoona Mirror
Bakersfield Californian
Billings Gazette
Boston Daily Globe
Boston Evening Globe
Bradford Era
Bridgeport Telegram
Capital Times
Cedar Rapids Evening Gazette
Charleston Gazette
Chester Times
Chronicle Telegram
Cumberland Evening Times
Daily Globe
Davenport Democrat & Leader
Decatur Evening Herald
Dunkirk Evening Observer
Emporia Gazette
Evening Independent

Freeport Journal-Standard
Galveston Daily News
Helena Independent
Idaho State Journal
Indiana Evening Gazette
Indianapolis Star
Iowa City Press-Citizen
Joplin News Herald
Kingston Daily Freeman
Lake County Times
Letherbridge Herald
Limon News
Lima News
Logansport Pharos-Tribune
Lowell Sun
Manitoba Free Press
Mansfield News
Montana Standard
Morning Avalanche
Nevada State Journal
New Castle News
New York Journal

New York News
New York Times
Oakland Tribune
Ogden Standard-Examiner
Olean Evening Times
Oshkosh Daily Northwestern
Portsmouth Daily Times
Post Standard
Salt Lake Tribune
San Antonio Evening News
Sandusky Register
Sioux City Journal
Sheboygan Press
Syracuse Herald
Twin Falls Daily News
Vidette Messenger
Waterloo Evening Courier
Winnipeg Free Press

Index

INDEX